My first million

A spiritual and material approach to the noble art of making money

Dear Mircea:

May you make many millions and share your wealth.

Love, Dually Sep 23

Ana Rodríguez

*To all those who wish to spend less time making money
and more time doing whatever they choose to do*

What our community says

I highly recommend that you read the following testimonials because... You could be one of them!

If the learnings we are about to share with you helped them, it is more than likely that their words bring light to some ideas, thoughts or beliefs you might not even be aware of, but, somehow, you were looking for.

Enjoy what these beautiful beings share from the innermost part of their hearts, which is their life changing experiences, way more meaningful than the mere fact of making some money.

Dear Ana,

I wanted to take a moment to express my deepest gratitude for the immense impact you have had on my life since joining your investment club. Before I met you, I never believed I was capable of investing or harnessing the power it holds. However, since becoming a part of your work and group, I have experienced a transformation that has empowered me in ways I never thought possible.

Your presence alone exudes strength and professionalism, yet you effortlessly manage to create an atmosphere of humanity and genuine connection. Your willingness to share your vulnerabilities has been incredibly inspiring and has fostered a sense of camaraderie among all the members. I have learned from you that investing is not just about money in the bank; it is about changing our money mindset and recognizing our own self-worth.

What sets you apart is your remarkable ability to understand the unique situations and challenges faced by each individual in the group. Your compassion and openness are qualities rarely seen in the world of finance. Your teachings have encouraged me to continually push myself and strive for excellence.

I eagerly look forward to our monthly meetings with the investment ladies. Through our collaboration, I have come to realize that we are a team—a team where we can rely on one another for support and guidance. This sense of unity and empowerment is something I never imagined finding in the realm of investing.

Ana, I am immensely grateful for having had the opportunity to know you. I genuinely wish that everyone could experience the guidance and presence of an Ana in their lives. Not only have you helped me increase my self-esteem regarding investing, but you have also shown me the true meaning of having an extraordinary human being by your side. Thank you, Ana, for being exactly who you are.

With all my love, Vero

Véronique Bourbeau, founder of *Run for Humanity*

Ana Rodríguez is an absolute beautiful lady. Gorgeous outside and, more importantly, inside.

Ana has a terrific brain and is a fantastic teacher - she has an amazing ability to simplify complex processes for easy comprehension.

Kind, compassionate, tolerant, Ana has the patience of Job - believe me, I've tested her big time over many years!

Ana loves to share - from her mastery of the stock market to her 10+ authored books - she is living life to the full and giving everyone a glimpse into what's possible.

Declan Dowling CEO Beliefelevators Ltd.

P.S. Ana gives a fantastic 'heart hug'!

Working alongside Ana has enabled me to not only increase my financial account, but also to increase my financial awareness, knowledge and my confidence. I love that Ana is always there to guide and support me through each step of learning the techniques and applying her teachings to increase my financial freedom, whilst still allowing me to be in control and make decisions that are aligned with my goals.

Ana is a fantastic facilitator and I am forever grateful for the freedom and awareness that she has provided, allowing me to have the financial freedom that I desire.

Amy, Conscious Success Ltd.

I met Ana 2 years ago and knew little about the stock market and nothing about options trading. Thanks to Ana and the people that she works with, that has all changed. I now make my living from trading options.

I retired in 2020 with no pension. I knew I had to find a way to create an income and thanks to Ana, I have done that. Her patient and methodical training have shown me how to identify strong companies whose shares are likely to increase in value and trade options on them. She showed me how to select companies whose share would be most likely to give me a supplementary income and other stocks that would be more likely to give me long-term growth and benefit from the power of compound interest.

It has been an interesting and profitable journey that I could not have made without the support of Ana and her team. Thank you Ana, I wish I had met you 20 years ago. 😊

Paul Butterworth, retired

I grew up in a family where money was always tight and ended up with a poverty mentality that remained with me throughout my life. As I walked to college, I used to dream about winning the lottery and what I would do with the money!!!

I am now a member of two investment clubs and also have a small investment account myself. The experience of being in the investment clubs has given me the courage to start investing by myself. The clubs are a safe environment in which to learn and grow your knowledge, share experiences and ask questions. I have made some very good friends in them and it is good to be around other people who have a shared interest in investing and growing their knowledge in this area. Ana supports the clubs very well and answers any questions patiently and willingly shares her knowledge for the benefit of all of us.

I have attended many training events where Ana is delivering the training. The methodology for choosing the stocks to invest in is well explained and logical. The emphasis is on value investing in stocks that meet the strict criteria and are worth investing in long-term. Ana has many years of experience in trading and explains complex issues in a way that makes sense and is easily understood.

By being part of the clubs I feel that I am investing in my long-term future for me and my family to help me to reach financial freedom. It also helps me to educate my children on a different mentality and hopefully escape from the poverty mindset that has pervaded my life. My hope is that the investments will allow my family to live a better life and allow me to be financially free when I am older. I will have succeeded if any of my children get to understand how the financial investing works and apply it in their own lives.

For myself, I would love to set up a philanthropic trust that is self perpetuating forever more by continuing to invest and use the proceeds from the fund for charitable causes such as modular housing, renovation of older derelict houses to get them back into use and support for women and families looking to escape from abusive and coercive relationships. I would name it after my father, who was a builder by trade. If I could get this off the ground then my life would be transformed! But the foundation stone (pun intended 😁) of this plan is first of all to understand the investment approach that Ana teaches and then apply it in philanthropic work.

Mae Sullivan, CEO

Ana: I think your trading is absolutely fantastic. You are an amazing trader and an amazing person and I've been privileged and honoured to learn your system under yourself and Owen, a system from which I can get an residual income and I can teach my children. Thank you so much.

The system that you have is the best system I've ever seen in my life and that's after been involved in many companies and businesses. I know I'll be doing this for the rest of my days and that's down to you and Owen and your guidance and being patient with me through the ups and downs. I've been involved in many different businesses and organisations and this is, by far, the best system I've ever seen.

A big part of trading is patience and discipline and I think you have all that. Your patience is unbelievable, like the way you wait for all the indicators to be in the right position. You also trade with a conservative view, which is brilliant, and teach to keep your buying power from 60 to 70%.

Thank you.

Paul, trader for 20 years

Freedom is one of my biggest values and that is exactly what Ana has given me in my life through her teachings and financial freedom vehicle! Ana has not only provided a vehicle to create generational wealth for me and my family, but she has taught me how to drive it too…

The consequences have been a significant upgrade in the quality of life, which has helped me become a better father and husband to!

Ana understands that true wealth is a composite of financial freedom, emotional freedom, mental freedom, physical freedom and spiritual freedom. The systema and her teachings are so complete it's perfect for everyone, from beginner to master.

Aaron, Conscious Success Ltd.

Ana's dedication and enthusiasm for her subject is inspiring. Her style of teaching, together with her commitment to personal development in general, creates an excellent environment in which to learn.

As the world around us evolves so quickly, it is important to have the right team in place for continuous development and Ana is ideally placed to provide that type of support. I look forward to working with her and sharing much success in the years ahead.

Andrew Morgan – Event Manager

I first met Ana in 2020 when discussing the possibility of running US Share Investment Groups with her. Since then, I have started five investment groups with Ana being one of the coaches.

Ana has a structured and logical way of working through investment data and a good eye for detail and number crunching.

She has the ability to break down complex strategies into simple stories making it fun for clients to learn and remember important points.

Ana has extraordinary patience by repeating processes until clients are able to understand and copy.

Really grateful to Ana for all the support she has given me and my clients.

Karen Newton, Wealth Coach

Disclaimer

We are not acting here as stockbrokers, broker dealers, or registered investment advisers. The stock market is a highly speculative arena. Many people lose money in the stock and options markets.

We don't recommend particular stocks, bonds, options, derivatives or securities of any kind. All price information pertaining to securities are subject to minute-to-minute market changes. If particular stocks are mentioned, they are mentioned only for illustrative and educational purposes.

The information in this book is intended to provide you with basic financial instruction regarding your personal investing and financial welfare. It is recommended that you seek a professional licensed stock broker and independent financial adviser prior to implementing any investment programme or any financial plan. However, we do not recommend the retention of any specific broker, dealer, advisers or financial planners.

We don't guarantee any results or investment returns based on the information you receive. Although we have used our best efforts to provide the most accurate and innovative option trading and investment strategies, we cannot promise your future profitability and do not promise verbally or in writing that you will earn a profit when or if you purchase stocks or options. Ultimately, all decisions are made by you and you are the only one liable for doing whatever you decide to do.

There is risk of loss in all trading and investing. Past performance is not necessarily a guide to future performance and all investment can go down as well as up. You should read the Chicago Board of Options Exchange booklet, entitled *Characteristics and risks of standardized options* before trading options. You should understand the risks in option trading including the fact that any time an option is sold, there is unlimited risk of loss, and when an option is purchased, the entire premium is at risk. In addition, any time an option is purchased or sold, transaction costs, including brokerage and exchange fees are at risk. No representation is made regarding the success of our recommendations or that any account is likely to achieve profits or losses similar to those shown, or in any amount. Any account may experience different results depending on the timing of trades and account size. Trading is risky, and many traders lose money. Before trading, one should be aware that with the potential for profits, there is also potential for losses which may be large. All opinions are subject to change without notice.

Without limiting the rights under copyright reserved above, no part of this book material may be reproduced, stored in or introduced into a retrieval system, or transmitted, in any form, or by any means (electronic, mechanical, photocopying, recording, or otherwise), without the prior written permission of the copyright owner of this material.

The author of this book does not dispense medical advice or prescribe the use of any technique as a form of treatment for physical, emotional or medical problems without the advice of a physician, either directly or indirectly. The intent of the author is only to offer information of a general nature to help you in your quest to become financially free. In the event that you use any of the information in this book for yourself, which is your constitutional right, the author and the publisher assume no responsibility for your actions.

THE LONG AND WINDING ROAD

What our community says.. 7

Disclaimer.. 15

Index 17

What's in it for you?... 19

Learn from my mistakes!... 23

Do you want to be a millionaire?...................................... 25

The trip to wealth.. 33

A 20 year plan to become a millionaire............................. 51

What's on the way of your wealth?.................................... 63

1.   **Investing for beginners**...................................... 75

    1.1. You can do it..85
    1.2 Introducing… Value Line!....................................96
    1.3. Picking quality companies................................. 101
    1.4. Picking high value stocks 138
    1.5. Buy low and sell high. Time horizon: 3-5 years.... 179
    1.6. Buy low and sell high. Time horizon: 18 months ... 182

2.   **Why the stock market** 185

    You deserve wealth. Or do you not?.......................... 195

3.   **Increasing the returns**...................................... 201

    3.1 Technical analysis 201
    3.2 Give me a break!... 239
    3.3 Buying cheaper: puts... 243
    3.4 Selling dearer: calls 281
    3.5 Accelerated RoI's: ride the waves 312

4.   **Increasing the returns even more: OPM**............ 317

     4.1 Margin and buying power 318
     4.2 Releasing buying power: lids.................................. 340
     4.3 Managing puts... 353

5.   **Mistakes I made** 389

6.   **Trick or treat**... 431

7.   **Real examples: bull, bear and both markets** 447

8.   **Consortiums vs going solo** 451

9.   **More advanced strategies** 459

10.   **Access to information** 467

11.   **FAQs** 477

12.   **Summary**... 497

13.   **Annex**... 499

15.   **Deepest gratitud to…** 505

16.   **Other books by the author**.................................... 507

17.   **Bibliography and links** 513

18.   **Notes**.. 515

If you don't find a way to make money while you sleep,
you will work until you die.
Warren Buffett

What's in it for you?

This book is about making money.

My expertise of wealth creation is in the stock market. Therefore, this is the field I will refer to because I have the experience, which means I know how to do it and, also, how *not* to do it.

Let's start by saying that making money in the stock market is really, really easy: buy low and sell high.

We can represent this basic and simple principle in a nice and neat figure as the one you will see at the turn of this page:

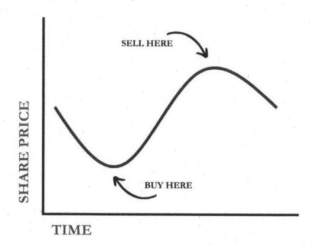

If it is this easy, why isn't everyone rich? Because YOU stand in the way.

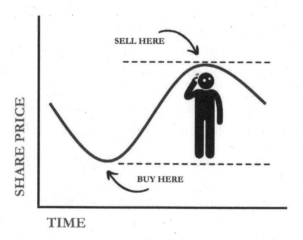

The way I see it, there are two main components in investing: psychology (us and our stuff) and mechanics (the practicalities of actual trading in the market).

When I started applying the mechanics, I achieved financial freedom in less than one year. Holding the wealth, though, proved to be not so easy and that's how the universe, in its infinite wisdom, gave me the opportunity to learn the lessons I needed to learn to be able not only to make money, but also to grow it and to keep it. It's time now to share these learnings with you hand in hand: both the psychology and the mechanics.

Psychology: we'll travel through the intricacies of our behavioural style, our beliefs about money and our relationship with it.

Mechanics: we'll go through the journey of making money in the market from zero to hero in a very simple, stepped approach in a way that makes sense to me, little by little so the foundations get to be strong.

I learned most of the mechanics that I'll share with you from TICN Ltd., a teaching company founded and CEO'ed by Owen O'Malley, my partner in business and life, to whom I'm deeply grateful

?

Learn from other people's mistakes.
Life is too short to make them all yourself.
Sam Levenson

Learn from my mistakes!

My journey to wealth has been a journey of discovery.

I used to think life was totally random, that stuff happened and some guys were just luckier than others.

Then, I realised that there were patterns that repeated themselves and, if we were awake enough to see them, we then had a say and could choose what to do with that information.

I have decided to come out of the closet, share my successes and my mistakes not only from a logical and mental point of view, but also from an esoteric and a spiritual perspectives.

Intelect, spiritualism and money: that's my offer.

As John Bogle said: *Learn every day, but eespecially from the experiences of others. It's cheaper!*

Please, google him so as to know why it would be worth your while to listen to this man's words.

This is what Warren Buffet said about him: *If a statue is ever erected to honor the person who has done the most for American investors, the hands down choice should be Jack Bogle.*

Start with the end in mind. If you want to be a millionaire, talk like one, act like one, work like one.

Bob Proctor

Do you want to be a millionaire?

Today is the 12th of February of 2023. I turned 57 one month and one day ago. Although I am not a millionaire yet, I am close enough to say with a high degree of certainty that I will be one this time next year.

My definition of millionaire is owning at least one million dollars or euros in cash or assets that can be turned into cash within a couple of days. Property, art, jewels... wouldn't be included here.

I have encountered numerous hurdles to get to the point where I am today and I feel this urgency inside to share them with you... to save you time!

This book is, of course, about making money. In particular, about the brick walls you encounter time after time, standing between you and wealth. Because, dear friend, making money is very simple. In my area, which is the stock market, it is as simple as buy low and sell high, as we stated before. The one-million-dollar question is: **why aren't we all millionaires?**

After decades of study, observation and action, I have come to the conclusion that there are many layers influencing our life experiences. I find the *we are all one* expression very meaningful now: the more we look inside of us, the more we can sense and understand the connection among us all.

I'm also starting to grasp the concept of *timelessness*. Although entropy keeps working on our bodies and we get wrinkles as the calendar moves forward, there is also this other inmaterial stuff that affects what we perceive as *the present moment*, in which nothing exists, yet everything can happen, that emanates from all the quantum soup that we add to with our thoughts and emotions, a soup whirling around in an omnipresent pot that contains all that is and all that could be.

Thank you for allowing me to go all philosophical! I promise you to stay very down to earth from here onwards. Or not. 🤔 We'll see.

Who doesn't like a good story, with a beginning, a middle and an end?

An uncomplicated way to contemplate events is to follow this temporal line of past, present and future, with a future that is nowhere and a present that turns into past the split second that it *is*.

Now, I am not so sure of this sequence of events happening in this order. What if in the past we imagined a future as if it had already existed and then we get to experience it in a present that will immediately turn into past? Then... The past is the future and the future is the past.

I feel quite confident now, though, that the experiences I went through were necessary so the vision that I had of my future when I was a little girl could happen.

If you approached me and ask me for some wisdom to share, I would suggest you looked into what you enjoyed the most as a young child, what your likes and gifts were and also what your challenges were.

In my opinion, those challenges came together with the gifts and by overcoming the aforementioned challenges, you grew. Sharing the experience with others by using your gifts is when fulfilment comes.

Just to pinpoint the start of my journey into wealth somewhere, I'll place it when my children were very young. They were born in 2000 and 2002, so you can picture a calendar in your head. In 2000, I was 34.

Some pre framing, though, to put things into perspective: At a very young age, thanks to the play both my money was a crucial part of the everyday life of our family unit.

My father would bring a thin manilla envelope every month that he handled to my mother. Every month, she opened it with hope and the light in her eyes would vanish almost immediately as she quickly counted the notes.

Those notes represented a fraction of what he was making. The rest, he would keep in the bank for... Well, he died and we still haven't figured out what was that emergency that kept us at bay from enjoying ourselves a little. No clue either what it would be like to live with less restrictions.

She would complain every month that there wasn't enough there for the kind of food he wanted to eat, and that prices kept increasing while the content in the envelops stayed the same. To no avail.

He would be fed as he wanted to and my mother and I ate what she could afford to buy with the remaining.

I won't even try to describe the fights, the swear words that I think would burn the paper you are looking at now as harsh as they were, the violence, the fear those scences created in me. The panic. The shivers of pure horror.

Looking back, I reflected on the fact that she would always comply with his demands on his menu, so, why would he bothered increasing the allowance, right? She would just shave the expenses off from our food and everything else, he didn't seem to care.

But it was only decades after that I would discover this disfunctional relationship between them. For whatever the reason, and we'll go into more detail as the story develops, they both fed the drama, dancing to the same tune, as if an invisible orchestra was playing it for their souls to move in rhythm with the music although, from the outside, it looked more like a lioness and a gazelle in a Roman circus. These are my memories, though, not reality.

Those few notes in the envelope didn't cover clothes, shoes or any amenities. To buy them, my mother would work in what she could: scwing, cleaning or looking after old people or children with special needs.

As for me, I was offered my first job at seventeen, when a neigbour knocked on the door and asked me to give her son private tuition. I already thanked Celia and her son Eduardo in my previous book and I won't miss the opportunity to thank them here again for the chance of exchanging my talent as a teacher by a tool that allowed me to have access to things and experiences I couldn't reach otherwise: money.

I haven't stopped making money ever since. What has radically changed has been the reasons behind it and, in particular, the emotions and energy that fuel the actions towards getting it.

I'm writing this book because I need to. I desperately need to put out there all the words that I have been keeping inside of me for so long, mainly not to annoy someone and to conform with what is considered rational. I'm done with playing small. I'm done with bottling up the genie inside of me. I'm done with walking on eggshells not to make others feel small. I'm done with listening to those who say there's no need for another book in times when people don't read anymore. I'm done with not fully follow what my heart wants. And my vision is that reading these words will awake the giant within you too.

My fingers strike this keyboard with the unshakeable determination of allowing my true self to flow, naked and raw. Very freeing! You try yourself with whatever speaks to you: singing, jumping, screaming, painting, cooking, gardening…

I would love that you could benefit from my experience so it can short-cut your journey to that place where your soul is pulling you towards. Because, let's face it, between our dreams and goals out there and the spot where we are stading here, it is normally time and money that stand in the way.

Making money takes time. It makes sense that if we can make money in a more efficient way, we will have the time (and resources) to walk our path faster.

I know that my experience can help you. I've cut a path in the jungle and faced many demons. Use my experience. Save time. Make more of your dreams happen. Dream bigger. Inspire by just being. Be you.

It wouldn't be very far fetched to say that most people would like to have more money. However, when it comes to individuals who consider themselves spiritual, it is quite common to find certain dissonance between such spirituality and money.

The famous verse from the bible «I'll say it again- it is easier for a camel to go through the eye of a needle than for a rich person to enter the kingdom of God! », Matthew 19:24, has had a big effect in a considerable number of mortals.

Even though a needle is a gate and a camel is not a dromedary, this idea that the doors of heaven can be closed for those who die in posesion of a lot of cash and stuff money can buy has been engrained in our operational system in such a way that, unconsciously, many of us have been devoted to keeping riches well away in an attempt to increase our chances of a nice existance in the afterlife. Just in case!

Everything I'll be sharing here is based on my interpretation of my experiences. As you read them, you'll filter them through your own. It's all good.

Please, bear in mind that my words are true to me and make sense in my own universe. It would be fantastic, that's the goal, that they would instill some aha moment, a little spark to light your own fire in your own universe.

Enjoy!

Money is like a sixth sense without which you cannot make a complete sense of the use of the other five.
W. Somerset Maugham

The trip to wealth

Imagine you are planning a trip to New York and that you have never been there.

You can go online (does anyboday use travel guides anymore?), find places you want to visit and shows or events you would like to attend.

When you set your feet on Liberty Island, you might discover that the statue of Liberty is taller than you expected, that the water line is closer than you thought it would be, that the place was too crowded for you to fully enjoy the experience of the visit or all the above.

However, the statue is there, on an island from where you can see the south of Manhattan.

What you didn't probably forsee was what it would feel like sitting down at the feet of the statue, the smells around you, the ideas that populated your mind while being there, the emotions flowing at arrival to this destination point you planned in advance.

Perhaps you had to delay the trip because something came up. Maybe you caught a cold the day before. Your suitcase arrived at your hotel two days later. It is a rainy day.

You fixed your destination and move towards it facing whatever came your way. When you got there, Ms. Liberty was bigger or fatter or greener than you expected, but… you got to see it!

The journey with wealth is no different: the long-term destination point could be making enough money for this trip to New York you always wanted to take or it could be resigning from your job. It is whatever you want it to be and as many destinations as you wish to get to are available for you.

Ralph Seger eloquently summarised this concept as follows: *An investor without investment objectives is like a traveler without destination.*

There will be hurdles in the journey and cots to be paid for. The question is: how will you face them? Will you give up even before you start? Will you head back at the mere sight of a tiny pebble under your foot?

The way we behave is hugely, if not fully, influenced by our childhood.

This is today. The future has not been written yet and we are the only ones to paint the picture of what we want it to look like. Since the thread of this book is money, we can start by have a clear vision of where we are… financially, the same way that we need to know what country we will be flying from to get to New York.

Let me be clear: *My wages are 3,650 a month* is not specific enough. We need to know also how much we are spending.

We can start with something simple. Don't panic if you don't know how to use a spreadsheet; a pen and a notebook will do.

I think this is a great moment to disclose that this book is not a self-help book, nor a *shelf*-help book, but a bootcamp book.

$$$

I know that it is just easier to just keep reading than to get up and do an exercise, but no one got to Liberty Island from the comfort of their sofa, right?

Exercise 1

Defining where we are

I can already feel some of you shaking at the mere thought of numbers in front of you. You can relax, because I'm going to make really easy. Just like an illiterate child, let's start with the ABC and, as you get more confident, you'll be able to write words, phrases, assays and even poetry. I like this example and you can tell, right?

Please, write down these two figures:

1. *This is how much I* **make** *a month*:

   ....

2. *This is how much I* **spend** *a month*:

   ....

$$$

If the first figure is greater than the second one, congratutions! Celebrate! We'll see what we can do with the surplus.

If the first one is less than the the second one, consider applying some adjustments.

If you don't have any idea of how much you make and/or how much you spend, dig into it, as scary as it may be.

Now it is when you monkey mind starts saying: *I can't imagine how expensive things are getting, my paycheck is smaller every time…* And I agree. It is what it is. Now: can we change something?

A comment that we usually hear about money is *I don't know where it went!* That's an easy question to answer! Optics. We need optics.

For one month, you are going to write down **all** your expenses. **ALL OF THEM**.

Whether you pay with cash, your watch, app, card, directly through your bank account or any other way, write all your expenses down. Yes: you can use your phone instead of a notebook, although there is something kinestetic about writing the old-fashioned way.

Be as specific as possible. For instance: if you buy groceries, review what you are buying. At least, divide in two columns: *Necessary* and *Treats*. It is my understanding that vegetables correspond to the first category and beer and biscuits, to the second.

This is a brilliant start. At the end of the month, you will have real figures that will give you clarity of where you are standing. As you add up more months, the picture will be clearer, as broken washing machines, unexpected taxes or wedding presents and holidays are included in the tally.

I am pretty sure that this simple exercise will help you make decisions that will benefit your financial health and maybe even your physical health. Maybe you can save a bit by switching off the lights you don't need, cancelling subscriptions you don't make use of, going out a bit less or just taking the dessert at home instead of having it at the restaurant.

At the end of the chapter, I'm sharing with you the first one my husband and I used. We were planning to build up our house and didn't know what mortgage we could afford, so we started by creating a dashboard to give us some clarity. Note: the biggest chunk of our expenses was travelling. We had no clue! A few years on, it turned to be our children's education. But that's another story.

With this very simple exercise you have learned a few things:

1. You know how much money is coming in and how much money is going out.

2. You know that, to make progress, the money coming out should be less than the money coming in.

3. You have learned about your expending habits and have already figured out a way of decreasing the flow of money going out but doing some cutting that won't change your lifestyle much, but, financially, it will make a big difference.

Exercise 2

Let's have fun

Close your eyes, breath deep a few times, until you feel calm, and ask yourself the following question: *What would I do if I had all the money I could dispose of?*

Open your eyes and start writing. Go big. Go crazy. There are no restrictions: if you want to rent the Eiffel tower to propose, write it down. Everything goes.

Feel free to use the space below:

....

....

....

....

....

....

....

....

....

....

While you comute or do the laundry or wait for the traffic lights to go green, keep thinking of other things you would do or buy if you had a bottomless bank account and add them to your list.

How does it feel?

Before you go asleep every night, visit one or more of those items in your list and *feel* yourself enjoying them. With all your senses.

What does it feel to be on a yacht in the Caribbean? What can you smell? Who are you with? Are you enjoying interesting conversations while seeing the sun go down? Are there dolphins swimming beside the hull of your boat? Can you hear the sea birds screeching? Can you feel the salt on your skin? Or the stickiness of the sunblock? Are you having a delicious meal? What is it you are tasting? What emotions are you feeling? Accomplishment? Empowerment? Joy? Gratitude? Love? Bliss? Abundance?

If this sounds like the law of attraction, it is because that's exactly what it is. There is a lot of science behind it, though. It works whether you believe in it or not, just like gravity.

Knowing how it works will allows to get some results or others, just like by knowing about Physics makes possible that something as heavy as an airplane flying, while absolutely none of its components can stay airborne by itself.

The exercise of practicing in our minds while in a relaxed state, involving all of our bodily senses is extremely powerful and is the first step of creation.

If you want some science, I'd invite you to read or watch some videos of Dr. Jean Pierre Garnier Mallet. He has published all the formulas that prove the existence of what he calls *the quatum double*. The experiments carried out over the years also prove his theory.

The way I understand it with very simple words is as follows.

To make things easy to see with our mind's eye, let's imagine that your quantum double (QD) looks exactly like you. It moves at lighting speed and, for that reason, you can't see it while awake. However, in that state in which we are right before falling asleep (alpha brainwaves), we perceive it and we engage in a conversation.

–Hey, dear QD –says your regular you– Can you, please, find me the quickest way to make more money a month?

–Of course! –answers your quantum double–. Give me details.

–Well… I want 1,000 more per month. In return – you continue–, I would like to do something related to writing, because I love it and I can do from home, in my own time. I write about topics that I already know a lot about and I will learn new things as well.

–How does that make you feel?

–Delighted, empowered, grateful, generous and wealthy.

–On my way! –your quantum double will say.

Your QD now has a clear vision of what is it that you wish to figure out, reach, invent, experience… What we know as *let me sleep on it.*

The QD moves at or faster than the speed of light and travels from your bed to the next quantum horizon, that is, the first stept towards you getting to your objective. It joins the first dot, to put it in Steven Job's words.

It could be meeting a school classmate you haven't heard of for a while who tells you about the presentation of this book happening in a week.

Your QD now scans all the possible outcomes of you attending this book presentation, that is, the possible futures if you get there one minute late, if you go to the toilette 30 seconds before or after, if someone spills a drink on you or not... Like *Sliding Doors* (Peter Howitt's movie).

There are millions of decisions we can take and each one is going to produce a different outcome in our lives. Each one will take us to different horizons.

What QD does at night (it also works during the day, don't you think) is that it visits all the possibilities. It sees the different futures and comes back to us with the one or ones that will bring us to our destination faster or easier... Or the opposite. It all depends on the commands.

That's why those who say that making money is easy will seem to attract it as if by magic and those who believe that money comes through very hard work will indeed work a lot to get it.

We'll get notions, inclinations, ideas, an *I don't know why, but* feeling that you need to go, say or do something, even if it doesn't seem to make any sense.

Those are the crumbs that your QD is leaving behind for you.

This way, you can work together with your QD, or a bunch of them, follow your intuition, or screaming clues that would be presented to you, and keep joining the dots for you to get there, whatever or wherever *there* is.

If you have this book in your hands, you were probably looking for some clues of what to make grow the money you have in your bank doing nothing, apart from shrinking year after year, or you got the notion of learning about finances for yourself or for your children to get an education in a topic that touches us all and no one ever taught us anything about. Perhaps you repeatedly saw yourself travelling the world and making money on the go by pressing a few keys on a keyboard or screen. Whatever the case, you are in front of the information you precisely wanted to get.

Exercise 3

To do in bed

Talk to your quantum double. Even give it a name, if you like.

It will go and travel while you are asleep anyway. However, you can direct it to go into the direction of paving the floor to reach the next goals you set and experiences you wish to have. If you don't share your ideas with it, it will go and use what your mind is very busy with: *what a big, fat cow you are, unable to eat less; work is horrible and workmates are a pest; I can't stand living with spouse anymore.* Whatever it is, your QD will find the way to get it: spare tire around your mid body, despiteful workmates, horrible spouse, a nightmarish job or the wonderful relationship or the house you always dreamt of if your thoughts are going this way. Whatever.

Write below the answer you wish to get when you wake up, or the desire you wish to fulfil or whatever you want to accomplish. Then, in the morning and every day after, follow the clues and take action!

$$$

Example of exercise 1:

My husband and I, when we planned to build our home, started tracking our money coming into the household and our monthly expenses as a financial starting point.

These are concepts we tracked at the beginning of our tiny financial self-learned education:

- Household
  - Food
  - Pets: food and veterinary
  - Electricity
  - Phone
  - Water and rubbish
  - Household (cleaning stuff, bulbs, etc.)
  - Clothes and shoes
  - Heating
  - Insurance
  - Taxes
  - Property taxes
  - Garden
  - Presents: birthdays, anniversaries, weddings, babies… Both within the nuclear family and outside
  - Others: things to be replaced or repaired

- Cars

  - Payments to buy a car, if applicable
  - Insurance
  - Maintenance
  - Fuel
  - Others: cark park, tolls

- Health

  - Consultations
  - Medicines or alternatives
  - Sports
  - Hairdresser and barber

- Education

  - Books, CDs, etc.
  - Courses
  - Others

- Leisure

  - Going out
  - Travelling
  - Cinema and entertainment
  - Other activities

- Others

  o Stuff outside the previous categories. If it repeated, it would get a new entry

Over time, as we became parents, the children's tab was added, including food if different to ours, education, clothes and shoes, nappies, health, leisure…

Do your own. It can be a lot more or less detailed, with the categories that suit you better. You can always modify it over time.

I would like to highlight that there was no entry whatsoever for *investment* and there was none either to give away. Those concepts weren't part of our reality. Live and learn!

Planning is bringing the future into the present
so that you can do something about it now.
Alan Lakein

A 20-year plan to become a millionaire

Let's start with a bit of action. We'll talk about mindset and all the rest of it later, but unless you can see that the numbers make sense, this could as well be another book about making money that will look nice on your shelf.

Which is NOT. It isn't! We already established that. This is a book that you can start applying NOW.

Let me tell you that one of my gifts is my ability to explain complex things in a very simple way that anyone can understand. Therefore… Feel free to relax.

I understand how tight for time we all are and how tough it could be to try and push new information into our fatigued brains.

Please, bear with me and, even if you suck at Math, look at the following formula, which is the path to making 1 million, as an example, yet easy to remember:

2,000

200

2%

20

1 MILLION

And this is how you read the formula to yourself: *If I start investing 2,000, add 200 per month thereafter and make it grow at 2% a month, I'll be a millionaire in 20 years.*

2% **a month** might be a bit of a stretch for you to believe that it can be done, as that amounts to a 26.82% compound per year.

Since 2012, I've been immersed in the stock market. This is my expertise, so, please, let me show you how a 2% on average per month is achievable.

Before you panic at the mere mention of *stock market*, let me assure you that <u>anyone</u> can make money in it, because we, humans, can learn anything we put our minds to learn.

I think we've heard it all when it comes to the beliefs people have about the stock market. Allow me to share a few of them here:

- You need a lot of money to invest
- It's very difficult and complicated
- It takes a lot of time
- It's risky
- It's a gamble
- You need a financial background

Other common beliefs our members have shared with us would be:

- It's for men
- It's for those who are good with figures
- It's a zero sum game, that is: if I win, that's because someone else is losing
- 20 years!

That being said, others' views are more optimistic:

- It's fun
- It's a great opportunity to make money easily
- It's the base of capitalism, so, long-term, you can't lose
- It's the easiest and more time efficient way to invest
- You can make money while you are sleeping
- You can live anywhere, as long as you have an Internet connection
- Anyone can do it from anywhere

Please, write down your own beliefs about the stock market:

....

....

....

....

....

....

....

....

....

....

....

They are just beliefs and perceptions and they are linked to emotions. They aren't necessarily true.

Taking investing decisions based on emotions proves to be not the best idea. I can affirm this as per my own experience and quoting no less that Mr. Warren Buffett, who shared in one of his AGM's that he never based his decisions to invest in anything else but facts.

To quote him: *Investing requires qualities of temperament way more than it requires qualities of intellect.*

For the moment, though, let's just focus on how it would have been possible to make a 28% profit (more than the 2% a month of our initial plan) in 2022, while the market fell nearly 20% in the same period.

Let me give you a two-paragraph crash course on buying and selling the market as a whole.

Paragraph 1: When people talk about *the market*, they normally refer to the Standard & Poors 500 index (SP-500), which is a measure of what 500 companies, representing all the industries, are doing. You can buy what is called SPY, which is an *index* that moves like the SP-500. In a nutshell, you can be buying and selling 500 companies spread over ca. 100 industries in one go.

Paragraph 2: If you look at the following chart of the SPY, you see some curves underneath. They are some *indicators* called *stochastics*. As a first approximation, you buy when they are underneath the line at 20 and start turning up and you sell when they are above the line at 80 and start turning down.

After this crash course, we are able to pick when to buy and when to sell. Would you agree with the following entry (buy) and exit (sell) points in the circles?

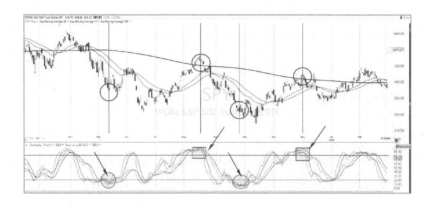

Excel time!

Relax... Let me read you the first bit so you understand where everything is coming from and, thus, following the next movements will be easy peasy.

After the crash course, we identified two points where the stochastics where under the lower line of 20 and pointed up, towards crossing the line upwards, as marked with circles in the image above, and two other points where the stochastics pointed down, crossing the upper line down of 80, identified with rectangles.

We placed our trades during those times, as summarised in the following table:

Date	Price	Action	Units	Money	Profit
12/08/2022	392	Buy	100	- 39,200	
18/08/2022	428	Sell	100	42,800	3,600
29/09/2022	363	Buy	118	- 42,800	
01/12/2022	407	Sell	118	47,988	5,188
Total profit					8,788
Total profit, %					22.4%

To make thing easy, we don't consider the cost of placing the trades. We use the closing price the days of consideration. Prices are in USD, $, whose symbol I prefer to omit so we can see the figures more clearly.

12/08/2022: A low point was identified. The price was 392 and we bought 100 shares. The cost was:

$$392 \; x \; 100 \; = \; 39,200$$

Since it is a **cost**, the negative sign is shown in the table.

On the 18/08/2022, a high point was identified. The price was 428. We sold all our shares at this price, thus:

$$428 \; x \; 100 \; = \; 42,800$$

Since our investment was 39,200, we have made 3,600 of profit.

Now, we have 42,800 to buy shares, which we used for our next trade, placed on 29/09/2022.

Because we have more money now, and, also, because the shares are cheaper, we can buy 118 (round figure). We then sold the shares at 407.

In short, our *investment* was 39,200 and we walk out with 47,988. Therefore, the *profit* would be:

$$Profit = 47{,}988 - 39{,}200 = 8{,}788$$

We made 8,788 out of 39,900. To express the profit as a percentage:

$$ROI = \frac{8{,}788}{39{,}200} x \, 100 = \mathbf{22.4\%}$$

We've made 22.4% in a 4-month period. In the meantime, what did the SP-500 do? It went from 392 to 407. Let's calculate the growth:

$$Growth = \frac{407 - 392}{392} x \, 100 = \mathbf{3.8\%}$$

Interesting: while the SP-500 gained a net 3.8%, by identifying the low and high points, with just one extra trade, a 22.4% profit could be made.

In this example, the market went up (*bull* market), but the same procedure can be applied in a *bear* market, that is, when it goes down.

Let's look at the same chart a few months before:

Clearly, this is a bearish period. However, applying what we have just learned, these would be results:

Date	Price	Action	Units	Money		Profit
27/01/2022	431	Buy	100	-	43,100	
04/04/2022	456	Sell	100		45,600	2,500
12/08/2022	392	Buy	116	-	45,600	
18/08/2022	428	Sell	116		49,648	4,048
Total profit						**6,548**
Total profit, %						**15.2%**

15.2% profit in a market that went from 431 to 428, that is, -0.7%.

$$Growth = \frac{428 - 431}{431} \; x \; 100 = \mathbf{-0.7\%}$$

If we consider the price when this trend started, signalled by the arrow on the left in the previous figure, the decrease of the SPY from the 5th of January to the 18th of August 2022 would be:

$$Growth = \frac{428 - 468}{428} x\ 100 = -9.3\%$$

Very interesting: while the SPY went **down** 9.3%, applying basic knowledge, a **15.2% profit** can be made in the same period of 7 months, which is a **2.2%** average growth per month.

During a bullish period, we made 22.4% in 4 months, which is **5.6%** on average per month.

And… Yes: In my experience, making money in bullish markets is easier than in bearish markets. It makes sense, doesn't it? Still, we can make money in bearish markets, which it could be something you didn't know one chapter ago.

In summary, you can become a millionaire by only investing 2,000 to begin with, 200 every month and making an average of 2% per month.

We've been talking about *shares*, which are pieces of companies. That's all they are! They are also known as *stocks* and *equities*.

When you own shares of a company, you are a partial owner of that company.

The birth of a share is called *IPO* (initial public offering). The buyers become shareholders and hold a portion of the company's ownership, along with the right to vote (in the case of *voting shares*) and the right to receive dividends, if the company does so.

Mostly, we deal with shares, although the principles we teach are applicable to other products, such as exchange-traded funds (ETFs), indexes, etc. This is jut a note; not being to give a presentation about these items won't stop you from making money.

Of all the hurdles you will need to face in this lifetime,
the hardest will be your self-imposed limitations.
Jan Hellriegel

What's on the way of your wealth?

We have have already established that we all have certain beliefs around money.

It seems pretty straightforward that money will escape us if we believe that rich people take advantage of others, that we will lose our friends if we have way more money than they do or that possible partners will love us only because of our size of our bank account. If we are holding onto these kinds of beliefs, we'll figure out a way to keep money far away from us.

There are many beliefs, however, that we are not aware of. Call it beliefs, experiences or spells. Or call it information travelling through our DNA, the news or through the ether.

Let me share with you a couple of examples, one with my mother and the other one with my father, that had a huge impact on my financial thermostat and my relationship with money and wealth.

My father's story

I have already related this story in my book *Mother: Goodbye!* In case you've read it, know I won't do a copy/paste.

Saying that my father, deceased in 1995, was an angry man would be an understatement. You could argue that it would be very much of a judgemental observation from my part. And I agree. However, it is my conclusion after 27 years of never seeing him laugh, observing a non-stop frown, hearing him yelling as well as in complete silence for full months on end.

His bursts of outrage could be triggered by me falling asleep with the little light by the bed on or by dropping something on the floor by accident or by forgetting to place a napkin by his plate. Huge arguments could start, last for hours and end up by him not talking to my mother and me for months at a time, in which we knew to be quite and just float around the house unheard and unseen.

From him, I learned that he had the power and the last say about money and that everything in the house belonged to him, even our knickers.

From him, I learned that he deserved more and I was to be last.

From him, I learned that it took many years to make a bit of money and that money was to be saved in the bank for a rainy day (that he didn't get to see).

From him, I learned to live very cheap, well below our finances.

From him I learned that love, mistreatment and fear go together.

From him, I learned studing was important to be *someone* in life. I also learned that he would get furious whenever he felt threatened by the mere idea of me doing better than him or knowing more than him.

He would never acknowledge any of my achievements, no matter how remarkable they would be. Fantastic manure for an unhealthy sense of selfworth.

The day he saw a poster I had prepared for my first and only scientific congress, a mere collection of eight sheets of white paper with black charts on a red background, I though the veins in his neck would explode and his eyes would pop out of his eye sockets.

He was a draftsman and felt very proud of preparing such posters and slides for doctors back in the day when these presentations had to be done by hand. He felt so superior to those *men with a degree*! He just couldn't take it that a nobody just off college like me could do his job in such a short time with very little effort.

It is my belief that that very day I took the decision to never accomplish more than he ever did so I wouldn't piss him off and wouldn't provoke such rage. A vow more than a decision. Or a decree. Whatever the word to define it, the Universe freaking heard me and complied!

Another event happened when I was way younger, about seven or so. I was visiting my aunt and my cousin and I were outside playing with other kids.

A black dog showed up and there I went, as an animal lover I am.

The dog, very big for my size, sitting on his ass, seemingly relaxed, moved its head up and open its mouth as I pet it on its head. It bit me. There was no blood, just scratched skin on both sides of my hand.

My cousin, a bit older than me and probably feeling responsible, took me to my mom and aunt. They washed my hand and put on a couple of plasters that didn't stick. In my mind, no big deal.

When we got home, my mother decided to share the news with my father, who went ballistic in a nanosecond and yelled for what it seemed hours, cursing left, right and centre, threatening with killing the dog, ashaming the mayor and who knows what other cataclysmic measurements because it cannot be happening that a dog bites a girl. *His* girl.

To the long list of more than thirty different animals that have bitten me, including geese, swans, a squirrel and a penguin, my encounter with that poor animal whose life was now at stake because of the rage of my father was meaningless.

I think that this was another moment in which I declared to the universe my commitment to never ever get any close to a dog so that my father wouldn't get furiously enraged and, at the same time, the dogs of the world would be safe from being put down by any mayor.

In the summer of 2020, while the roads were quite empty and many hotels were closed, my partner and I went for a road trip all the way from Spain to the Czech Republic.

On that trip, I decided to unbury my father from the hole that I put him in they day he died, at the top of a hill, under five meters of concrete duly delivered by cement mixers (all in my mind's eye).

And that's how I went back to that hill. The trees in the area had grown a lot and the slab of concrete was fully covered by tall grass and flowers.

This time, I summoned a convoy of JCBs that broke down the concrete and excavated until the box where my father had been kept captive was brought to the surface.

When the box was opened, I made him an inch tall. That way, I wouldn't be so scared of him, knowing that I could step on him if he started acting out as he used to.

With this tiny little creature on the outside of the boot of the car, I went on a holiday with my father for the first time since I was thirteen.

My body still behaved as it used to when in his presence or just thinking of him: sweat, freezing cold, shivering, short breath, scanning all around with my eyes as if searching for a predator.

Little by little, one kilometer after the next, these memories from my body subsided until I felt confident enough to allow him to grow up to four inches tall.

After the summer, already at home, I went for a walk to the beach. I was doing some exercise about abundance and, suddenly, I sensed that my father was on a cloud and, from up there, he said to me: *Because I love you, I agreed to teach you the way I did, so that you would learn what abundance is.*

Note that "because I love you" is written in the present tense. That's exactly how I heard it.

While alive, he never said good morning to me. I'm being literal here. Never. Hearing him say *I love you* was a shock. So much so that I sat down on the sand because my legs refused to hold me up.

This was the first time that I wore his shoes: he had agreed to show me what abundance was by being an actor playing a part portraying 0.0% abundance. It was his way to bring my attention towards wealth, abundance manifested.

Only a huge amount of love would agree to play such a part! He didn't gain much love from anyone, I can tell you. Sad.

That December after his message from the clouds, I received more than thirty thousand euros. I had never made so much money in one month.

The year after, 2021, more than ten times this amount.

Funnily enough, the biggest amount was received on the 24th of June, anniversary of his death. The transferred arrived while we were in a hotel, the night before we flew to Bali for two whole months, quite a definition of paradise.

The stopper that was keeping the genious in me from getting out of the bottle seemed to be gone.

I'm at peace with my father. I sense the inmense amount of love he had for me, so much that he accepted to live quite a miserable life, go through a death cried by nobody and not being missed by anyone once he was gone.

This is as good a moment as any for you to revisit your past and link events that happened while growing up with situations that repeat themselves over and over in your actual life.

It could be very painful. I know. You can also relax, sitting down or walking, and allow your mind to go back in time, expecting nothing, in the certainty that nothing bad can happen to you. It could be very helpful to have someone with you *holding the space*, as they say, that is, acting as your support as you allow yourself to express and experience all those emotions you have been keeping inside for sooooo maaaaany yeeeeears.

My mother's story

As I mentioned before, I wrote a whole book about my healing process after being brought up by someone who seems to tick all the boxes when it comes to narcissistic behaviour.

It took me many years to be in a peaceful state when thinking about her and even being in front of her.

When you grow up with a mother who is constantly telling you how good, pretty, clever and super dupper she is and requiring recognition every step of the way, you end up… Exhausted, to begin with.

Because she is the best, you have no other option but to be less good. Or the worst. However, not being a top-notch quality daughter isn't good for her job as a mother, so you need to learn to be as good as possible at the same time you never cast a shadow over her.

I know! Really tricky!

Managing mother's expectations and behaving as per her ever-changing standards was a spinning plate I was trying to keep up on one hand while the other hand was very busy keeping up the second spinning plate of making sure the studies my father facilitated showed up enough, but not so much as to surpass his own achievements or sense of self-worth, which was kept a secret. What a circus!

When I realised my mother exhibited a narcissistic behaviour, that it wasn't me going crazy with her narrative of stating one thing and the opposite at the same time, both the absolute truth as by her paramenters, I was in my early fifties.

At this moment, I see myself on the other side. Why do I say this? Because when I know that I will be sharing the same space as her I don't think about with with fear months in advanced as I used to. Also, because I don't get sick afterwards. Not that I would vomit; I mean, specifically, allergic rhinitis, sinusitis and herpes episodes. All of them.

To get where I am now, I went through three stages as detailed in my previous book, *Narcissist mother:*

goodbye! Three steps to stop living under the shadow of the woman who believes she owns you.

Please, let me summarise them here for you:

1. Discovery

   A major depression after my first child was born led me into a process of reviewing my life and deeply analising what I wanted for that baby. The answer came as *to create a safe environment for him so he can live true to his essence.* I had no idea how to do that because I had been brought up to live up to my mother's expectations. Not only that, those expectations were meant to serve her, not me. That's my reading, anyway.

   I learned that her behaviour ticked most of the boxes of what is know as Narcissistic Personality Disorder or NPD.

2. Despair and tantrums: I went from the victimism of why me, a sadness so deep and raw that physically hurt my insides to rage and everything in between, blame being the star of the emotions, all of them seasoned with tons of guilt for not fulfilling the loving daughter role.

3. Oneness: if I were in her shoes, I would behave exactly the same way as she did and still does.

I saw her as a little girl for whom I could feel nothing but love and enormous gratitude towards her for playing the role she plays in this lifetime so that my soul experiences the emotions that it decided to learn. Only a huge amount of love can agree to live a life as a narcissist so I could learn my lessons.

1. INVESTING FOR BEGINNERS

Investment success doesn't come from "buying good things",
But rather from "buying things well".
Howard Marks

In my previous book *Empowered*, there is a whole chapter dedicated to wealth.

From it, I am rescuing here the dictionary definition of wealth: *Wealth is abundance of valuable possessions or resources and it is also abundant supply.* That is, both material and non-material stuff.

We have already established where we are financially and where we want to get to. Congratulations!

The next step is your why.

It is **crucial** that you know the reason behind investing in shares to make more money. Obviously, this can apply to any way to increase your finances, but since I don't have experience in others, I'll stick to what I know best: the stock market.

I'm going to tell you the story of how I found my why.

As already mentioned, I underwent what professionals call *major depression*. It isn't necessary to go into many details. However, something needed to be changed in my life and since our children were still very young and I had a huge desire to spend as much time with them as possible, my husband and I agreed on me quiting my career as a chemist altogether.

Stop making money has never been an option for me, so I tried different ways. The turning point was when I heard Deepak Chopra (it was his own voice in the audiobook of *Seven Spiritual Laws for Success*) say to his children to meditate and make sure they knew what their path was… And not to worry about money because he would be there to support them financially.

I'm paraphrasing, but this idea turned to be my why: what I wanted the most was for my children to grow their natural gifts and talents and I figured that an education parallel to the regular one would help them get there.

This *parallel education* took the shape of personal development and regular attendance to seminars about topic that school or even university do not always cover.

Today, I kissed my sons bye at Catania airport, in Sicily, where we have attended *The Science of Consciousness* congress from Monday to Saturday.

We have attended together many other seminars and courses like T. Harv Eker's *Millionaire Mind Intensive*, Tony Robbins' *Unleash the Power Within*, *Wealth Mastery* and *Health Mastery*, TICN's *Making Money with Careful Planning* and *El Dorado*, a cruise with Dr. Joe Dispenza and Anita Moorjani and many others, some by themselves.

Chopra's words really went deep and I felt such gratitude… that I wished to be able to tell him live how big an impact they had had in my children as time moved on and… Guess what? I did! He was delighted.

This is one of those happenings that don't seem plausible and, yet, it exists in the field of infinite possibilities.

Before this big why of choosing the education I wanted for my children, I had others, such as:

- Leave my parents' home.
- Be independent from them and from anyone else (including possible future husbands).
- Travel.

Your turn now: what is your BIG WHY? Write it down here:

MY WHY

Any others?

....

....

....

....

Some ideas that people from our community have shared with us include:

- To show my parents they were wrong
- To pay off debts
- For my brother-in-law to feel envious
- To leave my job and tell my boss what I really think of him/her

- To retire somewhere warm by the sea
- To buy my parents a house
- To have time to enjoy life
- To afford the time to do things that bring me joy
- To inspire others
- To feel safe

I see wealth as an abundance of experiences that can be verey well enhanced by an affluence of money.

I see money as **freedom** and as currency that can buy many, many things, including health and time.

Of course, we all die and, of course, there's no website or shop in the world where you can buy minutes. However, money can buy you high-quality food that will improve your health and give you the capacity to hire people or buy machines that will do things for you, thus freeing you from spending time on them. Not only you can buy time by paying others to do stuff for you, but you also contribute to prosperity by making money move. If you don't move it, what's the point? You could as well fake an account with as many zeros as you like and just imagine you own all that money.

I'm sure you've heard many times that money is energy and, for that reason, it's meant to move. Let me highlight it for you:

Money must move

I must confess that this part I found a bit difficult to practice, since I thought that the more I saved, the more I would have.

I learned that this belief was not universal. At all! It was true for those of us who can be adjetivised as *hoarders* or *savers*.

From *Secrets of a Millionaire Mind*, I learned that there are four main personalities when it comes to our relationship with money and most mortals fall into one of these categories. Let me briefly outline them here for you.

1. *Savers* or *hoarders*: they (we!) tend to spend as little as possible and to focus on building an egg nest for a rainy day. We never spend more than we make.

   Our eyes automatically go to the right-hand side of the menu and to the label hanging from the clothes.

2. *Spenders*: quite the opposite to the savers, they love buying things (that, mostly, they don't need), oblivious of the limit in their credit cards.

They tend to incur in a debt that keeps growing and have no plan to sort it out.

3. *Avoiders:* they live as if money had nothing to do with them. They leave all the money issues to others and and ignore everything about it.

No clue how much gets in and out of the household.

4. *Monks:* for them, money is linked to an earthly plane that doesn't have much to do with them.

Their bodies need maintenance, which is a nuisance.

What type describes your behaviour towards money more accurately and why? Remember that no one is judging you and that there is not right or wrong answer.

....

....

....

....

Although there is no right or wrong answer, no need to be a genius to see that any of these behaviours seems to be healthy.

As for becoming a millionaire, I can't see any of the last three types getting there. Perhaps the savers stand a chance, but they get no joy out of money.

In case you wonder, yes, there is a very simple 'treatment' to heal from these 'ailments'. It's as simple to apply as an ointment; it just requires a bit of discipline: the splits.

This is how you can apply it: get all the money you make per month, I would recommend using cash, at least at the beginning, and divide it in percentages as follows or slightly different as it is more relevant to you.

If you can't afford to apply it to the whole monthly income, do it with part of it.

1. **50% household**

   Rent or mortgage, electricity, phone, heating, water, groceries (not treats), clothes (necessary clothes and shoes), car, etc.

   And… No: eating out or driving to a summer resort don't belong in here.

2. **10% investing**

   If you are a bit nervous about investing in the stock market or if you will be investing a small amount, in our chapter 8, *Consortiums vs going solo*, we'll show you how you can be in the market with as little as 150USD or equivalent in your own currency.

3. **10% learning**

   The knowledge you have accumulated and the skills you have have brought you so far. To reach further, you will have to learn something more or something new. You can also take advantage of the knowledge and experience of a mastermind group like our consortiums.

4. **10% medium- or long-term plans**.

   You decide how to use this money. My first goal was to travel with my son Jaime to London and then, with my son Mario… Which took me 6 years! After that, my targets were met faster.

5. **10% leisure**. Blow money.

   The name gives it away. Anything that gives you joy and is not necessary for subsistence.

   I found this the toughest. I forced myself to spend this money within a maximum of three months, because, otherwise, I would save it! Spenders would tend to borrow this split from future months.

6. **10% tithing**

You can give this money away to a person or organisation of your liking. *What we give away, comes back tenfold.*

Once you are well trained in this system, you can choose to give away time as well as or instead of money.

1.1. You can do it

I know! Lots of blah, blah, blah so far and we still have no idea of where to start investing in shares.

Even if we have no idea at all about shares or companies, we can always apply common sense. All we need to know is our desired outcome: to sell something at a higher price than we bought it for. In very simple terms: buy low and sell high.

Since this is what we want, how will we lose money?

It seems pretty clear that if we make money by buying low and selling hight, there are two possibilities of losing money (biggest worry of any investor):

1. If the company that we buy goes bankrupt, therefore, there is nothing to sell and we lose everything we invested.

2. If we sell at a lower price than what we paid.

Since these are the two ways of losing money, it makes sense to:

a) Choose companies that won't go bankrupt.

b) Don't sell at a lower price than we paid.

Applying these two simple rules, we'll make money in the market!

The million-dollar question, quite literally, is then: how to choose a company that doesn't go bankrupt?

As for selling at a lower price than we paid, that's simple: **don't** do it! Don't sell at a lower price than you paid for the shares when you bought them!

Shares will go up and down **all the time**. Forget about the romantic and hopeful idea that you are going to hit the jackpot and buy shares at the lowest price ever and see how they grow and grown up and up and up to the moon and beyond. Forget it.

You will be buying shares and you'll see them going down, then up, then down again over and over.

Your job is to be patient and remember that, long-term, good and strong companies go up.

Before we go into the details of how to choose a high-quality company, let me tell you what the two most important emotions to control are. This lesson costed me tens of thousands of dollars, so it is in your best interest to pay attention:

GREED

&

IMPATIENCE

Apart from these two emotions, investors tend to 'enjoy' the following rollercoaster:

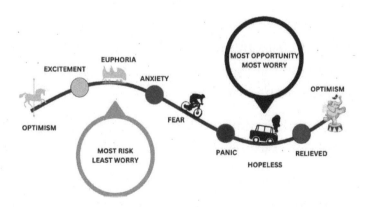

When emotions go up, intelligence goes down. This fact can be scientifically explained with brain wavelengths and hormones. In simple terms, you just need to remember a situation in which you were very _____ (worried, angry, sad, etc.). Be honest and admit that these are the times when you have said or done the stupidest things, right?

If you can't think of anything, close your eyes and go back to the last fight you've had with your spouse, child, parent, co-worker... Did you friendly and it a low voice discuss the disagreement and reached a conclusion peacefully or rather screamed at each other, called them names, got nowhere?

I know you were right and the other person was wrong, as it always is. In any case, can you imagine having to take the decision of investing in a company or another in such a state?

Although this could be a bit of an exaggeration, our fear to lose money could put us in a place where the stress is high and, therefore, our capacity to take sound decisions, compromised.

Another million-dollar question: how do we control our emotions?

What has helped me the most have been two ground-breaking techniques (I'm being sarcastic):

1. Breathing

   Clearly, with a spin, which consists on inhaling consciously, with the intention set into bringing the air to the heart and the focus on situations, people or circumstances that bring up the feelings of care, appreciation, gratitude or compassion.

   You can practice this simple exercise five minutes a day. It produces coherent waves, which can be seen on a screen and measured. These coherent waves strengthen our resilience, that is, our "capacity to prepare for, recover from and adapt in the face of stress, adversity or challenge". This is how the HeartMath Institute defines *resilience* and in their web page, where you can find a lot more about this phenomenon of brain-heart coherence which helps me not only to trade in a state of calm even if everyone is excited or freaking out, but also in every day life issues, like not ever getting pissed off when at the wheel, for instance.

   I must confess, though, that this is a work in progress and some people really know how to push my buttons.

2. Studying

   Applying the system –that I now know so well and that I'll be sharing with you here without hiding anything– to the very letter helps a lot. I mean: a lot. Studying the candidates to invest in applying the system, let me stress it, to the very letter, greatly contributes to my peace of mind and to keep a cool head.

When you apply a system that time has proved to work long-term and you focus on dealing only in what you have in front of you at a given moment in time, there is no space for excitement, fear, panic, optimism or any other emotion that would get on the way of you taking sound decisions.

I have had the priviledge and honour of listening to Warren Buffet and Charlie Munger live at their AGM[1] in Omaha, Nebraska, USA, 6 times so far. Me and between 35 and 50 thousand others, but still!

When Warren Buffet speaks, I listen. If you still don't know who he is or all you know is that he is very rich, I would suggest that you make it your business to learn more about him, because the more we imitate those who have succeeded before us, the more chances to succeed ourselves. Please, do reconsider your actual situation and hang out –virtually or in the flesh– with

---

[1] AGM stands for Annual General Meeting. Shareholders are welcome to attend the annual meetings of the companies they invest in.

those who have lots of what you want to get; money, in this case.

Warren doesn't do emotions when he decides to invest; Charlie Munger, either.

How come they don't have emotions around investing? Aren't they human? Do they have ink instead of blood and eat spreadsheets as food?

The last time I had the priviledge to see them live, they seem pretty human to me.

The reason why they don't do emotions is because they take their investment decisions based on facts, on a system that has proved to work. How well?

In their website, you can find Warren Buffet's letters to their shareholders. In his letter of February 2023, we can see the growth of the SP-500 vs Berkshire Hathaway's every year since 1965.

This is the summary over these 57 years:

1965-2022	Compounded annual gain	Overall gain
SP-500	9.90%	24,708%
Berkshire Hathaway	19.80%	3,787,464%

Let's decipher this table one bite at a time and, before that, let's make sure everyone understands what simple and compound interest means.

Simple interest: if you have one hen that lays one egg per day and you eat them or sell them, the simple interest is one egg per day (or seven eggs per week), that is, the growth per unit of time.

Compound interest: if you keep your eggs, let them hatch and grow to lay eggs, you will be collecting eggs from the initial hen **and** from the eggs that she laid. This is the interest on the interest; you are getting eggs from the initial mother hen and from her eggs that became hens and the next generations. In this case, you will get... Many more eggs per unit of time (that is, if you allow enough time for the birds to complete their life cycles).

You can watch the following video to learn more about simple and compound interest:

Compounded annual gain: this is the average growth per year including the growth of the previous years. The growth on the initial investment **and** on its growth.

We can see that, roughly, Berkshire's compounded annual gain is twice the SP-500's.

Translating to the hen and egg world, imagine that your hen and her descendants lay two eggs per day while your neighbor's lay one egg per day. After 57 years, you wouldn't only have twice as many hens/eggs/chicks as your neighbour, but so many more! Because this is exponential growth, that is, one that grows multiplying, rather than adding linearly.

That is the reason why the overall gain between 1964 and 2022 is 24,708% for the SP-500 and 3,7 million % for Berkshire.

You can now congratulate yourself because, apart from everything else you've learned so far, you have an idea of how much you can do on average per year in the stock market: if you invest in the SP-500, an average of 10% per year would make sense and 20% annual growth per year would also make sense if investing in Berkshire Hathaway.

Of course, what has happened in the past doesn't mean that it will repeat itself in the future, but it would be fair to say that it would be likely.

And, fair enough, if you were happy to make, on average, 10% a year or 20% a year, you could decide to invest only in the SP-500 or Berkshire, respectively. However, if you would like to make more... keep reading!

Now, we are going to get into the mechanics of making money in the market applying the system I have been learning and applying since 2012... Many hours a day! I have also been teaching it, which has helped me make simpler and simpler every time I go through the content of the seminar. Simpler and more practical.

All the attendess to every event and every webinar have given me feedback that I immediately apply into the teachings to make the concepts easier to grasp, understand and apply. From these pages, my deepest gratitude to you all.

To add to the pot, I will be structuring the matter we'll go through together in a slightly different way as I learned first with the view to offer more alternatives as to how far down the rabbit hole you wish to go in your journey through investing in the stock market. Together, we can make investment decisions as straight forward as you wish or apply as many strategies as you want and handle as little or as much theory and formulas behind the figures as your mind needs at every different level of learning.

1.2. Introducing... Value Line!

As we already know, the SP-500 includes 500 companies of different sizes in all the industries, which are approximately 100. Examples of different industries would be: automotive, food, financial services, real estate, technology, etc.

The SP-500 informs us of the average performance of all these 500 companies. Obviously, some will be doing better than others. If we had a way of measuring their performance and focus on the top ones, the average will be much higher.

Imagine you want to form a basketball team in a new town and your first step for the selection would be height. All you need to do is measure the height of each person, establish a threshold, and keep the, let's say, 100 tallest people. Simple!

The average height of this group of 100 will be, obviously, higher than the average height of the 500.

In the case of companies, we can do something similar, that is, to rank them for quality and get a selection of the best ones.

The equivalent of the measuring tape in the case of the basketball team would be the Value Line reports.

Value Line is a company that produces unbiased, conservative information about companies trading in the stock market. It produces 1,700 comprehensive reports of the top-quality companies, let's call them *pretty companies*, and up to 3,500 not so comprehensive reports on the subs on the bench, to continue with the analogy.

When you start reading Value Line reports, is like looking at sheep: they all look the same. However, the more time you spend with the sheep, the more you get to differentiate one from another.

Each company has its own character and type of behaviour. Just like people. After all, people manage them.

Over time, you will get to hold a pulse on each one of them, just like you get to know how your friends will behave or react under certain circumstances, just like each pet, although holding certain traits of its species, has that something unique that makes it *it* in particular; different and identifiable.

Out of a universe of thousands of stocks out there that we can trade, we are already fishing in the top ones by focusing on the 1,700 pretty companies that Value Line produces these comprehensive reports on.

Value Line started in 1931, two years after the beginning of the Great Depression, with the intention of offering investors information that could be trusted, with no bias or hidden agenda.

Not only past data are included in the reports, but also projections over the next three to five years, and a price estimated range for the following 18 months.

Their projections have been back tested since 1965, providing us with visuals to check how good they are at doing what they do.

Going back to our dear friends Warren and Charlie, they were asked about where to get information about possible companies to invest in and this is what they said:

Charlie: *I think the one set of numbers in America that are the best quick guide to measuring one business against another are the Value Line numbers.*

Warren: *I'd agree with that.*

Charlie: *That stuff on log scale paper going back fifteen years, that is the best one-shot description of a lot of big businesses that exists in America. I can't imagine anybody being in the investment business involving common stock without that thing on the shelf.*

This is what a Value Line report looks like:

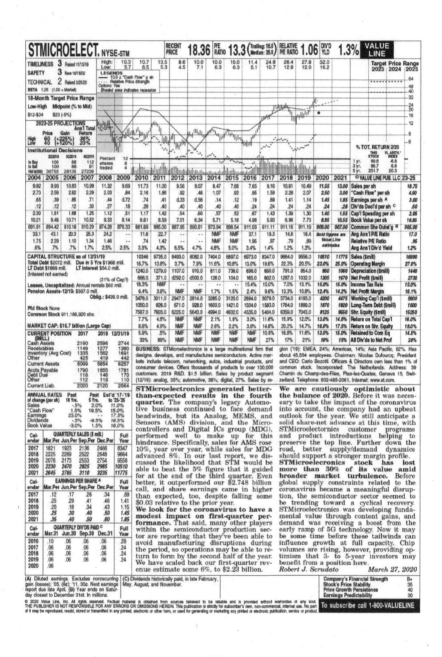

STMICROELECT. NYSE-STM

RECENT PRICE	18.36	P/E RATIO	13.3 (Trailing: 16.0 / Median: 35.0)	RELATIVE P/E RATIO	1.06	DIV'D YLD	1.3%	VALUE LINE

TIMELINESS	3	Raised 11/15/19
SAFETY	3	New 10/15/02
TECHNICAL	2	Raised 3/29/20
BETA	1.25	(1.00 = Market)

18-Month Target Price Range
Low-High Midpoint (% to Mid)
$12-$34 $23 (+5%)

2023-25 PROJECTIONS

	Price	Gain	Ann'l Total Return
High	60	(+225%)	36%
Low	40	(+120%)	23%

Institutional Decisions

	2Q2019	3Q2019	4Q2019
to Buy	100	68	112
to Sell	100	86	91
Hld's(000)	30753	28135	27239

High/Low monthly price range table (top):
| High | 10.3 | 10.7 | 13.5 | 8.6 | 10.0 | 10.0 | 10.0 | 11.4 | 24.8 | 26.4 | 27.8 | 32.0 | Target Price Range 2023 2024 2025 |
| Low | 3.7 | 6.5 | 6.5 | 4.5 | 7.1 | 6.3 | 6.3 | 5.1 | 10.7 | 12.8 | 12.0 | 16.2 | |

LEGENDS
— 10.0 x "Cash Flow" p sh
···· Relative Price Strength
Options: Yes
Shaded area indicates recession

% TOT. RETURN 2/20
	THIS STOCK	VL ARITH.* INDEX
1 yr.	59.5	-8.8
3 yr.	96.7	6.8
5 yr.	251.7	20.3

© VALUE LINE PUB. LLC 23-25

2004	2005	2006	2007	2008	2009	2010	2011	2012	2013	2014	2015	2016	2017	2018	2019	2020	2021		© VALUE LINE PUB. LLC 23-25
9.82	9.93	10.83	10.99	11.32	9.69	11.73	11.00	9.56	9.07	8.47	7.68	7.65	9.16	10.61	10.49	11.55	13.00	Sales per sh	16.75
2.73	2.58	2.82	2.29	2.03	.84	2.16	1.86	.92	.46	1.07	.93	.95	1.59	2.28	2.07	2.50	3.00	"Cash Flow" per sh	4.80
.65	.39	.85	.71	.44	d.72	.74	.41	d.33	d.56	.14	.12	.19	.89	1.41	1.14	1.45	1.85	Earnings per sh A	3.00
.12	.12	.12	.30	.27	.18	.28	.40	.40	.40	.40	.40	.24	.24	.24	.24	.24	.28	Div'ds Decl'd per sh C	.60
2.30	1.81	1.68	1.25	1.12	.51	1.17	1.42	.54	.60	.57	.52	.67	1.43	1.39	1.30	1.40	1.55	Cap'l Spending per sh	2.05
10.21	9.48	10.71	10.52	9.33	8.14	8.61	8.59	7.01	6.34	5.71	5.16	4.98	5.93	6.98	7.73	8.95	10.55	Book Value per sh	16.85
891.91	894.42	910.16	910.29	874.28	878.33	881.69	885.00	887.95	890.61	873.94	898.54	911.03	911.11	911.16	911.19	908.00	907.00	Common Shs Outst'g B	905.00
33.1	43.1	20.3	25.3	24.2	--	11.8	22.7	--	--	NMF	NMF	37.1	19.3	14.6	16.4	Bold figures are Value Line estimates	Avg Ann'l P/E Ratio	17.0
1.75	2.29	1.10	1.34	1.46	--	.74	1.42	--	--	NMF	NMF	1.95	.97	.79	.89		Relative P/E Ratio	.95
.5%	.7%	.7%	1.7%	2.5%	2.5%	3.3%	4.3%	6.5%	4.7%	4.8%	5.0%	3.4%	1.4%	1.2%	1.3%		Avg Ann'l Div'd Yield	1.2%

CAPITAL STRUCTURE as of 12/31/19
Total Debt $2072 mill. Due in 5 Yrs $1966 mill.
LT Debt $1899 mill. LT Interest $54.0 mill.
(Interest not earned)
(21% of Cap'l)
Leases, Uncapitalized: Annual rentals $60 mill.
Pension Assets-12/19: $597.0 mill.
Oblig.: $439.0 mill.

Pfd Stock None
Common Stock 911,186,920 shs.

MARKET CAP: $16.7 billion (Large Cap)

CURRENT POSITION	2017	2018	12/31/19
Cash Assets	2190	2596	2744
Receivables	1149	1277	1380
Inventory (Avg Cost)	1335	1562	1691
Other	425	419	442
Current Assets	5099	5854	6257
Accts Payable	1790	1855	1781
Debt Due	118	146	173
Other	112	119	110
Current Liab.	2020	2120	2064

	2010	2011	2012	2013	2014	2015	2016	2017	2018	2019	2020	2021		
	10346	9735.0	8493.0	8082.0	7404.0	6897.0	6973.0	8347.0	9664.0	9556.0	10510	11775	Sales ($mill)	16990
	16.7%	13.6%	3.7%	7.9%	11.6%	10.6%	13.0%	19.6%	22.3%	20.5%	23.0%	25.0%	Operating Margin	27.0%
	1240.0	1279.0	1107.0	910.0	811.0	736.0	695.0	650.0	791.0	854.0	950	1060	Depreciation ($mill)	1440
	666.0	371.0	d292.0	d500.0	128.0	104.0	165.0	802.0	1287.0	1032.0	1305	1670	Net Profit ($mill)	2730
	18.3%	NMF	--	--	--	15.4%	15.0%	7.0%	13.1%	15.0%	15.0%	15.0%	Income Tax Rate	15.0%
	6.4%	3.8%	NMF	NMF	1.7%	1.5%	2.4%	9.6%	13.3%	10.8%	12.4%	14.2%	Net Profit Margin	16.1%
	3478.0	3011.0	2947.0	2814.0	3285.0	3120.0	2694.0	3079.0	3734.0	4193.0	4200	4475	Working Cap'l ($mill)	5600
	1050.0	826.0	671.0	928.0	1603.0	1421.0	1334.0	1583.0	1764.0	1899.0	1870	1820	Long-Term Debt ($mill)	1600
	7587.0	7603.0	6225.0	5643.0	4994.0	4632.0	4535.0	5404.0	6359.0	7043.0	8125	9550	Shr. Equity ($mill)	15250
	7.7%	4.5%	NMF	NMF	2.1%	1.9%	3.0%	11.6%	15.9%	12.0%	13.0%	14.5%	Return on Total Cap'l	16.0%
	8.8%	4.9%	NMF	NMF	2.6%	2.2%	3.6%	14.8%	20.2%	14.7%	16.0%	17.5%	Return on Shr. Equity	18.0%
	5.9%	.5%	NMF	NMF	1.1%	--	NMF	10.8%	16.8%	11.6%	13.5%	15.0%	Retained to Com Eq	14.5%
	33%	89%	NMF	NMF	NMF	NMF	NMF	27%	17%	21%	16%	15%	All Div'ds to Net Prof	20%

BUSINESS: STMicroelectronics is a large multinational firm that designs, develops, and manufactures semiconductors. Active markets include telecom, networking, autos, industrial products, and consumer devices. Offers thousands of products to over 100,000 customers. 2019 R&D: $1.5 billion. Sales by product segment (12/19): analog, 35%; automotive, 38%; digital, 27%. Sales by re-gion ('19): EMEA, 24%; Americas, 14%; Asia Pacific, 62%. Has about 45,554 employees. Chairman: Nicolas Dufourcq; President and CEO: Carlo Bozotti. Officers & Directors own less than 1% of common stock. Incorporated: The Netherlands. Address: 39 Chemin du Champ-des-Filles, Plan-les-Ouates, Geneva 15, Switzerland. Telephone: 602-485-2061. Internet: www.st.com.

ANNUAL RATES	Past 10 Yrs.	Past 5 Yrs.	Est'd '17-'19 to '23-'25
Sales	-.5%	2.0%	11.0%
"Cash Flow"	1.5%	19.5%	15.0%
Earnings	23.0%	--	17.5%
Dividends	-.5%	-9.5%	16.5%
Book Value	-3.0%	1.5%	16.0%

Cal-endar	QUARTERLY SALES ($ mill.)				Full Year
	Mar.Per	Jun.Per	Sep.Per	Dec.Per	
2017	1821	1923	2136	2466	8347
2018	2225	2269	2522	2648	9664
2019	2076	2173	2553	2754	9556
2020	2230	2470	2825	2985	10510
2021	2645	2785	3110	3235	11775

Cal-endar	EARNINGS PER SHARE A				Full Year
	Mar.Per	Jun.Per	Sep.Per	Dec.Per	
2017	.12	.17	.26	.34	.89
2018	.25	.29	.41	.46	1.41
2019	.20	.18	.34	.43	1.15
2020	.25	.30	.40	.50	1.45
2021	.35	.40	.50	.60	1.85

Cal-endar	QUARTERLY DIV'DS PAID C				Full Year
	Mar.31	Jun.30	Sep.30	Dec.31	
2016	.10	.06	.06	.06	.28
2017	.06	.06	.06	.06	.24
2018	.06	.06	.06	.06	.24
2019	.06	.06	.06	.06	.24
2020	.06				

STMicroelectronics generated better-than-expected results in the fourth quarter. The company's legacy Automotive business continued to face demand headwinds, but its Analog, MEMS, and Sensors (AMS) division, and the Micro-controllers and Digital ICs group (MDG), performed well to make up for this hindrance. Specifically, sales for AMS rose 10%, year over year, while sales for MDG advanced 8%. In our last report, we discussed the likelihood that STM would be able to beat the 5% figure that it guided for at the end of the third quarter. Even better, it outperformed our $2.748 billion call, and share earnings came in higher than expected, too, despite falling some $0.03 relative to the prior year.
We look for the coronavirus to have a modest impact on first-quarter performance. That said, many other players within the semiconductor production sector are reporting that they've been able to avoid manufacturing disruptions during the period, so operations may be able to re-turn to form by the second half of the year. We have scaled back our first-quarter revenue estimate some 6%, to $2.23 billion.

We are cautiously optimistic about the balance of 2020. Before it was necessary to take the impact of the coronavirus into account, the company had an upbeat outlook for the year. We still anticipate a solid share-net advance at this time, with STMicroelectornics customer programs and product introductions helping to preserve the top line. Further down the road, better supply/demand dynamics should support a stronger margin profile. STMicroelecronics stock has lost more than 30% of its value amid broader global market turbulence. Before global supply constraints related to the coronavirus became a meaningful disruption, the semiconductor sector seemed to be trending toward a cyclical recovery. STMicroelectronics was developing fundamental value through content gains, and demand was receiving a boost from the early ramp of 5G technology. Now it may be some time before these tailwinds can produce growth at full capacity. Chip volumes are rising, however, providing optimism that 3- to 5-year investors may benefit from a position here.
Robert J. Scrudato *March 27, 2020*

(A) Diluted earnings. Excludes nonrecurring gain (losses): '05, (6¢); '11, 30¢. Next earnings report due late April. (B) Year ends on Satur-day closest to December 31st. In millions.
(C) Dividends historically paid in late February, May, August, and November.

Company's Financial Strength	B+
Stock's Price Stability	35
Price Growth Persistence	40
Earnings Predictability	30

To subscribe call 1-800-VALUELINE

When I saw one of these reports for the first time would be better described by something along the lines of WTF, but I will omit such a comment because I'm a lady.

The trick, as usual, is to eat the elephant one bite at a time (figure of speech; I prefer not to eat animals).

Keep reading and witness how easy it is to make sense of all this crammed information.

1.3. Picking quality companies

You will see what a wonderful system this is to quantify the quality of a company, because... There is no space for emotions!

The first time that I completed the evaluation of quality of a company, it took me more than 40 minutes. You will see how soon you will be able to evaluate both quality and price in a few minutes.

If you remember, we are now in front of 1,700 possible candidates for us to pick. Where to start?

With our group of tall candidates for our basketball team, we could start the selection process by asking them to run, to bounce the ball, etc.

In the case of companies, we'll study some parameters that, when put together, will give us a total score that will keep these companies to go to the next level or dismiss them.

For learning purposes, we can start by filling up the template in the next page the old fashion way, with a pen and the use of a calculator. Later, a spreadsheet can be used.

Remember: there is no space for emotions. We don't do fear! It all is about figures and no, you don't need to be a math nerd to go through this exercise.

When we first learned to read, we started with the letters; then, words and, at a further stage, phrases. Expecting a little child to write an essay its first week in kindergarten wouldn't be realistic.

Likewise, we can learn to fill up the template in a tiered approach. You can move to the next level whenever you feel ready.

Bear in mind that:

→ Each parameter is one component and one only. However, some are more important than others.

When you are looking for a partner, there are some characteristics you would love that person to be. For instance: kind, funny, handsome or pretty, tall, blond, of a certain age range, animal lover, travelling lover, fancy, respectful, good singer…

Wouldn't it be great to find someone who ticked absolutely all the boxes? With our two feet on the ground, we can honestly admit that *we* don't tick them all ourselves, so it's only fair that we pick those traits that we consider more important, like being kind and respectful. (Obvious to add "and single" and a few others non-negotiables).

→ Earnings (synonym of *profits*) is what drives share prices up long-term. Think of it: the whole reason for a company to exist is to make profits, that is, that the income in sales is greater than the expenses necessary to produce those sales.

How important do you think profits are when studying a company with the view to potentially invest in it? _____.

If you haven't answered "very", "very much", "extremely important", "crucial" or something along these lines, reconsider your answer.

→ Short-term, news move the share prices.

Someone who is a very calm and cool person, when something really good or bad happens, they could laugh and dance like crazy or scream in despair.

However, after a while, they will go back to their general tone of being calm and cool.

In March 2020, the news around the world made the share prices of most companies go down. However, after a few weeks or months, the great majority of them continued with their journeys as if March 2020 was only a bleep.

This is the template that we will be using to evaluate the quality of a company:

New Name: [_____] Date: [_____]

Q1 INDUSTRY RANK
Industry's potential for growth
relative to other industries

[____]

1-25 Ideal (4)
26-50 High Range (3)
51-75 Low Range (2)
76-100 Red Flag (1)

[____]

Q2 TIMELINESS
How fast will the price of the stock rise
relative to other stocks in the next 12 months?

[____]

1-2 Ideal (4)
3 High Range (2.5)
4-5 Red Flag (1)

[____]

Q3 SAFETY
How much volatility is there likely to be on the stock over
the next 12 months compared to it's long term trends?

[____]

1-2 Ideal (4)
3 High Range (2.5)
4-5 Red Flag (1)

[____]

Q4 DEBT
Debt as a % of capitalisation (Q4A / Q4B) * 100

[____] %

Q4A ($B)   **Q4B ($B)**

[____]   [____]

0-9% Ideal (4)
10-30% High Range (3)
31-50% Low Range (2)
51%+ Red Flag

Q5 BETA
Volatility of this stock relative to
movement of total stock market

[____]

0.95-1.1 Ideal (4)
0.94-1.2 High Range (3)
0.91-1.49 Low Range (2)
Other Red Flag (1)

[____]

Q6 GROWTH TRENDS
Q6a What has the company's sales [____] %
growth been in the last 5 years?
Q6c What has the company's earnings [____] %
growth been in the last 5 years?

15%+ Ideal (4)
11-14.99% High Range (3)
6.66-10.99% Low Range (2)
6.65% or less Red Flag (1)

[____]

5 Consecutive years of uninterrupted growth - Ideal(4)   Q6b Sales   [____]
4 Years of growth and
  Growth up in last 2 years - High Range (3)
  No growth in last 2 years - Low Range (2)
2 or more years without growth - Red Flag (1)   Q6d Earnings   [____]

[____]

Projected Revenues ($M)

Q6e		Ideal (4)	Range(3)	Range(2)	Flag(1)
Small less than $400m		15%+	13.6-14.9	12.1-13.5	12 or less
Medium $400-$3999m		12%+	11.1-11.9	10.1-11.0	10 or less
Large $4000m+		10%+	8.6-9.9	7.1-8.5	7 or less

Q6f Projected Sales [____] %

Q6g Projected Earnings [____] %

19-24 Ideal (4)
13-18 High Range (3)
7-12 Low Range (2)
0-6 Red Flag (1)
Total → [____]

Q7 MANAGEMENT
Q7a Are profits increasing? ☐
Q7b Is management solid & are they anticipating future trends? ☐
Q7c Have they handled past challenges? ☐
Q7d Are they operating smoothly without any pending lawsuits? ☐

4 Y's - Ideal (4)
3 Y's - High Range (3)
2 Y's - Low Range
1 Y - Red Flag

	Values	Multiply by	Total	Max
Industry Ranking		*		4
Timeliness		**		8
Safety		**		8
Debt		**		8
Beta		*		4
Growth Trends		***		12
Management		**		8
				52

The
Investment
● Club Network
TICN
Copyright TICN Ltd. 2002

40-52 Ideal (4)
27-39 High Range (3)
14-26 Low Range (2)
0-13 Red Flag (1)

TICN Guide

These are the parameters we will including in the template to assess the quality of a company:

Q1: Industry rank
Q2: Timeliness
Q3: Safety
Q4: Debt
Q5: Beta
Q6: Growth trends
Q7: Management

These parameters will be scored from 1, the minimum, to 4, the maximum.

As an example, we'll use STM. Gentle reminder: we are not telling you to buy anything!

We will use an old report, since the access to Value Line is via subscription.

Q1: Industry rank

This is the only parameter not included in the Value Line report. You can get it from the website. Although we are using an old report, for educational purposes, we will use the data as of today, which is the one available:

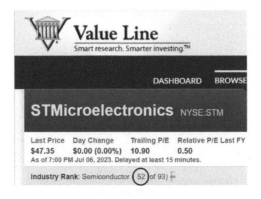

Tier I: Put the value in the cell and decide the score. In our example, because the industry rank is 52, the score is 2, between 51 and 75. Therefore, Q1 is 2.

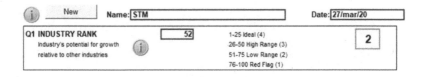

Tier II: Every week, Value Line updates the list of industries by growth potential, that is, which industries will grow faster relative to other industries.

Q2: Timeliness

STMICROELECT

TIMELINESS	**3**	Raised 11/15/19
SAFETY	**3**	New 10/18/02
TECHNICAL	**2**	Raised 3/20/20
BETA	1.25	(1.00 = Market)

<u>Tier I:</u> In our example, Timeliness is 3, therefore, Q2 is 2.5.

Q2 TIMELINESS	3	1-2 Ideal (4)	
How fast will the price of the stock rise relative to other stocks in the next 12 months?		3 High Range (2.5) 4-5 Red Flag (1)	**2.5**

<u>Tier II:</u> The Value Line Timeliness rank measures the probability of a stock to increase its price faster relative to the rest of the 1,700 stocks that Value Line produces comprehensive reports on, in the next 12 months. Its scale goes from 1, as the lowest, to 5, as the highest.

The way I visualise this parameter is as follows.

Imagine we have thousands of runners in a marathon. They all start running at the same time and they all compete in the same category, to make things simple.

The first 100 to cross the finish line, which are the fastest of them all, will get a gold medal, that is, the top score for timeliness (1). The next 300 runners crossing the finish line will get a silver medal, which would be the equivalent of 2 in timeliness. The next 900 runners, bronze and a 3 in the timeliness score. The following 300 runners, flowers and a diploma, which corresponds to a 4 in the timeliness score. The next 100 runners, they get a diploma, a 5 in the timeliness score and the rest of the runners up to 6,500, a thank you note.

$$100 + 300 + 900 + 300 + 100 = 1,700$$

The chosen 1,700 are those with a comprehensive report. The rest of companies out of 3,500 get a report, but with less data, like the one in the next page. Any other runner/company crossing the finish line later than the first 6,500 runners won't get report, diploma, flowers or anything… But they can keep competing to see whether they will classify in the next marathon.

CONSOLIDATED WATER NDQ-CWCO

RECENT PRICE	TRAILING P/E RATIO	RELATIVE P/E RATIO	DIV'D YLD
24.11	37.1	2.56	1.4%

VALUE LINE

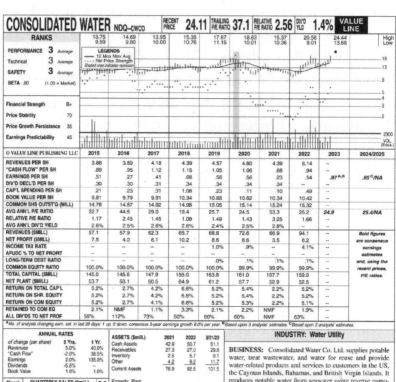

© VALUE LINE PUBLISHING LLC	2015	2016	2017	2018	2019	2020	2021	2022	2023	2024/2025
REVENUES PER SH	3.86	3.89	4.18	4.39	4.57	4.80	4.39	6.14	--	
"CASH FLOW" PER SH	.89	.95	1.12	1.15	1.05	1.06	.68	.94	--	
EARNINGS PER SH	.51	.27	.41	.68	.56	.56	.23	.54	.97 A,B	.95 C/NA
DIV'D DECL'D PER SH	.30	.30	.31	.34	.34	.34	.34	--	--	
CAP'L SPENDING PER SH	.21	.23	.31	1.08	.23	.11	.10	.49	--	
BOOK VALUE PER SH	9.81	9.79	9.79	10.34	10.88	10.62	10.34	10.42	--	
COMMON SHS OUTST'G (MILL)	14.78	14.67	14.92	14.98	15.05	15.14	15.24	15.32	--	
AVG ANN'L P/E RATIO	22.7	44.8	29.0	19.4	25.7	24.5	53.3	25.2	24.9	25.4/NA
RELATIVE P/E RATIO	1.17	2.45	1.45	1.09	1.49	1.43	3.25	1.66	--	
AVG ANN'L DIV'D YIELD	2.6%	2.5%	2.6%	2.6%	2.4%	2.5%	2.8%	--	--	
REVENUES ($MILL)	57.1	57.9	62.3	65.7	68.8	72.6	66.9	94.1	--	Bold figures
NET PROFIT ($MILL)	7.5	4.0	6.1	10.2	8.6	8.6	3.5	8.2	--	are consensus
INCOME TAX RATE	--	--	--	--	1.0%	.9%	--	4.1%	--	earnings
AFUDC % TO NET PROFIT	--	--	--	--	--	--	--	--	--	estimates
LONG-TERM DEBT RATIO	--	--	--	--	.0%	.1%	.1%	.1%	--	and, using the
COMMON EQUITY RATIO	100.0%	100.0%	100.0%	100.0%	100.0%	99.9%	99.9%	99.9%	--	recent prices,
TOTAL CAPITAL ($MILL)	145.0	145.6	147.9	155.0	163.8	161.0	157.7	159.9	--	P/E ratios.
NET PLANT ($MILL)	53.7	53.1	50.5	64.9	61.2	57.7	52.9	52.5	--	
RETURN ON TOTAL CAP'L	5.2%	2.7%	4.2%	6.6%	5.2%	5.4%	2.2%	5.2%	--	
RETURN ON SHR. EQUITY	5.2%	2.7%	4.2%	6.6%	5.2%	5.4%	2.2%	5.2%	--	
RETURN ON COM EQUITY	5.2%	2.7%	4.1%	6.6%	5.2%	5.3%	2.2%	6.1%	--	
RETAINED TO COM EQ	2.1%	NMF	1.1%	3.3%	2.1%	2.2%	NMF	1.9%	--	
ALL DIV'DS TO NET PROF	59%	112%	73%	50%	60%	60%	NMF	63%	--	

A No. of analysts changing earn. est. in last 26 days: 1 up, 0 down, consensus 5-year earnings growth 8.0% per year. B Based upon 3 analysts' estimates. C Based upon 3 analysts' estimates.

ANNUAL RATES		
of change (per share)	5 Yrs.	1 Yr.
Revenues	5.0%	40.0%
"Cash Flow"	-2.0%	38.5%
Earnings	2.0%	135.0%
Dividends	-5.5%	--
Book Value	1.0%	1.0%

Fiscal Year	QUARTERLY SALES ($mill.)				Full Year
	1Q	2Q	3Q	4Q	
12/31/21	17.1	16.7	16.4	16.7	66.9
12/31/22	19.6	21.1	25.1	28.4	94.1
12/31/23	32.9				
12/31/24					

Fiscal Year	EARNINGS PER SHARE				Full Year
	1Q	2Q	3Q	4Q	
12/31/20	.19	.11	.09	.17	.56
12/31/21	.06	d.10	.09	.16	.23
12/31/22	.15	.18	.05	.16	.54
12/31/23	.26	.22	.23	.17	
12/31/24					

Cal- endar	QUARTERLY DIVIDENDS PAID				Full Year
	1Q	2Q	3Q	4Q	
2020	.085	.085	.085	.085	.34
2021	.085	.085	.085	.085	.34
2022	.085	.085	.085	.085	.34
2023	.085	.085			

INSTITUTIONAL DECISIONS			
	3Q'22	4Q'22	1Q'23
to Buy	50	45	38
to Sell	30	44	36
Hld's(000)	6689	7462	7191

ASSETS ($mill.)	2021	2022	3/31/23
Cash Assets	42.9	50.7	51.1
Receivables	27.3	27.0	29.6
Inventory	2.5	5.7	9.1
Other	4.2	9.2	11.7
Current Assets	76.9	92.6	101.5
Property, Plant & Equip, at cost	136.1	139.8	--
Accum Depreciation	83.2	87.3	--
Net Property	52.9	52.5	56.3
Other	47.2	47.9	43.8
Total Assets	177.0	193.0	201.6
LIABILITIES ($mill.)			
Accts Payable	3.0	8.8	9.8
Debt Due	.1	.1	.1
Other	4.6	13.8	21.0
Current Liab	7.7	22.7	30.9

LONG-TERM DEBT AND EQUITY as of 3/31/23

Total Debt $.3 mill.   Due in 5 Yrs. NA
LT Debt $.2 mill.
Including Cap. Leases NA
Leases, Uncapitalized Annual rentals NA

Pension Liability None in '22 vs. None in '21

Pfd Stock None   Pfd Div'd Paid None

Common Stock 15,736,000 shares   (100% of Cap'l)

INDUSTRY: Water Utility

BUSINESS: Consolidated Water Co. Ltd. supplies potable water, treat wastewater, and water for reuse and provide water-related products and services to customers in the US, the Cayman Islands, Bahamas, and British Virgin Islands. It produces potable water from seawater using reverse osmosis technology and sells this water to a variety of customers, including public utilities, commercial and tourist properties, residential properties and government facilities. Consolidated Water builds and sells water production and water treatment infrastructure and manages water infrastructure for commercial and governmental customers. It also manufactures various water industry related products and provides services applicable to commercial, municipal and industrial water production, and treatment. In June 2023, Consolidated Water's subsidiary, Kalaeloa Desalco LLC signed a deal with the Honolulu Board of Water Supply to build and maintain a seawater reverse osmosis desalination plant. Has 223 employees. C.E.O.: Frederick W. McTaggart Address: Regatta Office Park Windward Three, 4th Fl, West Bay Rd, P.O. Box 1114 Grand Cayman KY1-110 KY. Internet: www.cwco.com.   E.B.

July 7, 2023

TOTAL SHAREHOLDER RETURN				
			Dividends plus appreciation as of 5/31/2023	
3 Mos.	6 Mos.	1 Yr.	3 Yrs.	5 Yrs.
27.99%	35.53%	41.05%	42.56%	68.68%

To subscribe call 1-800-VALUELINE

<u>Tier III:</u> Timeliness is calculated using the following components: the 10-year trend of relative earnings and prices, recent earnings and price changes and earning surprises. With the combination of all these known, actual data, calculations are made and a forecast of what the stock of consideration will be doing in the next 12 months in comparison to the rest of the top 1,700 companies Value Line produces reports on is reported as scores from 1 (the lowest) to 5 (the highest).

To get the most up to date timeliness score on a particular company, please, refer to the score on the dashboard rather than that of the pdf report, as the former is updated more often than the 13 weeks that takes for a new pdf report to be issued.

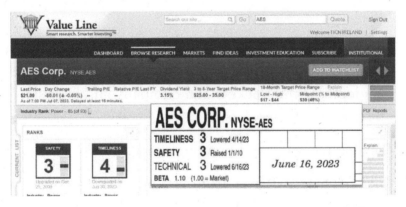

In this example, AES's timeliness was 3 when the June 16th issue came out, but downgraded to 4 on June 30th.

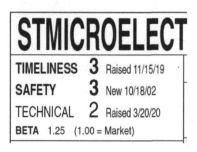

STMICROELECT

TIMELINESS	**3**	Raised 11/15/19
SAFETY	**3**	New 10/18/02
TECHNICAL	**2**	Raised 3/20/20
BETA 1.25	(1.00 = Market)	

<u>Tier I:</u> In our example, Safey is 3, therefore, Q3 is 2.5.

Q3 SAFETY	3	1-2 Ideal (4)	2.5
How much volatility is there likely to be on the stock over the next 12 months compared to it's long term trends?		3 High Range (2.5) 4-5 Red Flag (1)	

<u>Tier II:</u> Safety measures the total risk of a stock in comparison to others. In layman's terms, it measures the depth of the pockets of a company and how stable the price of the stock is.

The highest value is 1 and the lowest, 5.

<u>Tier III:</u> Safety derives from two parameters:

1. The financial strength of the company
2. The stability of the stock price

Financial strength of a company is a measure of its financial condition, that is, the strength of their balance sheet. It is reported on a scale that goes, from highest to lowest: A^{++}, A^+, A, B^{++}, B^+, B, C^{++}, C^+ and C.

The score of the stability of the stock price is based on a ranking of the standard deviation (a measure of volatility) of weekly percent changes in the price of a stock over the last five years. It is reported on a scale from a minimum of 5 to a highest of 100 in increments of 5 units.

Q4: Debt

```
CAPITAL STRUCTURE as of 12/31/19
Total Debt $2072 mill.   Due in 5 Yrs $1966 mill.
LT Debt $1899 mill.      LT Interest $54.0 mill.
(Interest not earned)

                                (21% of Cap'l)
Leases, Uncapitalized: Annual rentals $60 mill.
Pension Assets-12/19: $597.0 mill.
                        Oblig.: $439.0 mill.


Pfd Stock None
Common Stock 911,186,920 shs.

MARKET CAP: $16.7 billion (Large Cap)
```

<u>Tier I:</u> In our example, the total debt is 2,072 billion and the market capitalisation is 16.7 billion (we need to make sure we use the same units in both cases). When we divide the former by the latter and multiply by 100, we get a 12.41% debt ratio, which gives us a score of 3.

Q4 DEBT		12.41 %	0-9% Ideal (4)	3
Debt as a % of capitalisation (Q4A / Q4B) * 100			10-30% High Range (3)	
Q4A ($B)	Q4B ($B)		31-50% Low Range (2)	
2.072	16.700		51%+ Red Flag	

<u>Tier II:</u> The debt of a company is how much money they owe. However, what it is more interesting for us is to know how much money the company owes with respect to how much the company is worth.

Imagine you parents lent you 500,000, at a fantastic 0% interest rate. At this point in time, you owe them 50,000, which is **10%** of the total debt.

Your parents lent 100,000, at the same fantastic 0% interest rate, to your brother, who also owes them 50,000. This means he owes **50%** of the total debt.

Although you both owe 50,000, the ratio total debt to capital is 10% versus 50%, quite different!

<u>Tier III:</u> Market cap or market capitalisation is how much a company is worth at a given time. It is calculated as follows:

Market cap = number of shares ∗ share price

When share prices go down, the market cap goes down and viceversa.

When the ratio debt/market cap is high, a decrease in the share price can put the company at risk even if the debt stays the same.

Some companies, due to the nature of their business, carry a higher debt than others. When you see a debt that is consistently high over the years, look at the profits of the company over the same period. If the company makes profit with the high debt, that could be an indication that this high debt is due to the nature of the industry. You can also compare the data of other companies in the same industry.

Q5: Beta

STMICROELECT

TIMELINESS	**3**	Raised 11/15/19
SAFETY	**3**	New 10/18/02
TECHNICAL	**2**	Raised 3/20/20
BETA 1.25	(1.00 = Market)	

Tier I: In our example, beta is 1.25, therefore, Q5 is 2.

We assign the score of the range where beta fits first and we check starting by *ideal*, then *High range*... In our case, it fits in the 0.91-1.49 range.

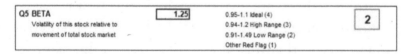

Q5 BETA	1.25	0.95-1.1 Ideal (4)	2
Volatility of this stock relative to		0.94-1.2 High Range (3)	
movement of total stock market		0.91-1.49 Low Range (2)	
		Other Red Flag (1)	

Tier II: Beta measures the volatility of the stock price in comparison to the market.

The way I envision what beta measures is as follows: we have a sample of all the seas in the world. Some will have very big waves and some will have tiny waves. We can give the arbitrary value of 1.00 to the average height of all the waves in the seas. In this framework, a sea with waves 0.95 will have waves shorter than the average and a sea with waves 1.20 will have taller waves than the average.

Thus, when the value of beta of a company is lower than 1.00, that means that the share price of that company moves up and down less than the average of all the shares in the market.

When higher than 1.00, the price of that stock moves up and down more than the average of all the shares in the market.

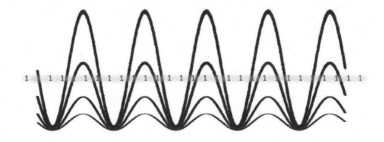

<u>Tier III:</u> If beta is, for instance, 1.05, it would fit in all the ranges, as 1.05 is included in all of them:

Ideal range (score of 4): beta between 0.95 and 1.10.

High range (score of 3): beta between 0.94 and 1.20.

Low range (score of 2): beta between 0.91 and 1.49.

Red flag (score of 1): beta lower than 0.90 or higher than 1.50.

We will assign the score of 4 to a beta of 1.05, because it is in the ideal range where 1.05 fits first.

The same way, 1.11 will be a 3; 0.92 will be a 2; 1.37 will also be a 2; 0.60 will be a 1; 1.65 will also be a 1.

Q6: Growth trends

Because this is the most important part on the evaluation of the quality of a company, as stated before, we will be studing this parameter in depth and in three parts:

Part 1: the average sales and earnings of the last 5 years.

Part 2: the consistency of the sales and earnings of the last 5 years.

Part 3: the projections of sales and earnings in the next 3 to 5 years.

ANNUAL RATES of change (per sh)	Past 10 Yrs.	Past 5 Yrs.	Est'd '17-'19 to '23-'25
Sales	-.5%	2.0%	11.0%
"Cash Flow"	1.5%	19.5%	15.0%
Earnings	23.0%	- -	17.5%
Dividends	-.5%	-9.5%	16.5%
Book Value	-3.0%	1.5%	16.0%

<u>Part 1, Tier I:</u> In our example, the average sales over the last 5 years was 2.0%, which means the score is 1.

The average earnings over the last 5 years was 0% (that's what - - means), which means the score is 1.

Q6 GROWTH TRENDS			
Q6a What has the company's sales growth been in the last 5 years?	2.0 %	15%+ Ideal (4) 11-14.99% High Range (3)	1
Q6c What has the company's earnings growth been in the last 5 years?	0.0 %	6.66-10.99% Low Range (2) 6.65% or less Red Flag	1

<u>Part 1, Tier II:</u> We prefer to see that the earnings grow at a higher rate than the sales.

A company selling more stuff –products or services– every year, on paper, seems like the way to go. If you have a factory that makes shoes, the more shoes you sell, the better... In principle.

What is more interesting, because is more profitable, is that you make those shoes, or whatever the product or service is, cheaper.

Considering that

$$Profit = Sales - Expenses$$

We either increase the sales or reduce the expenses to make the profit grow.

$$\text{Profit} = \text{Sales} - \text{Expenses}$$

$$\text{Profit} = \text{Sales} - \text{Expenses}$$

Part 1, Tier III: *Revenue is vanity, profit is sanity and cashflow is king.* Verne Harnish.

Revenue is the same as *sales* or *turnover*. It is also referred to as *top line*. Beware of those who brag about how much they've sold or how much their sales have increased: pure vanity.

Profit is also referred to as *bottom line*, that is, the most important bit of information of the performance of a company.

Cash or *cashflow*: we'll go into more detail when evaluating the price of a stock. There you go a teaser, though: *balance sheet*.

<u>Part 2, Tier I</u>: Here, we are assessing the consistency of the growth of sales and earnings.

To find out what the score is in each case, we will use the following code:

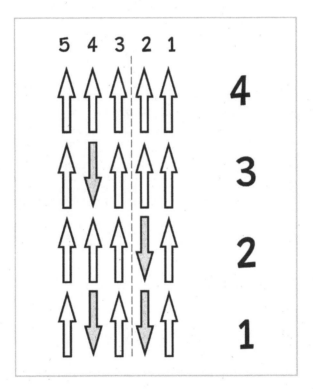

An arrow pointing up means that the value is higher than the previous year; an arrow pointing down means that the value is lower than the previous year. We've made these dark to stand out.

5 arrows pointing up: the score is 4.

1 arrow, and one arrow only, pointing down 3, 4 or 5 years ago: the score is 3.

1 arrow, and one arrow only, pointing down 1 or 2 years ago: the score is 2.

2 or more arrows pointing down, at any point in time: the score is 1.

In our example:

2014	2015	2016	2017	2018	2019	2020	2021	© VALUE LINE PUB. LLC	23-25
8.47	7.68	7.65	9.16	10.61	10.49	*11.55*	*13.00*	Sales per sh	*18.75*
1.07	.93	.95	1.59	2.28	2.07	*2.50*	*3.00*	"Cash Flow" per sh	*4.60*
.14	.12	.19	.89	1.41	1.14	*1.45*	*1.85*	Earnings per sh A	*3.00*
.40	.40	.24	.24	.24	.24	*.24*	*.28*	Div'ds Decl'd per sh C	*.60*
.57	.52	.67	1.43	1.39	1.30	*1.40*	*1.55*	Cap'l Spending per sh	*2.05*
5.71	5.16	4.98	5.93	6.98	7.73	*8.95*	*10.55*	Book Value per sh	*16.85*
873.94	898.54	911.03	911.11	911.16	911.19	*909.00*	*907.00*	Common Shs Outst'g B	*905.00*
NMF	NMF	37.1	19.3	14.6	16.4	*Bold figures are*		Avg Ann'l P/E Ratio	*17.0*
NMF	NMF	1.95	.97	.79	.89	*Value Line*		Relative P/E Ratio	*.95*
4.8%	5.0%	3.4%	1.4%	1.2%	1.3%	*estimates*		Avg Ann'l Div'd Yield	*1.2%*
6404.0	6897.0	6973.0	8347.0	9664.0	9556.0	*10510*	*11775*	Sales ($mill)	*16990*

Sales: ↑↑↑↑↓, one arrow pointing down within the last 2 years: the score is 2.

2014	2015	2016	2017	2018	2019	2020	2021	© VALUE LINE PUB. LLC	23-25
8.47	7.68	7.65	9.16	10.61	10.49	*11.55*	*13.00*	Sales per sh	*18.75*
1.07	.93	.95	1.59	2.28	2.07	*2.50*	*3.00*	"Cash Flow" per sh	*4.60*
.14	.12	.19	.89	1.41	1.14	*1.45*	*1.85*	Earnings per sh A	*3.00*
.40	.40	.24	.24	.24	.24	*.24*	*.28*	Div'ds Decl'd per sh C	*.60*
.57	.52	.67	1.43	1.39	1.30	*1.40*	*1.55*	Cap'l Spending per sh	*2.05*
5.71	5.16	4.98	5.93	6.98	7.73	*8.95*	*10.55*	Book Value per sh	*16.85*
873.94	898.54	911.03	911.11	911.16	911.19	*909.00*	*907.00*	Common Shs Outst'g B	*905.00*
NMF	NMF	37.1	19.3	14.6	16.4	*Bold figures are*		Avg Ann'l P/E Ratio	*17.0*
NMF	NMF	1.95	.97	.79	.89	*Value Line*		Relative P/E Ratio	*.95*
4.8%	5.0%	3.4%	1.4%	1.2%	1.3%	*estimates*		Avg Ann'l Div'd Yield	*1.2%*
6404.0	6897.0	6973.0	8347.0	9664.0	9556.0	*10510*	*11775*	Sales ($mill)	*16990*

Earnings: ↓↑↑↑↓, two arrows pointing down, the score is, therefore, 1.

5 Consecutive years of uninterrupted growth - Ideal(4)	Q6b Sales	2
4 Years of growth and		
Growth up in last 2 years - High Range (3)		
No growth in last 2 years - Low Range (2)		
2 or more years without growth - Red Flag (1)	Q6d Earnings	1

Part 2, Tier II:

In part 1 of the evaluation of growth trends, we measured the average, both for sales and for profits.

The way I understand part 1 and part 2 of the evaluation is as follows: Let's imagine we have a student whose grades during the last five years, from 0 –the lowest– to 10 –the highest– were as follows:

Year	1	2	3	4	5
Student 1	0	0	3	0	0
Student 2	3	4	5	6	7

In arrow language:

Student 1: ↑↓↑↓

Student 2. ↑↑↑↑

In both cases, the average score is 5.0, however, the consistency of the Student 2 is much greater than that of Student 1.

When considering the growth of companies, we prefer to see that they steadily keep growing year after year, rather than see them jump up and down. We like to see that they are consistently better year on year.

Part 2, Tier III: As we were saying in the last paragraph, we do love to see that companies consistently do better year on year both in sales and earnings. However, sh*t happens and this steady growth is very difficult to achieve, as we can establish when going through the 1,700 pretty companies.

Something to consider is that once you get an arrow down, it takes 5 solid years to wash it off the system. Thus, getting a score of 4 in growth trends is reserved only to the prettiest of the pretty companies.

Part 3, Tier I: This part 3 refers to what is the growth of both sales and earnings in the coming 3 to 5 years.

To punch the numbers in the cells, we need to know first what the size of the company is, which is given by the volume of projected annual sales.

Depending on the aforementioned volume of projected annual sales, we have three different sizes, all in USD:

Small: Up to 400 million

Medim: Between 400 and 3,999 million

Large: Greater than 4,000 million

The projected sales in the next 3 to 5 years in our example is 16,990 million.

2014	2015	2016	2017	2018	2019	2020	2021	© VALUE LINE PUB. LLC	23-25
8.47	7.68	7.65	9.16	10.61	10.49	11.55	13.00	Sales per sh	18.75
1.07	.93	.95	1.59	2.28	2.07	2.50	3.00	"Cash Flow" per sh	4.60
.14	.12	.19	.89	1.41	1.14	1.45	1.85	Earnings per sh A	3.00
.40	.40	.24	.24	.24	.24	.24	.28	Div'ds Decl'd per sh C	.60
.57	.52	.67	1.43	1.39	1.30	1.40	1.55	Cap'l Spending per sh	2.05
5.71	5.16	4.98	5.93	6.98	7.73	8.95	10.55	Book Value per sh	16.85
873.94	898.54	911.03	911.11	911.16	911.19	909.00	907.00	Common Shs Outst'g B	905.00
NMF	NMF	37.1	19.3	14.6	16.4	Bold figures are		Avg Ann'l P/E Ratio	17.0
NMF	NMF	1.95	.97	.79	.89	Value Line		Relative P/E Ratio	.95
4.8%	5.0%	3.4%	1.4%	1.2%	1.3%	estimates		Avg Ann'l Div'd Yield	1.2%
6404.0	6897.0	6973.0	8347.0	9664.0	9556.0	10510	11775	Sales ($mill)	16990

Because 16,990 million is greater than 4,000 million, we are dealing with a large company, in which case, we'll be comparing the growth of both sales and earnings with the highlighted figures as follows:

Projected Revenues ($M)

Q6e	16900	Ideal (4)	Range(3)	Range(2)	Flag(1)	
Small less than $400m		15%+	13.6-14.9	12.1-13.5	12 or less	
Medium $400-$3999m		12%+	11.1-11.9	10.1-11.0	10 or less	
Large $4000m+		10%+	8.6-9.9	7.1-8.5	7 or less	Large

The future projected sales and earnings can be found in the following table:

ANNUAL RATES of change (per sh)	Past 10 Yrs.	Past 5 Yrs.	Est'd '17-'19 to '23-'25
Sales	-.5%	2.0%	*11.0%*
"Cash Flow"	1.5%	19.5%	*15.0%*
Earnings	23.0%	- -	*17.5%*
Dividends	-.5%	-9.5%	*16.5%*
Book Value	-3.0%	1.5%	*16.0%*

Notice these figures are in italics: that means they are projections, rather than factual figures.

Q6f Projected Sales	11.0 %
Q6g Projected Earnings	17.5 %

<u>Part 3, Tier II:</u> Both estimates of sales growth and earnings growth refer to average annual compound growth, that is, the growth on the growth.

<u>Part 3, Tier III:</u> This is the formula to calculate the annual growth rate:

$$CAGR = \left(\frac{V_f}{V_i}\right)^{\frac{1}{t}} - 1$$

Where:

CAGR = compound annual growth rate
Vf = Final value

Vi = Initial value

t = time (in years)

Parts 1, 2 and 3 of growth trends put together

Let's do a quick review: we have studied the growth trends of sales and profits in three parts:

Part 1: the average during the last 5 years (past).

Part 2: the consistency over the last 5 years (past).

Part 3: the projections over the next 5 years (future).

By putting the three parts together, we get the overall score both for sales and earnings growth.

Adding all the scores we obtained when evaluating Growth Trends, we get a total of 13, which corresponds to a score of 3.

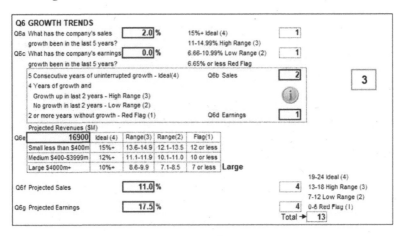

Q7: Management

<u>Tier I:</u> We will be answering four yes/no questions and, as usual, we'll make it very easy.

| 128.0 | 104.0 | 165.0 | 802.0 | 1287.0 | 1032.0 | *1305* | *1670* | Net Profit ($mill) |

Question 1: are profits increasing? We can use the same arrow system as for sales and earnings. In our example, ↓↑↑↑↓, which is a NO.

If they increase year on year, the answer is, definitely, a yes. If we are in front of a different case, use your common sense. For instance, if one year the profits have gone down but it would be a very small percentage, we could still answer yes if every other year is higher than the previous. If five years ago we get a down arrow and the other four years we get up arrows, I would still give it a yes.

Again, use your common sense. And, if you doubt, answer no.

Question 3: have they handled past challenges? Any company going through the lockdown times has handled a challenge. I always answer yes here.

Yet, again, once 2020 is a thing of the remote past, feel free to answer no, although I can't imagine a company not going through some challenges at some point.

Question 2 and 4: tick them and untick them and see if the **total score for quality** changes. Many times, it doesn't.

See more about the total score for quality in the next section, *Overall score.*

<u>Tier II</u>: Up until now, it all has been numbers. Therefore, zero room for interpretation. However, companies are living organisms consisting of stuff, machinery or otherwise, and, certainly, humans.

Under these premises, you and I now need to read the text and come up with our best interpretation to answer the following questions:

Question 2: Is management solid and are they anticipating future trends? That is, are they working soundly? Are they doing something to be one step ahead of what the future brings?

This is information that you would need to read, sometimes, between the lines and dancing around the financial poetry our dear Value Line analysts so lavishly endulge us with.

Question 4: Are they operating smoothly without any pending lawsuits?

The second part of the question, the one about the lawsuits, is normally no (I've only found one yes in the thousands of evaluations of quality I've done). If it were a yes, it would be clearly stated in the text of the commentary, with no need to do any archaeology work on our side.

As for the first part, the one about operating smoothy… Use your common sense. And, even at the risk of being annoying, when in doubt, asnswer no.

Tier III: Bear in mind that the commentary (the text) of the bottom right corner of the Value Line reports is:

1. Very eloquent, in absence of a better expression that more accurately describes the fact that the language is a bit convoluted.

2. Very conservative: no Value Line analyst will ever say *buy now! Not the right time!* or similar. They present the information as neutraly as they possibly can. In my opinion, and this is my opinion only, the

commentary tends to be more of a *the sky is falling over my head*/pessimistic type than merely neutral.

While doing my first tens of evaluations, I sort of freaked out when reading the commentary, as the words seemed to convey, to my unexperienced eyes, a lot of gloom and doom, even though all the numbers and projections didn't seem to align with my interpretation of what I was reading.

At this point, I take the doomsday comments with a pinch of salt and focus on some pieces of information that I deem to be very valuable, such as:

1. Percentage ownership of officers and directors: that means that the workforce has skin in the game, consequently, they are very interested in the company doing well. By the way: officers and directors are anyone working in the company, regardless of their job or position within it.

2. Buybacks: if the company is buying their shares back, that could be considered as an indicator of the good health of the company and its potential increase in share price.

3. Investments: when the cash goes down, it could very well be because the company has invested in buying another company, equipment, etc.

4. What is the clientele of the company? Some companies have only one main client, like a mothership, thus, there wellbeing will be heavily influenced by their mothership. (I'm using these terms for clarity only).

Overall score

Now that we have got all the scores for the different parameters we use to evaluate the quality of a company, we will be putting them all together to come up with the overall score for quality.

As we were saying before, some things are more important than others. When choosing a partner, kindness is more important than the colour of the eyes (for most people, anyway). In the case of the quality of a company, we already established that the most important item was the growth trends, in particular, the growth of the profits.

And because it is more important, we will be giving more weight in the overall score. Thus, the higher the importance of each parameter, the more weight we'll give it.

After using this system for decades, we think it makes sense to assign the following weights to each parameter, represented by the number of asterisks. The number of asterisks is equivalent to a multiplying factor we'll be using for each one of the scores.

In words we all understand: we'll multiply the score of each parameter by the number of asterisks, which represent the importance of such parameter.

In our example:

	Values	Multiply by	Total	Max
Industry Ranking	2	*	2	4
Timeliness	2.5	**	5	8
Safety	2.5	**	5	8
Debt	3	**	6	8
Beta	2	*	2	4
Growth Trends	3	***	9	12
Management	3	**	6	8
			35	52

The
Investment
Club Network
TICN
Copyright TICN Ltd. 2002

	TICN Guide
40-52 Ideal (4)	
27-39 High Range (3)	
14-26 Low Range (2)	**3**
0-13 Red Flag (1)	

Thus, applying the ranges for the overall score, our company is a 3 for quality. The maximum we can get is a 4 and, the minimum, 1.

Equally, the maximum we can get when evaluating the price is a 4 and that's why we call this evaluation process 4x4 System.

Out of the thousands of companies that we can buy shares in, we have now limited our choice to the ones with quality scores of 3 and 4 only out of 1,700. This could be as little as one to two hundred.

There are way less candidates to join our dream basketball team. Which is good, because they will form a better team.

Congratulations!

One chapter ago, you had no idea whatsoever of how to evaluate the quality of a company. Now, even if with the equivalent of training wheels in a bicycle, you are able to get a very good idea of the quality of a company making use of unbiased information.

Let's look now at another company so you can compare the one we've just evaluated with this new one.

Cheat. Copy what we've done before. Know that the process will get faster and faster as you repeat it... And you remember where to find the information in this sea of numbers!

Evaluation of quality: another example

Here is my invitation for you to evaluate the quality of CMPR. Please, do it. Practicing is the best way to learn.

Have you even seen anyone learning to swim from a book?

You can find the report and the mindmap in the Annex.

Comments on quality

If you haven't evaluated the quality of the company proposed as recommended in the previous section... You have another chance to do it. Come on! Break your *I'll do it later* habit! And this is coming from an author originally from a country famous for words such as *mañana* and *siesta*...

If you have done the evaluation, Congratulations! You've learned something new by practicing it, and, by doing so, but you have also started to create new neuronal pathways that will wire together the more you practice. Your brain is changing.

After studying these two companies, I am completely sure than you would pick the first one with no hesitation. One chapter ago, you might have no idea of where to start, and look at you now!

This builds confidence. And that's the point. It's not an emotion that morphs into who knows what, but a solid foundation to build our house of wealth. No space for guessing, hoping or praying.

Now that you are an expert in the making of evaluating the quality of a company using the 4x4 System, let's adventure ourselves into a nerdier sphere, which will help our confidence grow even stronger.

1. When you see a *d* in front of a number, that means *deficit*, negative. Certainly, not something we want to see. However, some companies are seasonal and some particular quarters are negative due to the nature of the business although the full year can be always positive.

2. It is very difficult to score 4 for quality. And remember how long it takes to clean up the effect of an arrow pointing down (↓) when measuring the growth trends of sales and earnings. Five years, no less!

3. In the accounts that I am involved in, we work with qualities 3 and 4. However,

4. make sure you know where the 3 is coming from (see red flags underneath).

5. Each parameter in the evaluation is important. Nevertheless, some are more important than others. Remember that being kind (or respectful, or integrous, or faithful) carries more weight than the colour of the hair (if any) when finding a partner.

6. Remember that the most important item is the growth trends of sales and earnings. Out of the two of them, earnings.

7. Earnings, which is the same as profits, is, pretty much, the reason for a company to exist.

8. Consider applying the same principle to yourself: is your quality as a person growing?

9. Red flags: I prefer to go through my red flags at the end of the evaluation of both quality and price, as they apply to the overall view of a company.

10. The Value Line reports are updated every 13 weeks, which means that there is a new report every quarter. In the meantime, you can check any news events on their website.

11. When conducting the evaluation of quality, you could use the following values directly from the

dashboard, as they are updated more frequently: price, timeliness and safety.

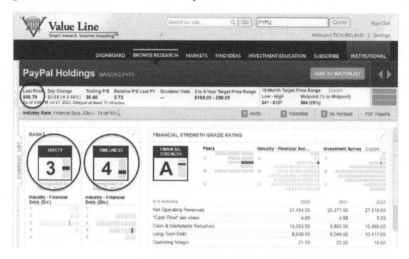

1.4. Picking high value stocks

The whole point of the exercise we are about to do is to find good value, that is, products on sale.

Our products are shares. What do I mean by shares *on sale*? That they are cheaper than they normally are while the quality stays the same. Yes: like on Black Friday or June sales, you can buy the same stuff at a lower price.

To the uninformed individual, a decrease in a stock price could mean (based on nothing substantial, really) that the company is going bust. But you are now an informed individual and you won't have an opinion, but you will base your conclusions on facts.

Do you remember our dream basketball team? It has now moved one step forward. We have gotten rid of the slow movers (in evaluation of companies' lingo, the ones with a score of 2 or 1) and the participants are ready for the next test: price.

How much are we ok with paying for these quality players? You would agree with me that the lower we pay for them, the better for us.

In the world of picking stocks to invest in, we'll be focusing on the parameters listed below. No need to freak out if you don't know what they mean, because everything is learnable and we have already experienced that we can fill up an evaluation template quite easily.

Nonetheless, be open and happy to learn something new: that means you are creating new neuronal connections (neuroplasticity), which has wonderful effects in your mind and body.

P2: Dividends
P3: Estimated price appreciation
P4: Sales vs earnings
P5: P/E ratio
P6: Buy and sell ranges
P7: Reward to risk ratio

P2: Dividends

Cal-endar	EARNINGS PER SHARE A				Full Year	Cal-endar	QUARTERLY DIV'DS PAID C				Full Year
	Mar.Per	Jun.Per	Sep.Per	Dec.Per			Mar.31	Jun.30	Sep.30	Dec.31	
2017	.12	.17	.26	.34	.89	2016	.10	.06	.06	.06	.28
2018	.25	.29	.41	.46	1.41	2017	.06	.06	.06	.06	.24
2019	.20	.18	.34	.43	1.15	2018	.06	.06	.06	.06	.24
2020	.25	.30	.40	.50	1.45	2019	.06	.06	.06	.06	.24
2021	.35	.40	.50	.60	1.85	2020	.06				

<u>Tier I:</u> We need two figures here as follows:

1. Last year's earnings per share

2. Last year's dividends

Let's divide 1. by 2.

If we get more than 0.5, we give it a score of 4.

If we get less than 0.5, we give it a score of 1.

1. **Last year's earnings per share = 1.15**

2. **Last year's dividends = 0.24**

$$\frac{1.15}{2} = 0.58 > 0.24$$

P2 DIVIDENDS					Yes, Ideal (4)	
E.P.S		P2a	1.15	Are last year's dividends		4
Last year's dividends		P2b	0.24	less than 1/2 of E.P.S?		
				No, Red Flag (1)		

<u>Tier II:</u> Those who love formulas are happy now. Those who are more visual, no clue what has just happened.

Because an image is worth more than 1,000 words, imagine that the earnings per share (the profits of the company per share) are represented by this rectangle and a line showing the middle.

We want the dividends to be **below** the line in the middle.

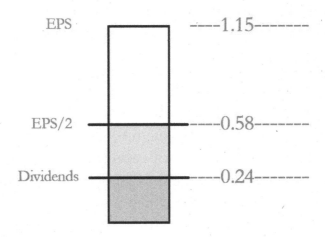

The dividends of last year (0.24) are less than half the earnings per share (0.58).

<u>Tier III:</u> Companies report their earnings every quarter. The way to report them is *earnings per share*, to refer it to a unit so we can compare like with like.

Stating that an orchard produced 5,000 liters of cider gives us less information than if we say that an orchard produced 60 ml of cidre per apple. This information provides a much clearer picture of how much each apple is producing.

With those profits, companies can do... Whatever they want, really. Some give part of those profits to the shareholders. That's a *dividend*.

Part of those profits will be used to make the company grow and produce more stuff or produce it more efficiently or both.

When companies pay a dividend, we will receive it in our accounts passively, that is, doing NOTHING. Well, we do have to do something: buy the shares! But once they are bought, we will receive a payment directly in our account every time the company pays dividends, which could be, typically, once, twice or four times a year.

If companies decide to pay dividends, we, as investors, are very happy with it, why not. However, we prefer that those dividends are no more than 50% of the profits, because, as shareholders that we are, we understand that most of the profits stay within the company and are invested into its growth.

To calculate a more precise dividend, instead of using the one that corresponds to the whole last year, you can add up the dividends paid the last four quarters.

Thus, for example,

Cal-endar	QUARTERLY DIVIDENDS PAID c				Full Year
	Mar.31	Jun.30	Sep.30	Dec.31	
2019	- -	.056	.056	- -	.11
2020	- -	- -	- -	- -	- -
2021	- -	- -	- -	- -	
2022	- -	.021	.020	.019	.06
2023	.022	.033			

If we use the dividends of last year, that would be 0.06 dollars per share; if we use the last four quarters, it would be 0.09:

$$0.020 + 0.019 + 0.022 + 0.033 = \mathbf{0.09}$$

P3: Estimated price appreciation

```
2023-25 PROJECTIONS
                          Ann'l Total
          Price   Gain     Return
High       60    (+225%)    36%
Low        40    (+120%)    23%
```

Tier I: We need to answer a very simple question: the projections of the highest value, are they greater or less than 15%?

The 36% of our example is greater than 15%. Therefore:

P3 ESTIMATED PRICE APPRECIATION				
Projected % growth of the high high stock price 5 years forward	P3a	36.00	Is it over 15% per annum?	Yes, Ideal (4) No, Red Flag (1)	**4**

Tier II: The estimated price appreciation sounds quite fancy, doesn't it? Nevertheless, all it means, in regular everyday words, is: How much, percentagewise, is the price going to grow in the next 5 years?

Tier III: The question of Tier II is a tricky one, because it refers to the *compound* growth.

Our standard of growth over the next 5 years is that we want the share price to, at least, double in this period.

What should the compound growth be for the share price to double in the next 5 years?

If we don't remember from our school days the formula of compound interest, nowadays we have the Internet, which, within a fraction of a second, *reminds* us that such a formula looks like this:

$$V_f = V_i \left(1 + \frac{r}{n}\right)^{nt}$$

Where:

V_f = the final price (twice the price today, in our case study).
V_i = the initial price (the price today).
r = the rate of growth (precisely what we want to calculate).
n = number of times the interest is applied per time period. In our case, 1, as it is applied once per year.
t = number of time periods elapsed. For us, 5, as we are considering a 5-year period.

Since we want the initial price, V_i, to double, then the final price, V_f, should be twice the initial price:

$$V_f = 2V_i$$

Making substitutions in the formula,

$$2\,V_i = V_i \left(\frac{r}{1}\right) x^2$$

$$2\,V_i = V_i \left(\frac{r}{1}\right)^{\frac{1*5}{t}} - 1$$

$$2V_i = V_i \left(1 + \frac{r}{1}\right)^{1*5}$$

$$2 = (1 + r)^5$$

$$\sqrt[5]{2} = 1 + r$$

$$r = \sqrt[5]{2} - 1$$

$$r = 0.1487$$

To get the percentage, we just need to multiply by 100, and that's when we obtain, therefore, 14.87%.

Rounding it up, we get 15%, which is the magic number: when the estimated price appreciation is 15%, the share price will double in the next 5 years. If it is higher, the price will increase even more. Happy days.

P4: Sales vs earnings

ANNUAL RATES of change (per sh)	Past 10 Yrs.	Past 5 Yrs.	Est'd '17-'19 to '23-'25
Sales	-.5%	2.0%	11.0%
"Cash Flow"	1.5%	19.5%	15.0%
Earnings	23.0%	- -	17.5%
Dividends	-.5%	-9.5%	16.5%
Book Value	-3.0%	1.5%	16.0%

Tier I: We need the average sales over the last 5 years and the average earnings over the same period.

Past 5 years: in our example, 0% for earnings and 2.0% for sales.

Earnings grow faster than sales? NO. 0<2.0.

Future 3-5 years: 17.5% for earnings and 11.0% for sales.

Earnings to grow faster than sales? YES. 17.5>11.0.

Then, we will compare the expected sales and expected earnings in the future 5 years:

One YES and one NO gives us 2.5, rounded to 3 by the spreadsheet.

P4 SALES Vs EARNINGS			
% of annual sales in past 5 years	P4a	2.00	Earnings growth faster than sales?
% of annual earnings in past 5 years	P4b	0.00	2 Yes = Ideal (4)
			1 Yes, 1 No = Range (2.5)
Projected % of annual sales growth in next 5 years	P4c	11.00	2 No = Red Flag (1)
Projected % of annual earnings growth in next 5 years	P4d	17.50	Earnings growth faster than sales?

3

<u>Tier II:</u> The best possible scenario of the sales growth and earnings growth is that both increase year on year with the earnings growing faster than the sales.

Intuitively, you can figure out yourself that this ideal scenario would mean that our company is selling more stuff (products or services or both) every year and the profits are getting greater every year because they can do things better, faster, with less expenses, more efficiently...

<u>Tier III:</u> This measurement is self-evident, so I don't have much to add as a Tier III but the same quote we used before: *Profit is sanity*, whichever way you want to put it.

What is profit? the amount of money a company makes by selling stuff (products and/or services) after substracting all the expenses they need to pay for to produce those products and/or services. In very, very short: the bottom line.

P5: P/E ratio

2015	2016	2017	2018	2019	2020	2021	© VALUE LINE PUB. LLC	23-25
7.68	7.65	9.16	10.61	10.49	11.55	13.00	Sales per sh	18.75
.93	.95	1.59	2.28	2.07	2.50	3.00	"Cash Flow" per sh	4.60
.12	.19	.89	1.41	1.14	1.45	1.85	Earnings per sh A	3.00
.40	.24	.24	.24	.24	.24	.28	Div'ds Decl'd per sh C	.60
.52	.67	1.43	1.39	1.30	1.40	1.55	Cap'l Spending per sh	2.05
5.16	4.98	5.93	6.98	7.73	8.95	10.55	Book Value per sh	16.85
898.54	911.03	911.11	911.16	911.19	909.00	907.00	Common Shs Outst'g B	905.00
NMF	37.1	19.3	14.6	16.4	Bold figures are		Avg Ann'l P/E Ratio	17.0

Tier I: We get the Avg Ann'l P/E ratio of the last 5 years, add up the five values and divide by five to get the average.

Then, we compare this average with the actual P/E ratio.

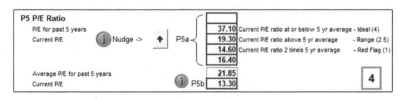

In our example:

P5 P/E Ratio						
P/E for past 5 years						
Current P/E	(i) Nudge ->	↑	P5a	37.10	Current P/E ratio at or below 5 yr average	- Ideal (4)
				19.30	Current P/E ratio above 5 yr average	- Range (2.5)
				14.60	Current P/E ratio 2 times 5 yr average	- Red Flag (1)
				16.40		
Average P/E for past 5 years				21.85		
Current P/E			(i) P5b	13.30		4

<u>Tier II:</u> *P/E ratio* is equivalent to *price to earnings ratio.* The price of a share divided by the profits that that one share produces.

It is our preference that the actual P/E ratio is lower than the average P/E ratio of the last five years. That is very likely to mean that the value now is better, as it will take us less time to get our investment back. Let's go a bit further into this concept.

In everyday life, we are probably more used to *earnings yield* than we are to P/E ratios and, surprise, one is the mathematical inverse of the other.

Example of earnings yield: if we have a house for which we paid 500,000, we rent it, and our tenants pay 40,000 a year, the yield would be:

$$Annual\ yield,\% \ = \ \frac{40,000}{500,000} \ x \ 100 = 8\%$$

We can read this as: *Every year, we get 8 for every 100 that we invested.*

If we go to a more natural environment, if we invest 500 per tree in an orchard and we get 40 every year per tree planted, that's, again, an 8% annual yield or annualised return on investment.

When turning the equation around:

$$P/E, years = \frac{500,000}{40,000} = 12.5\ years$$

We can read this as follows: *It will take me 12 and a half years to get my investment back out of the profits I make a year.*

From the equation, we can deduct that the higher the earnings or the lower the price, the less time it will take us to get our investment back.

Now that we understand the concept, let's go to shares.

In our example, the P/E ratio is 13.3.

P/E RATIO	**13.3**	(Trailing: 16.0 Median: 35.0)

The P/E ratio is one of the most widely used parameters used to value companies.

What are the implications? How do we read this? The P/E provides an indication of how much the investors are willing to pay for a stock based on its current earnings. A high P/E suggests investors are willing to pay higher per unit of earnings, which indicates optimism about future growth. When the P/E is low, it could indicate both that the market holds low expectations on the future growth of the company or that the stock is undervalued.

<u>Tier III:</u> According to Investopedia, and as seen in the previous section: *In general, a high P/E suggests that investors are expecting higher earnings growth in the future compared to companies with a lower P/E. A low P/E can indicate either that a company may currently be undervalued or that the company is doing exceptionally well relative to its past trends.*

The kind of stock we love to invest in are currently undervalued high-quality companies. In our experience of investing in high-quality companies, low P/E ratios tend to indicate, indeed, that a company is undervalued (it's cheaper than it should be) or it is doing much better than it used to be doing.

Hence the importance to keep a record of past P/E ratios of the companies we are interested in or are already holding.

To put things into perspective, let's see what the P/E for our dear friend the SP-500 has done since the late 1800's:

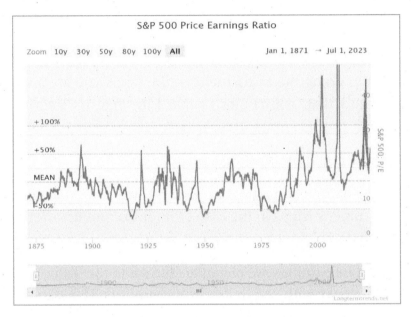

When the P/E of the SP-500 reaches peaks, that could be interpreted as a sign of the market being oversold, like in 2000 (dot com bubble) or 2008 (sub prime mortgages). In these times, the shares in the SP-500 exhibit prices higher than their true value.

There are minimums in 1942 (WWII), the 70's (oil crisis), the recession of the 80's and, more recently, massive lockdowns around the world starting in March 2020. These were fantastic times to buy shares at low prices.

Please, note that for the first 120 years, the VIX was trading mainly between 10 and 20. However, for the last 30 years, the VIX has been living between 15 and 45.

When doing the assessment of the price, you are going to find that, sometimes, Value Line reports the P/E NMF (no meaningful figures).

There could be three reasons for this:

1. That the company has been trading for a very short time, such as in the case of an initial public offering (IPO).

2. The earnings are negative (shown in the Value Line report with a *d* in front, remember? The *d* means *deficit* –minus–.

3. The earnings are very small in comparison with the share price.

P5: Buy and sell ranges

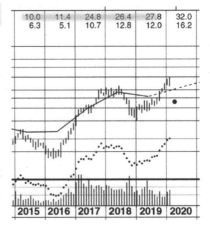

Tier I: As usual at this level, we'll just fill up the cells with the information that it is required.

To calculate the **average high**, we add up the highest prices of the last 5 years and divide by 5.

In our example:

$$\frac{10.0 + 11.4 + 24.8 + 26.4 + 27.8}{5} = 20.08$$

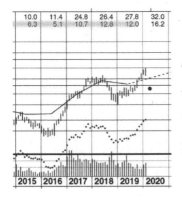

To calculate the **average low**, we add up the lowest prices of the last 5 years and divide by 5.

In our example,

$$\frac{6.3 + 5.1 + 10.7 + 12.8 + 12}{5} = 9.38$$

To calculate the **average EPS** (earnings per share), we add up the EPS of the last 5 years and divide by 5.

2014	2015	2016	2017	2018	2019	2020	2021	© VALUE LINE PUB. LLC	23-25
8.47	7.68	7.65	9.16	10.61	10.49	11.55	13.00	Sales per sh	18.75
1.07	.93	.95	1.59	2.28	2.07	2.50	3.00	"Cash Flow" per sh	4.60
.14	.12	.19	.89	1.41	1.14	1.45	1.85	Earnings per sh A	3.00
.40	.40	.24	.24	.24	.24	.24	.28	Div'ds Decl'd per sh C	.60
.57	.52	.67	1.43	1.39	1.30	1.40	1.55	Cap'l Spending per sh	2.05
5.71	5.16	4.98	5.93	6.98	7.73	8.95	10.55	Book Value per sh	16.85
873.94	898.54	911.03	911.11	911.16	911.19	909.00	907.00	Common Shs Outst'g B	905.00
NMF	NMF	37.1	19.3	14.6	16.4	*Bold figures are*		Avg Ann'l P/E Ratio	17.0
NMF	NMF	1.95	.97	.79	.89	*Value Line*		Relative P/E Ratio	.95
4.8%	5.0%	3.4%	1.4%	1.2%	1.3%	*estimates*		Avg Ann'l Div'd Yield	1.2%
6404.0	6897.0	6973.0	8347.0	9664.0	9556.0	10510	11775	Sales ($mill)	16990

In our example:

$$\frac{0.12 + 0.19 + 0.89 + 1.41 + 1.14}{5} = 0.75$$

The future **estimated high stock price** can be calculated in two steps as follows:

Step 1: We divide the **average high** by the **average EPS**, which gives us the **average high P/E ratio.**

$$\text{Average high P/E ratio} = \frac{20.08}{0.75} = 26.77$$

2014	2015	2016	2017	2018	2019	2020	2021	© VALUE LINE PUB. LLC	23-25
8.47	7.68	7.65	9.16	10.61	10.49	11.55	13.00	Sales per sh	18.75
1.07	.93	.95	1.59	2.28	2.07	2.50	3.00	"Cash Flow" per sh	4.60
.14	.12	.19	.89	1.41	1.14	1.45	1.85	Earnings per sh A	3.00
.40	.40	.24	.24	.24	.24	.24	.28	Div'ds Decl'd per sh C	.60
.57	.52	.67	1.43	1.39	1.30	1.40	1.55	Cap'l Spending per sh	2.05
5.71	5.16	4.98	5.93	6.98	7.73	8.95	10.55	Book Value per sh	16.85
873.94	898.54	911.03	911.11	911.16	911.19	909.00	907.00	Common Shs Outst'g B	905.00
NMF	NMF	37.1	19.3	14.6	16.4	Bold figures are		Avg Ann'l P/E Ratio	17.0
NMF	NMF	1.95	.97	.79	.89	Value Line		Relative P/E Ratio	.95
4.8%	5.0%	3.4%	1.4%	1.2%	1.3%	estimates		Avg Ann'l Div'd Yield	1.2%
6404.0	6897.0	6973.0	8347.0	9664.0	9556.0	10510	11775	Sales ($mill)	16990

Step 2: We multiply the **average high P/E ratio** by the **projected EPS**, which gives us what we were looking for all along, which is the **estimated high stock price** (the highest value the shares will trade at in the next 3-5 years provided everything else were kept the same).

$$\text{Estimated high price} = 26.77 \times 3.00 = \mathbf{80.31}$$

We now need to calculate the **estimated low stock price**. Again, this is a two-step process.

Step 1: We divide the **average low stock price** by the **average EPS**, which gives us the **average low P/E ratio**.

$$\frac{9.38}{0.75} = 12.51 = Avg\ low\ \text{P/E}\ ratio$$

Cal-endar	EARNINGS PER SHARE A				Full Year
	Mar.Per	Jun.Per	Sep.Per	Dec.Per	
2017	.12	.17	.26	.34	.89
2018	.25	.29	.41	.46	1.41
2019	.20	.18	.34	.43	1.15
2020	.25	.30	.40	.50	1.45
2021	.35	.40	.50	.60	1.85

Step 2: We multiply the **average low P/E ratio** by the **EPS for last year**, which gives us the **estimated low stock price**.

$$12.51\ x\ 1.15 = \mathbf{14.38}$$

We now have an estimation of what the highest price of the stock can be in the next 3 to 5 years and an estimation of what the lowest price of the stock can be in the same time period.

Low = 14.38
High = 80.32

Substracting the highest from the lowest and dividing the result by three will give us three equal chunks or slices that we can call *sell range*, *hold range* and *buy range*.

1. Sell range: the highest part. When the shares trade between its limits, we could consider selling them.

2. Hold range: the middle part. When the shares trade between its limits, we could consider doing nothing wih them, but to hold on to them.

3. Buy range: the lowest part. When the shares trade between its limits, we could consider buying them.

$$Slice\ size = \frac{80.32 - 14.38}{3} = 21.98$$

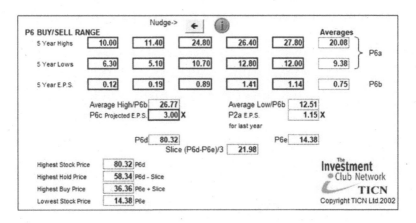

Tier II: As we already mentioned, what makes share prices move up long-term is the earnings (the profits).

We could say that the earnings are the energy that makes share prices move up and down: the more energy, the higher prices can reach.

To calculate the average high, low and EPS of the last 5 years is very straightforward.

Our next goal is to estimate what the **highest** and the **lowest** share prices will be in the future considering the factual information we have from the past and the estimated *energy* Value Line is giving us for the future.

1. Estimation of the **high stock price**: we know that price/earnings is the same as P/E. If the price is the average highest price, when we divide this highest price by earnings, we will, therefore, have the **average highest price/earnings**, which we can call **Avg high P/E ratio** (the highest P/E ratio).

2. By multiplying this parameter by the **projected EPS**, we get the **estimated high stock price.**

$$\frac{(avg\ highest)\ Price}{earnings} x \frac{(projected)\ earnings}{share} =$$
$$= \frac{(avg\ highest)\ Price}{share}$$

3. Estimation of the **low stock price**: Just like we did for the high price, we multiply the **average low price** by the same *energy*, the **EPS**. This multiplication will give us the **average low P/E ratio**.

4. Now, to estimate what's the minimum that his **average low P/E ratio** is going to go to, we will multiply it by a conservative factor: last year's earnings. Why? Because they have just happened, so, in a scenario in which the earnings won't grow, we 'd be stuck with what we got last year. (Please, bear in mind these calculations are estimations and we need to establish the assumptions).

$$\frac{(Avg\ low)\ Price}{earnings} \times \frac{(last\ year's)\ earnings}{share} = \\ = \frac{(avg\ low)\ Price}{share}$$

We now have the highest price and the lowest price we can expect in the future 5 years with the available information we have now and the projected EPS Value Line is giving us.

It's now time to calculate the slices.

If you are a mathematics lover, you will figure out that substracting the low from the high and dividing by three you will get the size of the slice and all you have to do now is to add that slice to the lowest price and then again to get the intervals for buying, holding and selling.

If your love is elsewhere, the best example I have come up with to explain the slices is as follows.

Imagine you have a desk or piece of furniture at home and you wish to build three shelves on top of it.

Just humour me and let's use the data from our example even if the dimensions don't make sense. Thank you!

Because we are all very good at *diy*, we will do the calculations on a paper first. Our drawing would look something like this:

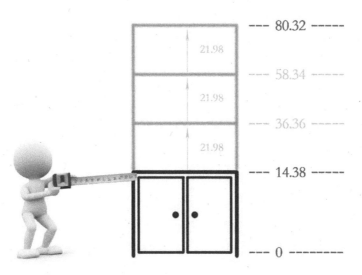

Easy, peasy, right? We measure the top of the desk and the total height and then divide by three, which gives us the height of each shelve.

Tier III: When doing these calculations, we need to use our common sense.

We can punch numbers on a spreadsheet, but when the figures are funny, we need to be able to understand what the figures are showing us.

The desired outcome is to stack the odds in our favour for the share prices to go up rather than to go down, even though they can always go down, anyway.

With this exercise, we want to do everything in our hands to be in the range of prices where the probability of the share price to go up is higher than the probability of the share price to go down.

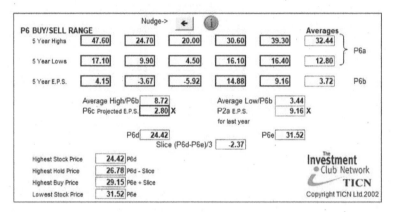

Please, pay attention to the EPS: they are all over the place!

These calculations were made on the Value Line report of U.S. Steel Corporation (ticker symbol X) dated 3rd of March of 2023.

If you are intrigued and you read the commentary of older reports, you will find that two reasons converged: the *higher stell demand across most markets* and *the addition of*

Big River Steel, which the company (X) acquired in January of this year (Value Line report of December 3rd, 2021).

P7: Reward to risk ratio

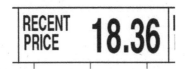

| RECENT PRICE | 18.36 |

Estimated high price = 26.77x3.00 = **80.31**

<u>Tier I:</u> The estimated high price minus the current price gives us how many dollars the price can go up.

P7 REWARD/RISK RATIO						
Estimated high price P6d	80.32	Current Price	P1	13.30	A divided by B =	61.90
	minus			minus		
Current Price	P1	13.30	Estimated low price P6e	14.38	3 or more = Ideal (4)	4
	A	67.02	B	-1.08	Less than 3 = Red Flag (1)	

The current price minus the estimated low price gives us how many dollars the price can go down.

We divide the former by the latter and get a number. If equal or greater than 3, we give it a score of 4; if less than 3, we give it a score of 1.

$$13.30 \; x \; 3 \; = \; 39.9$$

The current price times 3 is lower than the calculated high price of 80.32. The condition to get a score of 4 is met.

Tier II: In the *stacking the odds in our favour*, when buying a stock, we want to be as close to the bottom as possible, as that means we are buying as cheap as possible (by the way, forget about buying at the lowest price ever and selling at the highest price in history. For-get-it).

Ideally, we want to see that the price can go up at least three times the amount of dollars that it can go down.

Even if you are not the most visual person of the world, chances are that you can *see* here what we have been calculating and talking about mathematically:

In this example (ASGN), the shares are trading below the low calculated price. Even if we consider the lowest price in Value Line's the 18 months projection at this moment, we can see, literally, that there are probabilistically more chances of the shares to go up and down in the future, although, yes, of course, we know that shares go up and down all the time.

<u>Tier III:</u> Again, sorry about that, you will sometimes have to use your common sense. In particular, when there are negative figures in the calculations. We are not working with absolute values here, but with the real values.

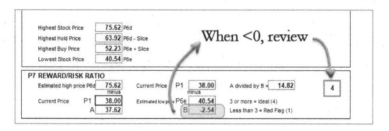

In this example here, we would get a score of 4. Notice that there is a negative value, due to shares being trading below the lowest projected price.

When we divide 37.62, which is the difference between the price today and the highest price:

$$\frac{37.62}{-2.54} = -14.8$$

The spreadsheet takes the absolute value, which is greater than 3:

$$/-14.8/ = 14.8$$

However, since the shares are trading at 38.00, for the reward to risk ratio to be 3:1, we would need the price to at least triple, that is, to go to 114.00, which is above the calculated highest price of 75.62.

In summary, in this scenario, the score should be 1.

Overall score

As we did for quality before, now that we have got all the scores for the different parameters we use to evaluate the price of a company, we will put them together to come up with the overall score for price.

In this case, we will give dividends only one asterisk, as we consider dividends to be less important than the rest of the parameters, all of which get the highest weight, that is, three asterisks.

In our example,

	Value	Multiply by	Total	Max
Dividends	4	*	4	4
Estimated Price Appreciation	4	***	12	12
Sales V Earnings	2.5	***	7.5	12
P/E Ratio	4	***	12	12
Reward/Risk Ratio	4	***	12	12
			48	52

Completed By	Ana R.

	TICN Guide
40-52 Ideal (4)	
27-39 High Range (3)	
14-26 Low Range (2)	4
0-13 Red Flag (1)	

Thus, applying the ranges for the overall score, our company is a 4 for price. Let's remember that the maximum we can get is 4 and, the minimum, 1.

Since, in our example, we had got a 3 for quality and we have now got a 4 for price, the overall score of our example company, as of the report dated 27th of March 2023, is:

SMTC 2023 03 27 **3 x 4**

Out of the 3 and 4's for quality companies that we have encountered –between 100 and 200–, in my experience, we can find no more than a 20% of them at a good, nice, low price. Of course, sometimes there will be more and sometimes there will be less.

And… Time to celebrate!

Not that long ago, you had no idea of how to evaluate what the quality of a public company, subject to be purchased by you and now, you have a lot to say about the quality **and** about its price. Wow! You've come a long way!

The way would have been even longer if when you first put your hands on this book you had not even ever thought of investing in the stock market because... (You know what: all the negative beliefs associated with the poor stock market that has done nothing to you!).

For our example, I chose a fundamentally strong company (the *fundamentals* are the money related bits and pieces, the finances, of companies. By the way, I've just realised so far I've never used the word *businesses*!).

I also chose SMTC as of the report of March 27, 2020 because I knew beforehand that we would get a 4 for price and that would be great for your learning.

Evaluation of price: another example

As a present, I will give you a company which, although fundamentally strong, we would consider it as *expensive*, as its score for price is lower than 4: ORLY.

This is the summary of its evaluation of quality and price that you can use as a cheat sheet. You can find its Value Line report in the Annex. The Industry Rank was 60 when the evaluation was made.

Quality score

	Values	Multiply by	Total	Max
Industry Ranking	2	*	2	4
Timeliness	4	**	8	8
Safety	4	**	8	8
Debt	4	**	8	8
Beta	1	*	1	4
Growth Trends	4	***	12	12
Management	3	**	6	8
			45	52

	TICN Guide
40-52 Ideal (4)	
27-39 High Range (3)	**4**
14-26 Low Range (2)	
0-13 Red Flag (1)	

Price score

	Value	Multiply by	Total	Max
Dividends	4	*	4	4
Estimated Price Appreciation	1	***	3	12
Sales V Earnings	2.5	***	7.5	12
P/E Ratio	2.5	***	7.5	12
Reward/Risk Ratio	1	***	3	12
			25	52

	TICN Guide
40-52 Ideal (4)	
27-39 High Range (3)	**2**
14-26 Low Range (2)	
0-13 Red Flag (1)	

Comments on price

How does it feel to confidently discard a company because it is too expensive? A decision made on real, actual figures, rather on the comments of your brother-in-law or your work colleague who heard somewhere that this stock is going to do a killing in a few months, so much so that you will be able to retire. Empowering, right?

Please, allow me to add some further information that I find particularly useful.

1. Value Line assigns analysts to the different companies based on seniority. Thus, the bigger, more complicated businesses to analyse are signed by the most experienced analysts, which will produce issue after issue on their assigned companies for years.

   I don't know about you, but this gives me even more confidence in the quality of the information.

2. We have stated that an average compound estimated price appreciation of 15% over a period of 5 years will make the stock price to double over this period. The higher it is, the more chances to increase our share price more and more.

   And when everything ticks the boxes and we get to see double digits also in the low estimated price appreciation, this is what our faces look like: ☺

3. When the total debt to market capitalisation is high, look also at the short-term debt (next 5 years). If this short-term debt is lower, you might still consider investing in this company short-term.

4. Working capital: is the difference between the current assets and the current liabilities.

Examples of current assets (assets expected to be converted into cash or used up within one operating cycle —usually, one year—): cash, accounts receivable (money owed to the company by customers), inventory (goods ready for sale and raw materials), prepaid expenses, short-term investments (that can easily be converted to cash within a short time frame), property plant and equipment (PP&E. Land, buildings, machinery, vehicles…), intangible assets (patents, trademarks, copyrights), investments (stocks, bonds, long-term notes recivable), long-term investments in affiliated companies, deferred tax assets (tax benefits that can be used to offset future tax liabilities), natural resources (oil reserves, mineral deposits, forests…), goodwill (excess of the purchase prices of an acquiered company over the fair value), leasehold improvements (enhancements made to leased properties that increase their value and utility), research and development assets…

Examples of current liabilities: accounts payable (money owed to suppliers or vendors), short-term loans, accrued expenses (expenses incurred in and not paid yet, like salaries), unearned revenue (payment received upfront), current portion of long-term debt, income tax payable (owed to the government), dividends payable (declared and not yet paid), debt, deferred tax liability, pension liabilities, lease obligations, etc.

This information will help understand better the commentaries, as you will be able to identify if certain information will be an asset or a liability.

5. Book value. Or liquidation value: if the company were to be sold, how much will it get back per share? 3:1 would be an acceptable ratio between trading price and book value; however, the closer the trading value is to the book value, the better.

6. When Warren Buffet worked for Benjamin Graham, he used to take the P/E ratio, multiply it by the price of the book and find companies that showed a figure below 22.5 when doing this calculation.

7. A quote from Mr. Buffet: *Price is what you pay. Value is what you get.*

Red flags

Over the years, at a very high cost, I've learned what a company can get away with and what can't.

Some of my decisions are an absolutely no-go territory; others, I would consider going there under under very precise circumstances.

In case it wasn't clear enough, let me stress the fact that I've learned these lessons at a very high financial and emotional cost. Judging by the fact that I am exposing myself with the good, the bad and the ugly, I'm sure you can infer that I do feel empowered... And much wiser!

I must admit I made most of my mistakes when I was at the very left of my personal Dunning-Kruger. If you have never heard of it, please, allow yourself to spend a few minutes learning about it because, once you understand it, you are a lot less likely to take (stupid) decisions while being on the left of the curve.

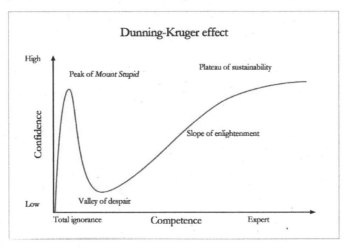

What this graph tells us is that when we learn something about a topic we knew nothing about, we tend to feel overconfident, to put it midly.

As we learn a bit more, we realise we don't know as much as we thought and that there is still so much to learn! Sort of the well known *I only know I know nothing.*

As we acquire more knowledge and experience, our level of competence increases gradually until the time comes when we could be considered experts in the matter.

Those getting there tend to continue learning and practicing their skills.

Ideally, they would also keep an open mind in case some new developments take place that would bring light to aspects they thought they knew everything about, but it might not be the case.

This latter paragraph shares both wishful thinking and reality. My point of view, anyway.

Yes. The red flags. Here they go:

1. Not having a full, comprehensive, Value Line report: no way.

2. Having a full, comprehensive report but timeliness has been suspended.

I would still look at this company if I've known it for a long time (do you remember the sheep?) and if the account is large and I have no other candidates. In this case, the investment will be planned as short-term and the allocation –we will talk about it at a later stage– will be smaller than the rest of positions of *pretty* companies.

As a teaser, know that *asset allocation* is, in plain clothes terms, how many eggs to put per basket.

3. Negative earnings: consistent negative earnings is a NO-NO.

   A company would be granted with a second look if the negative earnings happen only seasonally, like the 2nd quarter of each year every year, but the total earnings per year are positive and sound.

4. 3x3: never for small accounts (<200,000). In large accounts, a deep valuation will be made before deciding to invest in a 3x3.

   This valuation is a bit over the level of this book.

5. 2x3, 2x4: forget about them.

6. Score of 1 for quality: I don't think that's compatible with being one of the 1,700 *pretty* companies. At least, I've never encountered one.

7. Companies with Value Line reports of less than 5 years: NO-NO.

   For me, no less than 15 years.

8. Less assets than liabilities: for the novice, I'd say this is a hard NO.

   With more experience, there would be cases in which this situation is planned to be reversed in the foreseeable future and the reason for it could be a new acquisition, for instance, which requires money.

9. $P/E = NMF$. That means either negative earnings or tiny earnings in comparison with the share price.

10. Price higher than 100. My definition of small account is less than 200,000. Even at 200,000 or above, I stick to shares trading at a maximum price of 100. Of course, plus/minus a few dollars.

    More information about this when we talk about asset allocation.

11. I would strongly recommend picking companies in industries you understand and like.

Does all this mean that you are supposed to evaluate your companies once every three months? YES.

Do you expect to have a good relationship with your lover if you only talk to them once a year? No, right? Then, do the same with your businesses: know about them, just like you want to know about your lover's life.

However, I would hardly recommend that you don't fall in love with any stock in particular: you are not being unfaithful if you sell it, nobody dies if you had it for quite some time and now it's time to let it go. Becoming attached to some shares is doing emotions. AND WE DON'T DO EMOTIONS when trading.

1.5. Buy low and sell high. Time horizon: 3-5 years

Little summary of what we have learned so far. I'm using figures from 1965 until 2022 and I'm rounding them figures a bit, so they are easier to remember:

1. The market, as SP-500, grows at an average of approximately 10%.

2. Berkshire Hathaway grows at an average of approximately 20% a year.

3. We know now how to pick companies of high-quality at a good price by using the 4x4 System.

4. Value Line reports provide an estimation of the price appreciation, that is, the annual compound growth of the pretty stocks.

With the above information, it seems obvious that all we need to do for our investments to grow faster than 20% a year on average is to invest in companies with a projected total annual return higher than 20%.

Some examples:

2025-27 PROJECTIONS				2025-27 PROJECTIONS		
	Price	Gain	Ann'l Total Return		Price	Gain	Ann'l Total Return
High	95	(+290%)	41%	High	30	(+115%)	23%
Low	50	(+105%)	21%	Low	18	(+30%)	10%
2026-28 PROJECTIONS				2026-28 PROJECTIONS		
	Price	Gain	Ann'l Total Return		Price	Gain	Ann'l Total Return
High	85	(+270%)	39%	High	110	(+180%)	31%
Low	60	(+165%)	27%	Low	70	(+75%)	17%

All we would need to do would be:

1. Pick a company (or more) with a projected annual return greater than 20%.

2. Study its quality and make sure the score is 4 or 3.

3. Make sure we are ok with the reason/s why the score is 3 instead of 4, if that were the case.

4. Confirm that there are no red flags.

5. Buy the shares and establish the exit point.

6. Remember not to be too greedy and miss the exit point because Value Line said the shares will get to 90 and they are *only* trading at 88, for example.

7. Sell the shares when they have reached the exit price you have decided upfront.

Note: Value Line's projections might change over time. Either up or down. If up, you could adjust your exit point to a higher value. If down, you could adjust your exit point to a lower value that still meet your calculations.

Not all our children grow to be as tall as we thought they would. Same with shares: some will grow more than others. In this case, the average is what matters.

1.6. Buy low and sell high. Time horizon: 18 months

Value Line also provides estimations for the low and high prices within the next 18 months.

You can apply everything we said in the previous section, but, instead of using the 3-5 years horizons, use the 18 months'.

Be aware that this short-term projections move more than the long-term projections.

Be also aware that you can't go to the stock market and buy and sell as if you were in a grocery store. We need a *broker*, a person between us and the market.

This broker could be a physical person in a brokerage firm that you communicate with directly or it could be an execution platform. This latter is what we use.

Our broker is Planner Securities LLC and no, we don't get any commission from them. Planner provides a platform to trade, called *Alphaplan*, and we, the users, can do and undo from that platform. Would we need some assistance or even place a trade via phone, we can call them and they will assist.

They use an *intelligent router* that scans the market and finds the best prices for us. These prices are set by the different *market makers*.

Every price has two parts: the *bid* and the *ask*. The difference between them is called the *spread*. Pretty much, the market maker makes his or her salary (mostly *his*) from the spreads.

Don't worry if you don't know what bit is the bid and which one is the ask: when you buy, you buy at the highest price; when you sell, at the lowest price.

Think of what happens when you go to the bank to buy some currency: there are two prices. When you buy the currency, they give you as much as you can buy at the highest price of the two; when you come back from your trip, they will buy the money you didn't use at the lowest price of the pair; the bank always makes money on the trades.

The tighter the spread, the better for us, because we get to buy cheaper and sell dearer.

2. WHY THE STOCK MARKET

The intelligent investor is a realist who sells to
optimists and buys from pessimists.
Benjamin Graham

I don't know about you, but when I was growing up, I didn't receive any formal financial education.

My father was the breadwinner of the household and he made his money working at an office. It's a simplification, but you get the idea.

As for my mother, since whe needed or wanted some more money that the few notes in the manilla envelope she got monthly, she found herself some jobs here and there.

From both of them, I learned that they way to make money was to exchange it for our time, doing whatever activites we could do and others benefitted from. In short, time = money. There were bosses and people working for them and the members of my family belonged to the second group, the people working for bosses. Many years later, I learned the word *employee* and its implications.

Many of my family members had farms: they grew animals and plants and sold them for money. I loved the fact that they could choose at what time they would go to this or that field to do whatever activities were to be done. They worked for themselves.

What I considered a bit off putting was that they didn't take any holidays ever and that they needed to know pretty much everything having to do with the farm, because there was no one else to ask for training or support, apart from the occasional hand given by a neighbor.

In the case of the shops in our neighborhood, they provided us with stuff (clothes, shoes, food, hair cuts) and we paid for that stuff. They used to have people working for them, who came and went, but the owners seem to be there, in the shop, all the time, day after day. After all, they were business owners.

I did know the concept of shares, bonds, funds… But the same way that we all know pear trees, tapeworms or prostrate glands: we know they designate things that exist, have a fair idea of what they relate to, but wouldn't be able to tell them apart from similar items in a line up.

I didn't fully embrace the concept of *money can work for me* until my late 40's.

Those who have their money work for them are called *investors*.

Looking at this world from a bit of a distance, the basics don't seem too distant to my uncles and aunts putting potatoes in the ground and reaping a crop a few months later.

The planting couldn't be whenever, but at a certain time of the year. The potatoes would grow if no cataclysmic events happened until the time of cropping: not too early, not too late. If things didn't go according to plan, it would be time to wait for another year, so we knew that, long-term, there would be potatoes.

My family learned the skills and how to read the cues Nature provided. They learned to pick the right variety of potato, the type of soil, the moment to plant, the moment to do some maintenance and the moment to pick the tubers.

Same with shares: we now know how to choose pretty companies in industries we understand and like, of good quality that we can buy when they are at a good price, allow them to grow and, then, collect the growth when they are ripe.

With these four ways of making money in my head and not expecting to inherit much, win the lottery or marry into riches, and valuing free time greatly as well, I realised as follows:

	Money	Time
Not working	✘	✔
Working for others	✔	✘
Working for oneself	✘ or ✔	✘
Owning a business	✘ or ✔	✘
Investing	✔	✔

Interesting: the most likely way to having both money and time happens to be investing...

Once you know it, it's so evident! The only way to have money and time is to have money growing by itself. In the field, that means that the potatoes grow by themselves, without you having to be there holding them with your hands and watering them every hour. They just grow by themselves when they are in good soil, there is rain and the sun does its thing.

If our cheap shares of pretty companies belong to fundamentally strong companies, they have no other option but to grow.

In the meantime, we can use our time (our life) to do whatever feeds our souls.

Let me share with you this chart put together by a very conciencious and thorough researcher, colleague of ours, Bruneau Joseph. It is a comparison of different investments:

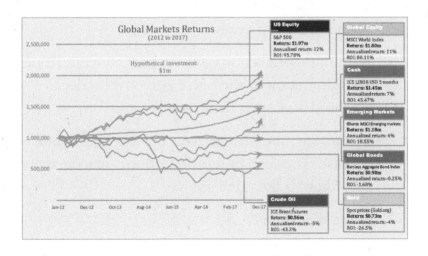

As we can see, the SP-500 outperforms global equity, cash, emerging markets, global bonds, gold and crude oil.

Below, some characteristics of investing in the US stock market I can share from my own experience.

1. Lifespan

   According to the Bureau of Labour Statistics, only 30% of the businesses survive after 10 years, with only 25% surviving after 15 years.

   Our *pretty* companies have been publicly traded for more than 20 years.

   According to the Small Business Administration, 50% of the businesses fail the first year and 95%, within the first 5 years.

   With these predictions, my deepest congratulations and admiration to the brave person who decides to go ahead and open their own business!

   By the way, the main reason for this failure rate is, in case you are interested, poor management, according to the same source.

2. Asset allocation

   In our system, we tend to allocate 5% per position and around 10% per industry, which means that the risk is well spread out (the allocation for really strong companies could be higher). When you have a business, this type of spreading the risk isn't always possible.

3. Experience

We only invest in companies with a proven record of decades long. These businesses have been through ups and downs and they are still standing. That means that their management teams know how to do their job.

4. Time

When we trade in a highly *liquid* market (this means that there are always buyers and sellers) like the US market, we can buy the best companies in the world in seconds.

In one of the companies that I worked for, a good profit would be 10 to 12% a year. To get to that figure, a team of people had to work 48 weeks of 40 hours per week per year. The average on the SP-500 is 10%; all you would have to do would be to buy an index that mirrors the SP-500 and… Wait.

5. Abundance

If you invest in art, you know that a piece of art is unique (unless limited series). If we consider property, I agree that there are a lot of them, but each one of them is unique, even if only because two identical properties couldn't be place on the exact same spot.

Also, if you buy one house, no one else can buy it. However, it doesn't matter how many shares someone buys, there will still be available for you as many as you wish to buy.

6. Liquidity

You an sell all your portfolio and have the money back in your bank in two days. Try to sell a property in 2 days at a fair price.

7. Convenience

You can trade the market from anywhere in the world if you have a device and an internet connection or a telephone line.

8. Assets/rent

We haven't talked about this bit yet. However, know that, in our system, we can use our shares as *assets* in the sense that they produce an income, that is, they put money into our pockets.

Gold, for instance, doesn't produce anything.

9. Easy

I hereby confess my absolute ingnorance on how long it takes to learn and be an expert in any other kind of investments. I do know, though, that learning to invest in the stock market at a basic level can be done in a weekend.

10. Cheap

If you invest by yourself, you can start investing as little as 500USD. If you invest in one of our clubs or consortiums, it could be as little as 130USD per month, with no upper limit.

11. Wide offer

We only invest in the US markets because this is the biggest market in the world, with thousands of companies to choose from.

All the top companies in the world trade in the US. Any company can be trading in their own country, but, if they are good enough, they will be traded in the US stock market as well.

The amount of money into buying and selling shares, although it obviously changes, is in the hundreds of millions every day, which makes this market very liquid.

In a low liquid market, it could take minutes (or more) to get your trades filled. I have seen this in the Brazilian stock market: orders populated the tapes… To be filled a long while later or not at all due to lack of buyers or sellers. In the US market, the orders get filled almost immediately.

12. The big danger

According to Tony Robbins' *Unshakeable*, the biggest danger of the stock market is NOT to be in it.

What are people afraid of? Losing money in the market. Tony Robbins' answer to this fear: *The stock market has never taken a dime from anybody. You take out your dime by selling.*

In a 20-year period, the S&P 500 produced an 8.2 percent return. If you were out of the market for just 10 of the best days … your return was cut in half, from 8.2 percent to 4.5 percent.

Important lesson: **stay** in the market **long-term**.

I've made money working for others (for 20 years), working for myself (as a photographer), from my own business (MLM) and I now live off the stock market.

Full disclosure: my personal accounts produce enough income to pay the bills. However, I love writing I love teaching and welcome any income that comes from these activities or any other. Could I do it for free? I could, but I choose not to because we, humans, get a lot more benefit from whatever it is when we pay for them... And it's fair.

You deserve wealth. Or do you not?

I briefly mentioned in the previous section that I worked in the corporate world, as a photographer and in an MLM (multi level marketing). I made money in all three, nevertheless, not as much as I could have.

In my humble opinion, I didn't make more money simply because, deep down, I thought I didn't deserve it.

1. First job at a company: even though I was the youngest worker with a university degree that signed a permanent contract and I was promoted within a short time after getting the job, facts that could have been considered as strong clues supporting that my work was good, there was this little voice telling me that I could have and should have done better and more.

I also believed a workmate of mine telling me that since I was doing the same things over and over, it made perfect sense to always get the same wages. It never crossed my mind, back then, that by doing the same things over and over, I was becoming more proficient, faster, wiser and a master; I was able to do more stuff better in a shorter time, which meant more profits for the company. Why not earning more??

2. Second job at a company: For doing the same job as my counterparts in other countries, I was being paid a lot less, and I mean it: less than half.

How did they get away with it? Because I allowed it. Not only I was being paid a lot less for the same work than others, I wasn't paid **at all** for about one and a half years, since my wages were being used to pay my co-workers'.

I allowed that. I know: crazy.

3. Photography: I love photography, joined a photography group more than 20 years ago, had my own studio at home, spent hundreds of hours taking photos and developing them in my dark room and on the computer.

I used to take pictures for others and just give to them as a present. Mostly, I just got a thank you.

Same idea: because money was not exchanged and they didn't appreciate my little pieces of art because they didn't know how much work went into the photos.

When I decided to go more professional and get paid, it was wonderful... when the clients came to me directly after seeing previous work of mine and it was also painful when I *tried* to sell services. I hated, as strong as a word this is, to sell myself, I guess because I felt pushed to explain how good I was and how much more the clients could get out of my work compared to others'.

4. MLM: Multi level marketing. If you take it as a business, your work consists on building a distribution network of high-quality products.

   It was a very toughening period in that I did a lot of things outside my comfort zone. Very good learning experience that I won't do again.

5. Stock market: As I said before, I became financially free only months after I started trading. I was at the stupidity peak in the Dunning Krugger effect chart. Making money couldn't be that easy, right?

   It took me five years in university plus one doing research to have access to monthly wages for which I was selling a minimum of 180 hours of my life per month plus all the time required to do them, like commuting, getting ready, buying working clothes, a car... And, now, in 3 to 5 hours a month I can do twice as much as my wages? What? Too good to be true!

And... *voilà*! Let's go back to real life as I believed it was, that place in which making money was tough and it took very long hours.

My journey through the aforementioned Dunning Krugger chart was slow and emotionally costly. The learning curve benefitted not only from the thousands and thousands of hours I put into learning the 4x4 System theoretically, practically and teaching it, but also from working in myself. The *know thyself... And you should have the power* proved to be so true!

6. Writing and teaching (nowadays): I have written more than ten books in two languages. I wasn't talking about them for the same old *story*: not worth it, not good enough. I don't hold those statements as true anymore.

   I wrote *story* in italics because I wish to bring your attention to it: everything you tell yourself, or your monkey mind says to you is nothing else but a story. Most likely, a story someone else told you, you made it your own and you have been living your life according to that story. When is now a good time to change the narrative? Is that really you? The good son or daughter who works as a _____, just like daddy before you? Who married and has children because that's what's you are meant to do?

Time is ticking. Do you want to live someone else's idea of who you are supposed to be to make them happy or try something different… without guilt?

Growing up, we belief everything that comes in through our senses is the truth because we have no filters. As mentioned in previous books of mine in more detail, it has to do with the way our brains work: the main wavelengths that it produces till the age of approximately seven are similar to those under hypnosis, thus why we don't question the existence of a being such as the Tooth Fairy (or a mouse if you are in Spain), which will come at night and leave some money for the removal service of our milk teeth.

We also believe that we are good at running or suck at Math, that we sing like an angel, that we will never amount to anything, all of which we make true, whether we were born with a gift for running, numbers, music or whatever the discipline that just needed to be nurtured for it to shine.

From my days in school, I remember how the girls who were good at, let's say, art, but didn't have a brain for languages were sent to English private tuition rather than to an extra curricular art class. Why? So that they could become… mediocre.

You might believe in God, the Universe, the Consciousness, the Field, the Source or whatever word you want to use to design the creative intelligence. Even if you don't, call it agnostic or atheist, you do believe in Mother Nature. It's in your face all the time!

Bring a cat to your mind, or any other animal of your preference. Imagine that we condition the cat to live underground, as if it were a mole. You might think this is ridiculous, probably failing to recognise that you have been an accountant all your life, to say something, who dances with your feet under the desk even while stuck to your chair punching numbers in your computer.

Whatever number of days ahead of you, what do you *really* what to do with them?

Wealth is a stated of mind and having money is just part of it. I strongly recommend you say ¥€$ to wealth in all areas. Mean it!

And take action!!!

3. INCREASING THE RETURNS

It does not take money to make money.
Robert T. Kiyosaki

3.1 Technical analysis

Time to take our players to the basketball court. So far, they have proved to us that they are tall and that they can run fast. We want to hire them cheap and perhaps sell them to another team when they are at the top of their careers and invest in other younger promises.

Let's consider that we want to buy some shares. Because Value Line gives us the short-term price projections (18 months), we already have quite a clear idea of when share prices are close to the lowest point in this time frame.

Since we are already more advanced students, we can refine the *entry point* (that's what's called the point at which you enter the position. In easy words: when we buy the shares) by *reading* the charts.

It's not reading like a book, but more like traffic signs.

Ready for the adventure?

Charts

Two axes: the one at the bottom (x-axis or abscissas) shows time and the one standing (y-axis or ordinates) shows price.

Since the inception of the stock market (the New York Stock Exchange, NYSE, started trading back in 1792), all charts have in common that they are never straight lines, rather sort of waves that move up and down ceaselessly.

Please, make sure you stick this concept to your brain: share prices move up and down all the time. I'll say it again: **share prices move up and down** all the time. Why is that? Share prices change all the time due to the confrontation, so to speak, between offer and demand, which translates into a chart with a trajectory that shows ups and downs.

During this *confrontation*, certain levels show spots in which there is an unbalance between offer and demand, which we call *support* and *resistance*.

Support: in times where there is more selling than buying, the interest for selling significantly decreases, thus reaching a minimum point that, most likely, has happened in the past.

Resistance: in times where there is more interest in buying than in selling, there comes to a point where a maximum point is reached, resistance, where the tables turn and a higher interest in selling starts to happen.

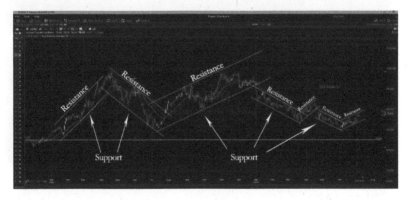

The balance between the forces of buying and selling is very delicate and it only takes a little unbalance to shift the share price movement.

Trends

When joining the support points, we get the *support line.*

When joining the resistance points, we get the *resistance* line.

The channel in between both lines is the *trend.*

Trends can go up, down and sideways. Sometimes, they also get the shape of a flag.

Case 1: up market

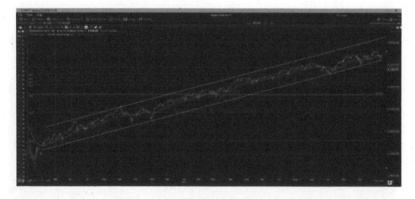

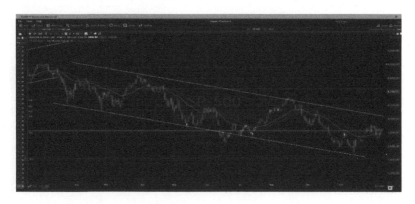

Case 2: down market

Case 3: sideways market

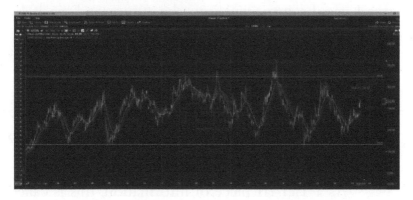

Flag pattern

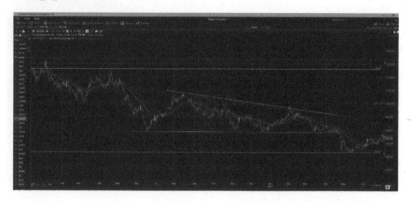

Very often, once a wave has been formed, a trend can be projected into the future and, as if by magic, the chart will travel from the bottom, support, to the top, resistance, from where it will start it trip down to support again.

It seems quite magical, doesn't it? How does the price know to start turning at a precise point? It has to do with human behaviour.

As a Tier III piece of information, this is called *The Elliot Wave Theory.*

But before we talk about Mr Elliot, let's rewind a few centuries, to the 12th century, no less.

It was in 1170 when a Leonardo Fibonacci was born to an Italian merchant. After his trips in the north of Africa —Egypt, mainly—, he published a book on calculus, thus introducing in Europe one of the big discoveries in Mathematics: the decimal system and the use of number zero. I can't even imagine how to do calculations with Roman numbers. Can you?

$$LXV + XII = LXXVII$$

versus

$$65 + 12 = 77$$

Fibonacci is very well known by the series that has his name, in which each number is obtained by the addition of the two previous numbers of the series: 1, 1, 2, 3, 5, 8, 13, 21, 34... It's a curious series that exhibits the following behaviours:

1. When dividing one number by the **next** one, the ratio tends to 0.618 (known as φ).

2. When dividing one number by the **previous** one, the ratio tends to 1.618 (know as Φ).

You got it! The golden ratio, everpresent in the natural world (biology, geology, galaxies, etc.) and also in those made by intelligent beings, like art, music or architecture. Why do we humans like this ratio? Because it creates harmony.

But... What does this have to do with the markets? Good question. And this is when we fast forward to the 20th century and revisit Mr. Elliot.

In the 1930s, Ralph Nelson Elliot studied 75 years' worth of yearly, monthly, weekly, daily, hourly and 30-minutes charts across various indexes.

He wrote several books, one of them being *Nature's Law*. In this text, Elliot says that the universe is governed by rules, as without those rules, there would be chaos. These rules applied all the time (like gravity, for instance); therefore, when we know how those rules work, we can predict future events.

Now! The juicy bit: since the markets are a human invention and humans are part of Nature, humans' behaviour is also governed by rules that create repetitive patterns in the markets.

He observed that there were recurring fractal wave patterns in the stock price movements related to changes in investors' sentiment and psychology. NB: **not** on the fundamentals of the companies.

Once we learn them, we can use them to predict what will happen.

Aha moment: whatever happens will happen again in the future.

Elliot establishes that there are certain patterns shown by anything that exhibits a pattern of growth and decay, such as the financial markets.

His theory identifies impulse waves that establish a pattern and corrective ones that oppose the larger trend. In easy words: even if the trend is up, there would be down movements and even if the trend is down, there will be up movements. And the prices of the correction are more likely to happen at the Fibonacci levels.

Let's see an example with the SP-500. From March 2020 until January 2022, the SP-500 followed an uptrend.

When drawing the Fibonacci tool from the lowest to the highest point, we get the different prices that are more likely to happen when the correction takes place, that is, stepping stones on the way down.

Let's now see what really happened:

Note: perfection doesn't exist. But we can see that the levels are pretty accurate.

By the way, the <u>main</u> setback levels, which we can't hardly see on the figures because the numbers are tiny, are as follows:

% setback	Market setback, approximately
30.20%	1/3
50.00%	1/2
61.80%	2/3

What this means is that when prices go up, they will come back down 1/3 or 1/2 or 2/3 of the increase. Can you imagine the psychological effects?

After euphoric cycles, fear cycles will take place and they will happen in predictable patterns.

This tool allows to foresee where the setbacks are likely to happen after a bullish period.

We've mentioned the word *fractal*. That means that there are trends within trends, that the same behaviour of prices going up and down can be

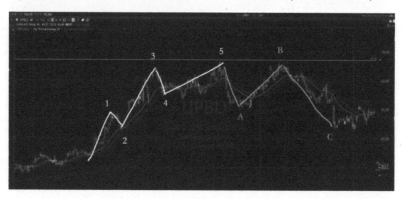

observed when we zoom in and when we zoom out, that is, independently from the time scale we are using.

This is what the Elliot waves look like: 5 legs on uptrends (1 to 5) and 3 on downtrends (A, B and C).

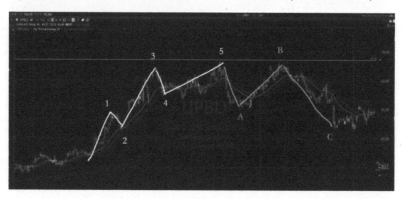

On the way up, there are 5 movements: impulse, setback, impulse, setback back and last impulse. The correction consists of 3 movements: down, up and down again. An Elliot wave, therefore, consists of 8 movements, which is one cycle of the stock market.

There are certain rules to identify the Elliot waves:

1. Wave 2 cannot setback more than 100% of wave 1.
2. Wave 4 cannot move close to wave 1.
3. Wave 3 cannot be the shortest wave.

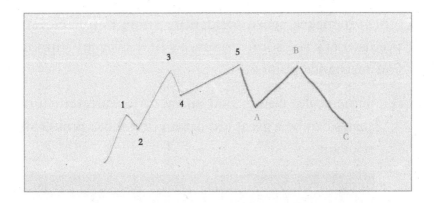

I am pretty sure you are starting to figure out how these waves are relevant to us: because we can ride them!

So far, we have learned to buy low and sell high, in time frames of 18 months or 3 to 5 years.

Now that we know how to ride the waves, we could go in and out of our positions within a shorter period of weeks or a few months, thus increasing our returns.

At this point, though, you might be thinking: *looks pretty easy when you see the lines, but it's something completely different when you face a chart that's naked!*

And you are right! If you draw a line every time the price changes, we could end up tracing those lines… every day, which is not helpful, really.

It makes sense to identify some more relevant points. Let's see some criteria to find relevant support and resistance points:

1. Time scale: points that show up at different time scales can be a great indication that those points are relevant.

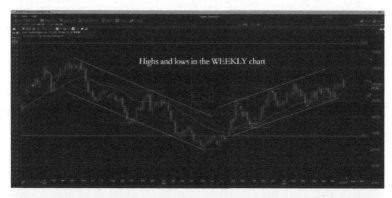

Highs and lows in the WEEKLY chart

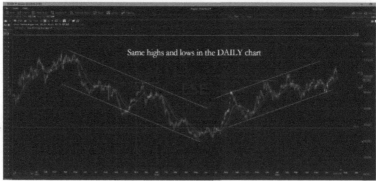

Same highs and lows in the DAILY chart

2. Volume: at prices at which there has been many trades, chances are that, in the future, many trades will take place at those levels again.

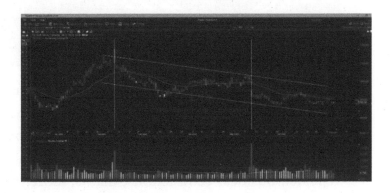

3. Number of rebounds: the more times a level is reached, the more relevant it is

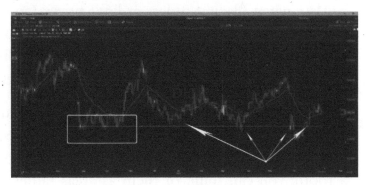

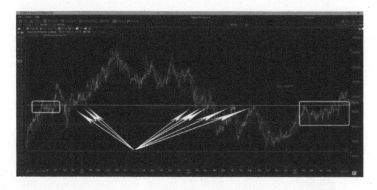

4. Round numbers: since many *derivatives* (financial products derived from an asset, which is called the *underlying asset*) are made available at certain prices only, those prices tend to be benchmarks for repeated business transactions, that is, more trades are placed at those prices. These trades of the derivatives have an impact in the price of the underlying asset.

   Also, when placing orders at limit prices (you can program your trading platform to get an order triggered at a particular price), it is way more likely that those limit prices are round than with decimals.

5. Please, be aware that the trend lines will be just a fair approximation, as the support and resistance points are not fixed on stone. Allow a bit of wiggle room; you can think of them as areas rather than thin lines where prices would rebound like a ball at an exact point. *Ain't gonna happen.*

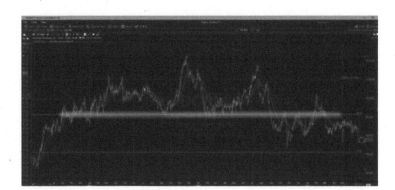

6. Supports will be resistances and resistances will be supports. Please, look at the previous charts and confirm this statement. Thank you.

7. As stated before, when a correction is due to happen, using the Fibonacci levels can help us identify relevant support points on the way back.

8. There are patterns within patterns independent of the time scale.

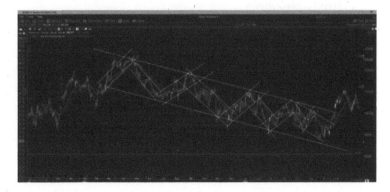

Japanese candlesticks

Japanese candlesticks, or just *candlesticks*, represent what the price of a share has done in an established time frame.

Candlesticks are not the only way to represent the movements of trading prices. It is, however, the one more widely used.

They are useful to show, at a glance, the range of prices and the volatily during the time period of consideration.

Thus, by looking at yesterday's candlestick of something traded in the market, we can tell:

1. The price when the market opened, called *open price*.

2. The price when the market close, called (you got this!) *close price*.

3. The maximum price reached during the day (because, in this example, we are considering yesterday's –one day– candlestick). This is call *high*, what else.

4. The minimum price a trade was made, which is called *low*.

Candlesticks have two parts: the body (the rectangle) and the wicks.

The colour of the candlestick and its body fillep or not gives us information about a movement up or down in the time frame of consideration and also in reference to what happened the day before (the net change).

Tier I:

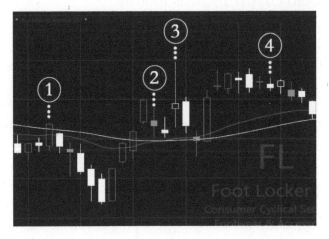

Note: The red candles look white and the green ones, grey.

1. Green, empty candle: It's an up period and higher than the previous period.

2. Green, full candle: Up period, lower than the period immediately before.

3. Red, empty candle: It's a down period, higher than the previous period.

4. Red, full candle: It's a down period, lower than the previous one.

Tier II: Depending on the geometry of the candlesticks, we could classify them as follows:

1. Indecision candlesticks

   Characterised by small bodies and small wicks.

   They indicate a certain equilibrium between the offer and the demand, doubt, waiting for events to unfold. They show small movement in the share price.

   An extreme case of indecision candlesticks is the *doji*, with no body: open and close prices are the same or nearly the same.

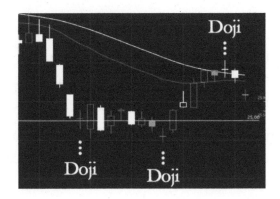

2. Impulse candlesticks

They show a long body, thus showing a remarkable difference between the open and closing prices.

They are known as *marubozu* (shaved head) when they don't have one or both wicks.

Prices move more than they normally do. It can be a sign of panic or euphoria, which in creases volatility.

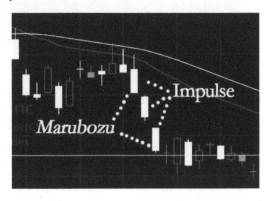

3. Rejection candlesticks

The wick on one side is quite long in comparison with the body. They usually have the shape of a hammer.

They show that the price has gone far, but came back, which indicates that that price has been rejected, which indicates confusion.

These candlesticks are known as *karakasa* (umbrella).

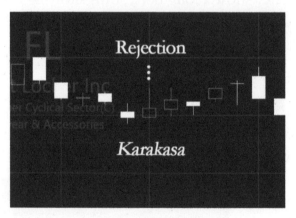

<u>Tier III</u>: The sentiment associated with the pattern developed throughout a day is carried to the next day. For that reason, when considering a string of candlesticks, we can see certain patterns that tend to indicate different things.

There are hundreds of these patterns, although many of them are just combinations of the basic ones.

What's important is the psychology behind these patterns.

Be aware that all candlestick patters apply to short periods; it takes time for a trend to develop.

Let's look at the most significant ones:

1. Hammer candlestics, karakasa: if the wick points down, it means the inferior level is rejected; if it points up, that the upper level is rejected.

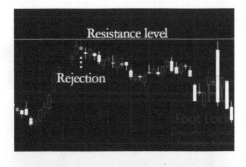

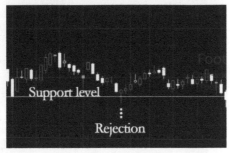

The implications are even more significant when they appear at the support or resistance levels.

2. Engulfing patterns: it's a combination of two candlesticks, the second one's body being bigger than the first one, and of different colours (implying one moves one way and the other one moves the opposite way and opposite to the previous trend).

This pattern also shows there is a rejection, but rather than appearing over one period, it needs two.

An engulfing pattern, in fact, is equivalent to a hammer:

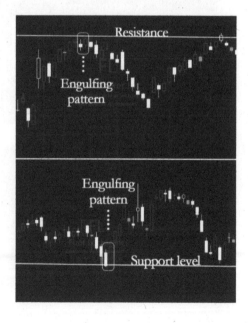

An engulfing pattern happening at support or resistance also means, like a hammer pattern, a rejection.

Again, this is a short-term pattern.

Indicators: Stochastic oscillators

Before we dive in the deep end, let's touch of what *indicators* are.

As the name suggests, indicators are tools that provide an idea of what is likely to happen based on what has happened so far.

When we see the sign of the green man walking, we read it as an indicator of *it is safe to cross*. Still, we could get run over by a car.

There are many indicators. We will just go through four of them that give us very valuable information.

The first one is the stochastics.

Tier I: The *stochastic oscillator* is an indicator used for generating overbought and oversold signals.

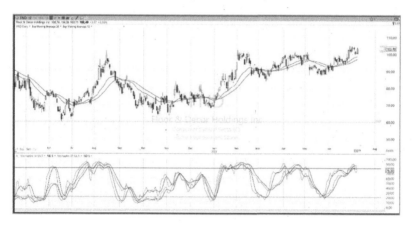

Its values go from 0 to 100. Measures greater than 80 indicate that an asset is *overbought* and measures lower than 20 indicate that the asset is *oversold*.

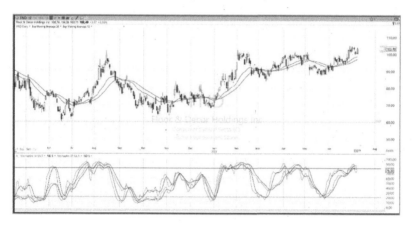

By the way, what are *overbought* and *oversold*?

Overbought: it means that many shares have been bought, which could be translated into *high demand*. Because of this high demand, the price is higher than the real value of the asset.

Oversold: when shares are sold at a fast pace, this could be considered as *high offer*: there is a lot of product in the market, therefore, the price goes down, even below the fair price or real value of the stock.

Tier II: A stochastic oscillator is a momentum indicator that compares a particular closing price to a range of its prices over a certain period or time.

In practice, when the stochastics slide below the 80-line, that could be considered as an indication of the asset being overbought. In easy words: time to sell. Or consider selling, at least.

Likewise, when the stochastics surpass the 20-line, that could be considered as an indication of the asset being oversold, that is: time to buy or consider buying.

Our favourite settings for the stochastics are as follows:

Stochastics	
Plot style	Line
%K	5
Average type	Exponential
%D	5
Average type	Exponential
Period	14 days
Period	35 days

As you can see, we use stochastics at 14 days and at 35 (%K) plus their 5-day moving averages.

Tier III: This the formula for the stochastic oscillator for a period of 14 units of time:

$$\%K = \frac{C - L_{14}}{H_{14} - L_{14}} \times 100$$

Where,

%K = The current value of the stochastic indicator
C = The most recent closing price
L_{14} = The lowest price traded of the 14 previous periods
H_{14} = The highest price traded during the same period

Indicators: RSI

<u>Tier I:</u> The *relative strength index* (RSI) is a momentum indicator that measures recent price changes. It moves between 0 and 100 and provides a short-term buy and sell signals, as it indicates the overbought and oversold levels of an asset.

In practice, RSI levels below 30 indicate an oversold condition (that the shares are cheap). Likewise, levels above 70 suggest that the asset is overbought (overvalued, expensive).

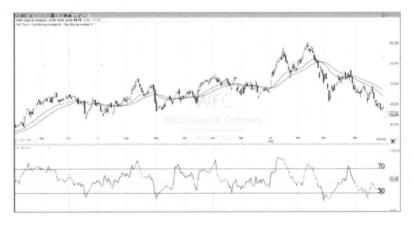

<u>Tier II:</u> The RSI looks at the pace of recent price chages to determine whether a particular stock is about to rally up or is ready to be sold.

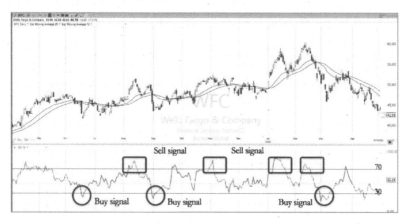

In practice, when the RSI dips down the 70 level, this could be considered as an indication of the stock being overbought, therefore, it would make sense to consider selling.

When the RSI surpases the level of 30, that is a bullish sign; in other words, time to consider buying.

The RSI crossing the 30 and 70 lines is rarer than the stochastics crossing the 20 and 80.

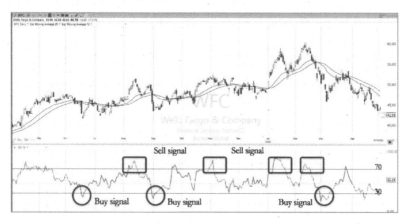

Our favourite settings for the RSI are as follows:

RSI	
Plot style	Line
Period	14 days

As you can see, we use RSI at 14 days.

Tier III: This is the formula to calculate the RSI:

$$RSI \; = \; 100 - \left(\frac{100}{1 + RS} \right)$$

Where:

RSI = Relative Strength Index
RS = Average gain/average loss

Indicators: Moving averages

Tier I: The moving average (MA) is an indicator that is calculated to smooth out the price data by creating a constantly updated average price.

My favourite ones are the 10-day MA (10 DMA), the 20-day MA (20 DMA) and the 200-day MA (200 DMA).

The 10-day MA, to take one as an example, is the average of the stock price over the last 10 days.

The longer the period, the slower the fluctuations of the curve representing it.

The dotted line is the 10 DMA and the continuos one, the 20 DMA.

Takeaways:

1. Considering the pair 10 DMA/20 DMA, when one crosses the other, that indicates a change in trend.

2. When riding on top of the pair 10 DMA/20 DMA, the trend is up; when the prices are below the pair, the trend is down.

3. Prices tend to the mean. The 200 DMA shows a price that will, very likely, be achieved in the future.

Tier II: Moving averages are used to identify the trend direction of a stock or its support and resistance levels, which is equivalent.

We always use the exponential moving average (EMA) rather than the simple moving average (SMA).

The exponential moving average is a weighted average, thus, gives more importance to the stock price in more recent days.

<u>Tier III</u>: the formula to calculate the EMA is as follows:

$$EMA_t = \frac{x_t + (1 - \alpha)x_{t-1} + (1 - \alpha)^2 x_{t-2} + \cdots + (1 - \alpha)^t x_0}{1 + (1 - \alpha) + (1 - \alpha)^2 + \cdots + (1 - \alpha)^t}$$

Where,

EMA=Exponential Moving Average
t= time period
x=close price
(1-α)=smoothing factor

Note that the closer we are to today, the higher the weight of the price. In simpler terms: prices are more relevant the closer they are to the present moment, which makes sense.

Indicators: MACD

<u>Tier I</u>: The *moving average convergence divergence*, MACD is an indicator that shows the relationship between the 26 exponential moving average (EMA) and the 12 EMA of a share price.

The difference between this *main line* resulting from substracting the 26 and the 12 EMAs and the 9 EMA called *signal* is plotted as a histogram.

Thus, we'll have:

1. The main line, which represents the difference between the 26 and the 12 EMAs.

2. The signal line, which is the 9 EMA of the plot.

3. The histogram, which corresponds to the difference between the main line and the signal line.

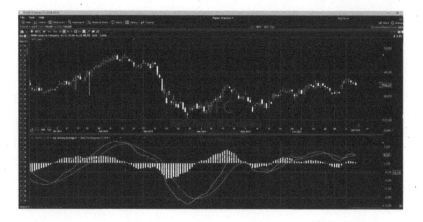

Being very practical:

1. When the 26 and 12 EMAs touch, the main line is at the 0 level. If you think of it, this is obvious, because if the EMAs touch, there is no difference

between them, that is, the difference is zero. (The 12-day EMA is represented by the dotted line).

2. The further we are from zero, the bigger the difference between the main line and its 9 EMA, which means that the main line is still accelerating.

Tier II: We have introduced the MACD 12 26 9 because this is the most widely used. It corresponds to half a month and a full month of trading days worth. However, it can be used with different time frames depending on the trader's preferences.

For instance, in our groups, we use the following settings:

MACD	
Plot style	Histogram
Short	10
Long	35
Average type	Exponential

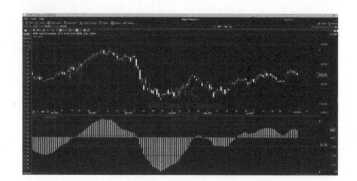

This indicator is very versatile. We can use it to determine trends and detect oversold and overbought points.

Let's see how we can use this indicator to our advantage:

1. When the main line crosses the zero level, this could be an indication of a change in the trend.

2. When the fast EMA (12 days) crosses on top of the slow EMA (26 days), that could indicate a downtrend.

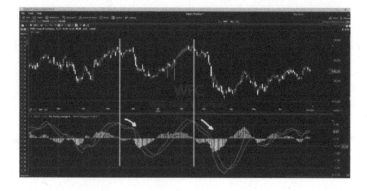

3. Equally, when the slow EMA (26 days) crosses on top of the fast EMA (12 days), that could indicate an uptrend.

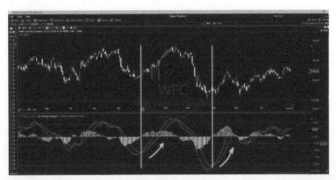

Before we continue with this list, we need to define *divergence* and *convergence*.

<u>Divergence</u>: it happens when the price chart shows **new maximums in an uptrend** and the MACD main line doesn't follow suit, that is, it goes down.

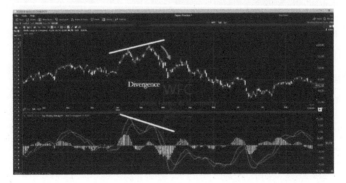

When there is divergence in an uptrend, that means that this uptrend is losing momentum and, therefore, a downtrend could be about to happen.

We call this *hidden weakness.*

<u>Convergence</u>: it happens when the price chart shows **new minimums in a downtrend** and the MACD main line goes up.

Convergence

When there is convergence in a downtrend, that means that this downtrend is losing momentum and, therefore, an uptrend could be about to happen.

We call this *hidden strength.*

<u>Tier III:</u>

The formula of the MACD 12 26 is as follows:

$$MACD = EMA_{12} - EMA_{26}$$

3.2 Give me a break!

> *You are not given a dream unless you*
> *have the capacity to fulfil it.*

> Jack Canfield

That's some information to take in, isn't it?

After reading this chapter up until now, it wouldn't be surprising to start going those thoughts that we are so familiar with: *I can't! This is too difficult! Too much information. I'll never wrap my head around it all! This is not for me. I'm not good at numbers. What's the point?*

Breaking news: if this is the way you normally think, take a look around and confirm you wish to stay at the same point you are now or, rather, you would like to learn something new that will take you to an unfamiliar place where you can find <u>everything</u>, as they say: *Everything you want is on the other side of fear* (Jack Canfield again).

Time to breath deep until your heart and your brain are in coherence, that is, working in unison.

Think of all the things you've learned so far and you had no idea. I am confident that the skills in this book are not so challenging to learn as it was reading and writing when you were 5 or 6 years old.

The difference between back then and now could be, though, that when you were younger, there was not a shadow of a doubt that you could do anything your little friends could do. However, you might be comparing yourself to someone else and how far you are from that ideal person. Or, even worse, you might be comparing yourself to an idea of yourself someone else has!

Let me show this concept in the shape of a made-up fable, probably based on the fact that, growing up, I read Aesop's fables book many times.

Once there was an ugly bird, big, clumply and covered by fluff where there should have been feathers.

—You should be like me —said a peacock giving the ugly bird a few spare feathers from its tail. The ugly bird held them tight under its wing, so, now, he couldn't fly.

—You should be like me —said the penguin showing the ugly bird how to walk. And off went our bird limping badly because he couldn't walk with the cuteness of the penguin.

—Wow! I'd love to be like the ostrich! —said the ugly bird to itself and quickly grabbed a couple of huge ostrich feathers in its beak, thus not being able to talk.

For months, it carried around the feathers of the peacock and the ostrich while limping around, not being able to walk comfortably, fly gracefully or even talk. It was so busy carrying all these things while perfecting its limp that it didn't realise that, underneath, it had grown to be a beautiful, gorgeous, elegant bird. Let's say a swan, for the sake of a well-known story.

Our true greatness and beauty lie within us

Little reflection here: you can learn anything you wish to learn, no matter what the speed is. Question: any child of your school never learned to ready or write? Some would be dyslexic and some would be poets; still, they all learned, right?

This course is designed so you can add levels of knowledge at your own speed. When you feel comfortable swimming a width of the swimming pool, you might try to go a full length, first by the wall and later, in the middle lane. Don't worry if others swim full lengths in the middle of a deep pool to begin with: maybe they can't cook and you are a brilliant cook.

Please, accept an invitation to write down skills you are very good at, whether innate or learned. None is too small.

....

....

....

....

....

....

....

....

....

3.3 Buying cheaper: puts

A bit of recap of what we've learned so far:

☞ Pick high-quality companies.

☞ Pick good value companies (high-quality and low price).

☞ Plan to buy low and sell high in a 3- to 5-year window.

☞ Plan to buy low and sell high in an 18-month window.

☞ Refine the entry points by using charts and indicators.

Look at you! **Celebrate!**

Time to go one step further: buying shares cheaper than they are (legally!).

Yes: there is a trick. You might want to own the shares, yet, applying the strategy I'm about to tell you, you could end up not even owning them.

Intriguing, right? Or not, if you ever heard about *put options*.

Now, you can keep reading or have a break watching this short movie:

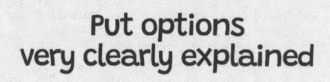

Put options
very clearly explained

... and the possible outcomes
we can encounter

Not long enough for popcorn, but enlightening, I hope.

Before watching this video, you might have not ever heard about *put options*. No problem: you'll get very well acquainted with them!

Some of you might have heard about *buying* put options and would run a mile from this chapter.

However, we will be talking about *selling* put options, so stay put.

This is the principle: We have chosen a company of good quality which is at a low price and the charts and indicators confirm we are in the right area to enter this position, that is, to buy the stock.

When you **sell a put option**, you give the buyer the option to <u>sell the shares to you</u> at an agreed price between the moment of the sale and a determined time in the future.

Put options are only traded in multiples of 100 shares. These packages of 100 shares are called *contracts*. Therefore, selling 2 contracts of a put option is equivalent to selling a put option on 200 shares.

Imagine you sell car insurance. A female client in her 50s goes to your desk and says: *I want to fully insure my car today (1ˢᵗ of January) till the end of the year (31ˢᵗ of December at close of business –COB–) for 30,000. How much is it?* And you give her a price. Let's say 2,100, which is 7% of the total amount insured. The client is happy because she knows that whatever happens to her car, she can go to your desk and ask you for a 30,000 refund no questions asked.

Your potential client now is a male in his 20s who drives a motorcycle. He wants to insure his vehicle for 14,000. Same time range. In this case, you quote him 2,000, which is 14.3% of the amount insured. Why would you charge him more? Because there are more probabilities of him claiming the insurance than the lady above, and that's why you increase the price of the insurance, called *premium*.

> **The more probabilities of an event to happen, the higher the premium.**

As buyers, the lady and the young man can claim their insurance money from you any time between the day the signature of the contract and the following 31st of December at COB.

Possible scenarios during this year in which your clients can exercise their right to claim the policy any time, no questions asked:

1. The clients don't crash, therefore, they never claim the insurance money. You get to keep the premium. It seems you've made money out of thin air, because all you did was to receive money for... Signing some papers. However, you are rendering a service, that's why you are paid for. If your clients do not require your services, that's their choice.

2. The clients do claim the insurance money: you pay them. It is their prerogative to exercise their right to claim the insurance at any time. As an insurer, you should have the money to pay your clients. Bear in mind that many clients would have paid you and never claimed their insurance money, so you would have a nice nest egg that builds up in a compound fashion. To avoid that all your clients show up at your office the same day claiming for their money, you would have been clever enough to find different types of clients, more of those with a low risk profile, and you will sell the insurances expiring at different points in time, to minimise the probabilities of all the contracts being exercised at the same time.

After the 31st of December at COB in our examples above, neither the lady nor the young man can go and ask for the insurance money because the contract would have expired.

Let's now go to a stock market scenario. We will use CVS as an example.

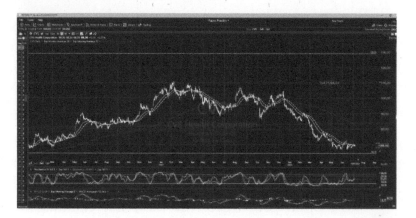

We could buy the shares today at 69.36 (11th of July 2023) or we can sell a 70 put option for August, which means that if the option is exercised, we would be buying them at $70 per share.

You might think: *That sounds a bit silly, since we can buy the shares $0.64 cheaper today!* And you would be right... If only you hadn't forgotten about the premium.

The premium is $2.78, ergo even **if** we pay $70 in the future, the net price would be $67.22 as follows:

Price	Premium	Net
69.36	0	69.36
70.00	2.78	67.22
Discount		-3.1%

What just happened? We've just discovered **we can buy shares at a discount in the future.**

Tier I: If you wish to buy CVS at a discount, you would *sell to open* (STO) a number of *contracts* you decide of the *70P* for *August*.

Bear in mind that you will invest $7,000 per contract (1 contract = 100 shares, each share = $70).

As a beginner, though, we would recommend that you sell puts with 4 to 6 months till expiration. We've chosen August for a teaching reason you will see in the next Tiers.

Tier II: There are many strikes you can choose from and many expiration dates.

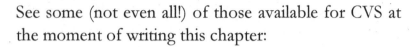

See some (not even all!) of those available for CVS at the moment of writing this chapter:

Price 69.36	14th July	jul-23	28 July	4 Aug	11 Aug	Aug	Aug 25	Sep	Nov	Jan 24	feb-24	jun-24	jan 25
Strike	3	10	17	24	31	38	45	66	129	192	220	346	556
60	0	0.02	0.03	0.15	0.2	0.27	0.3	0.5	1.17	1.58	2.02	2.88	4.55
61	0	0.01	0.05	0.2	0.26		0.39						
62	0	0.02	0.07	0.27	0.33		0.49						
62.5		0.03				0.51		0.81	1.75	2	2.53	3.45	5.15
63	0	0.04	0.1	0.37	0.39		0.62						
64	0.01	0.06	0.14	0.52	0.61		0.77						
65	0.03	0.12	0.21	0.68	0.79	0.9	1.03	1.29	2.36	2.85	3.15	4.3	5.95
66	0.04	0.21	0.35	0.9	1.06		1.21						
67	0.1	0.37	0.55	1.19	1.22		1.45						
67.5		0.5				1.67		2.05	3.15	3.7	4.05	5.25	7.1
68	0.22	0.65	0.85	1.56	1.68		1.96						
69	0.47	1.05	1.32	1.95	2.12		2.3						
70	0.97	1.55	1.76	2.5	2.62	2.78	2.84	3.15	4.3	4.75	5.15	6.4	7.95
71	1.63	2.32	2.45	3.03	3.3		3.4						
72	2.52	3.05	3.15	3.43	3.95		3.95						
72.5		3.5				4.25		4.6	5.7	6.1	6.45	7.55	9.15
73	3.4	3.8	4.1	4.45	4.55		4.7						
74	4.2	4.8	4.95	5.3	5.35		5.4						
75	5.1	6	5.7	6.2	6.2	6.25	6.25	6.3	7.15	7.55	7.95	9.05	10.5
76	6.5	6.8	6.95	7.05	7.1		7.1						
77	7.3	7.75	7.9	7.75	8		7.9						
77.5		8.4				8.48		8.65	8.85	9.4	9.7	10.55	12.15
78	8.5	8.8	8.9	8.7	9		8.85						
79	9.5	9.6	9.75	9.65	9.65		9.7						
80	10.5	10.6	10.6	10.65	10.9	10.65	10.65	11	11.35	11.5	11.65	12.3	13.5
81		11.6	11.55	11.9	11.85		11.65						
82	12.5	12.5	12.85	12.6	12.6		12.75						
82.5						15.5			13.05	13.5		14.25	15.3
83	13.35	13.8	13.85										
84													
85	15.5	15.8	15.55	15.85	15.85		15.85	15.8	15.65	15.55	15.9	16.2	17.15
87.5						18.3					18.2	18.48	17.15
90	20.4	20.8	20.8	20.8	20.8	20.8	20.8	20.8	20.85	20.65	20.15	20.8	19.2

The row with the numbers 3, 10, 17, etc. show the number of days till expiration.

The bulk in the middle is the premiums.

Since the shares are trading at 69.36, every strike above that price (from 70 onwards) will produce premiums that include both *real value* and *time value*.

Underneath, we will only have time value, as the real value will always be zero.

What is time value and real value? Movie time:

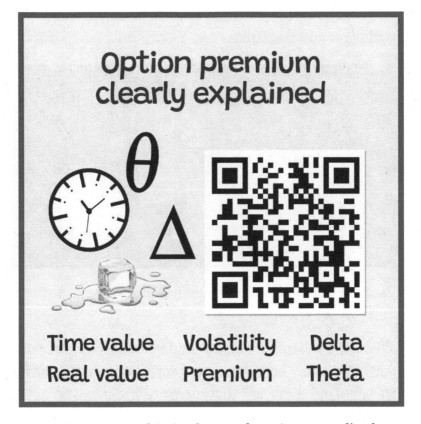

I suppose this is the perfect time to talk about birds and bees.

The premium of an option has two components: **time value** (also called *extrinsic value*), which is always

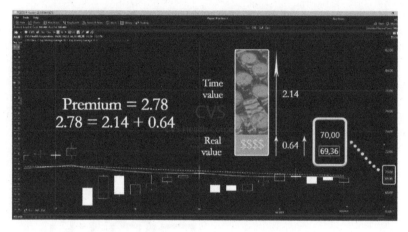

>0 (always greater than zero) and **intrinsic value** (also called *real value*), which is ≥0 (greater or equal to zero).

Intrinsic value: For a put option, the intrinsic or real value is the difference between the price the shares are trading at and the strike.

Imaging you wish to buy bananas and you are not in a hurry to get them.

There is a a banana person who sells this fruit in your neigborhood. The price, as expected, depends on offer and demand. Let's say that the price today is 48.

You approach the banana person and ask them how much they would give you today to buy the bananas within the next three months at a price of 50. You wouldn't want to pay more and you are up to making a deal.

Since the price today is 48 and you will be buying them at 50, you obviously expect the banana person to give you a minimum of 2, which is the real value: the bananas can be bought at 48 and be bought at 50. Those 2 are real.

The banana person offers you 5. And you do your calculations: *I can make 5 on an investment of 50. That is 5/50 times a 100… 10% return on investment (RoI). Since the time frame is 3 months, I'll be making 10%/3=3.33% RoI per month. If I end up buying the bananas at 50-5=45, I'm happy too, because they are at a good price even at 48 and I'll be buying them at a discount of 3/50 times 100 =6%. Either way, it's worth my while.*

Since the banana man is giving you 5 and 2 of them are the real value (the difference between the price today and the strike), the other 3 are what's called:

Time value: No rocket science!

$$Premium = real\ value + time\ value$$

Since we know the premium (5) and the real value (2), the time value is 3.

The futher the expiration date, the higher the time value. Common sense. It's not linear, but common sense, nevertheless.

Again, it's all about probabilities: as a seller of vehicles' insurance, the premium your customers will pay you will be smaller when they are insuring 3 months than when they are insuring a whole year. The whole year will have a discount, though: it won't be 4 times the premium corresponding to 3 months. Keep this in mind for the next tier in options.

In your mind, it doesn't make sense, as it seems that the seller, the banana person, will potentially be selling you bananas at 45 in the future when he is selling them today at 48; it seems he is losing 3.

If we wear the banana man's shoes for a bit, we'll see that he is thinking:

a) *If the banana price drops in the next three months, I will still be able to sell them to this poor son of his mother at 50. After all, it's a cheap enough insurance. Celebration!*

b) *If the banana price goes up, I'll by making more money anyway, so happy days.*

Going back to our CVS example, if we plot the time value of all the premiums, this is what we get:

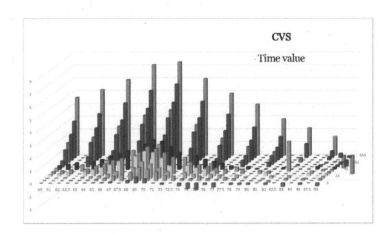

As we can see, the time value increases as time increases, as expected. We can also see that the time value is higher closer to the trading price.

If we plot the time value *per day*, this is what we get. By the way, the time value per day is calculated by dividing the premium by the number of days till expiration.

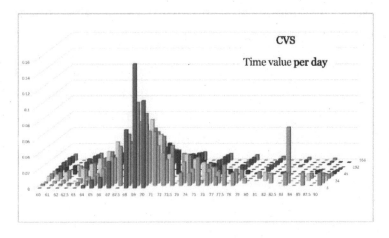

The maximum time value per day is higher the closer we are to expiration.

We can also see some time value at strikes far from the trading price. Yes: this happens quite frequently. These higher points (high volatility) that seem to deviate from the trend are called *the smile*. Our dear friend Rick Langer trades there (his strategy is different to what I'm describing in this book) and he does very well taking advantage of these smiles, because he is a great trader. His strategies wouldn't be advised for beginners, though.

As stated before, the most popular options are those expiring the 3rd Friday of the month. These options are called *monthly options*.

Some companies, like CVS in our example, also trade *weekly options,* which, no brainer, expire on a Friday, other than the 3rd one of the month. There is more liquidity in the monthly options.

When we look at the time value of the next month out for CVS put option premiums, that would be August, this is what we get when we plot the time value of the different available strikes:

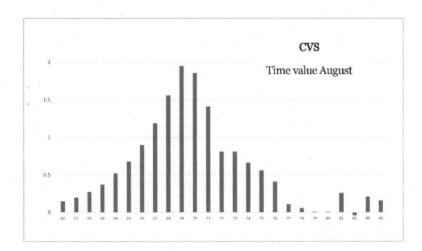

The maximum time value corresponds to the strike closer to the trading price. As a reminder, the share price is 69.36, therefore, 69 is the closest strike.

If the share were trading at 69 exactly, we would say that the 69 strike would be *at the money* (ATM).

Any strike underneath the ATM strike is considered *out of the money*, OTM (for put options) and any strike above the ATM is called *in the money*, ITM (for put options).

It is important that you know that the highest amount of time value is given by the ATM option (or the one closest to it). Is that a coincidence? No: that's because...

> **The more probabilities of an event to happen, the higher the premium.**

And the highest probabilities are always closer to the trading price. Logically.

At this introductory stage of **selling** put options, you will be able to:

1. Sell a put in a company that you want to buy.

2. Set the price that you will be accepting the shares at provided they are assigned to you. This is called *strike price*.

3. Set the expiration date of the options you are *writing* (same as STO).

4. Have the money to buy it.

5. Receive a premium, or option income, that's yours forever and ever.

6. You can use this premium to buy shares, either these ones you sold a put on or others.

We'll go through all the possible scenarios later. At this point, let's just consider two possible outcomes:

Put outcome #1: The shares don't get put to you. You don't have the shares, but you get to keep the premium, which you can use to buy any shares.

Put outcome #2: The shares get put to you, that is, you get to buy them at a discount price if you compare with the price you would have paid the day you decided to sell the put.

Comparing with the insurance examples and not being sexist, but just basing the most likely outcomes on statistics:

Outcome 1: The biker had an incident and claims his money. You, as the insurer, pay him. In stock market terms, the market makes you buy the shares you sold puts on. Why would it be happening? Because the shares are trading at a lower price than the strike. The share price *crashed*, if you will, so they dump them onto you. They have the right to do so and that's the reason why they bought the insurance from you in the first place (I'm oversimplifying here for the sake of clarity, but you get the idea).

Outcome 2: The lady's car is as spotless as it was on day one (I might be pushing my limits here…). No accidents, no incidents, not even a scratch. She won't claim any more from you. Happy days. In stock market terms, the share price didn't crash, didn't end up below the strike, so no need to dump the shares on you.

Most of the time, the put options won't be *assigned*, they won't be put to you, until expiration, even if the price goes or stays below the strike during the time the contract is open. But know that shares can be put to you early, before expiration, because those are the terms of the contract.

Not all companies offer put options. Only the strongest ones. In our case, all our 3x4's and 4x4's offer options.

The most popular **expiration dates** are the third Friday of every month. Options will expire at COB of the markets, which is 4 pm in New York, 9 pm in London, 10 pm in Central Europe, 6 am of the following day in Sydney.

By the way: this is now (summertime). Please, check the equivalences of the country where you are in winter and summer.

Going back to the two outcomes listed before, you might question yourself what to do next.

a) If you end up having the shares being put to you, in short, you have the shares now, you are *long* in those shares. Let them grow! Review the Value Line report and, if they are still shares of high-quality, keep them and decide the exit price, just like we learned before.

b) If you didn't have the shares put to you, you have the cash you had to buy them plus a bit extra from the premium, which allows you to buy more shares. You can decide to sell another put on a stock that is of high-quality and at a good price now.

We have been considering one stock only, but you can sell more than one put at a time on different companies, obviously. Even on the same company at different strikes or expiration dates, but that is something you would do later, when you have more experience.

If you are getting acquainted with selling puts, this is what you could consider as a beginner:

Tier I:

What stock

1. A company you understand and like.

2. Good quality (3 or 4).

3. Good value for money (good, low price).

4. Appropriate price for our asset allocation (we mentioned 5% of account value per company and consider a bit higher when you have more experience and you really know well a strong company you would like to have more of). Make sure you have the money to take delivery of the shares.

5. Charts showing we are at a low point.

6. The indicators showing the price is at support and very likely to move to the next resistance.

What strike

7. Next available strike up.

(We can be more adventurous as we get more confident).

What month

8. To begin with, I would say pick expiration dates at least 4 to 6 months ahead of you.

9. Make sure you spread the allocation evenly over the different months.

How does put premium move with share price?

10. Share price and put option premium move in opposite directions. In other words, when the share price goes up, the put option premium goes down and viceversa.

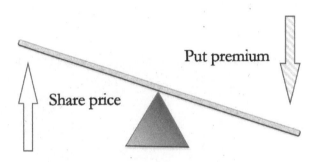

As an approximation, for every $1 that the share goes up, the option premium goes down $0.5. Conversely, for every $1 that the share goes down, the put premium goes up approximately $0.5.

The exact amount that the put option premium moves per dollar that the shares move is given by *delta*, one of *the greeks*, or values designed by Greek letters that give us information about the different components of the premium.

Thus, delta, Δ, is the cents that the option premium goes up or down for every $1 that the share price goes down or up, respectively (in the case put options, since premium and share price move in opposite directions).

Let's see a real example:

Deltas for put options show a negative sign, pointing to the fact that they move in the opposite direction to the assets.

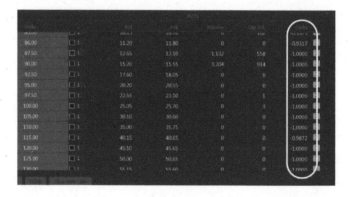

The price closest to ATM is $75 since the shares are trading at $74.64 (as expected, CVS has moved up since I started writing this section).

Thus, with the share price moving from $75 to $76, the option premium will decrease by 0.5034; from $76 to $77, by 0.5915. Again, the more ITM, the closer to $1, until we reach a point where the increase in the share matches the increase of the option income 1 to 1.

What if?

1. *The share price has gone down since I sold the put!* No big deal. Whether you would have bought the shares or sold a put, share prices will always go up and down.

2. *The share price has gone up, they didn't get put to me and I wanted them so badly!* Since, as we know, share prices will go up and down all the time, you'll get this one in the next down. Stop moaning.

   This is **put outcome #1**: The shares trade at a higher price than the strike and the put is not assigned, that is, the shares are not put to you.

3. *The shares got put to me and they have gone down.* Deal with it: share prices will always go up and down. Consider buying more at a lower price to bring the average price down.

4. Is this a good moment to rethink about how we don't do emotions when trading? I think so.

   Individual who cannot master their emotions are ill-suited to profit from the investment process. Benjamin Graham, Warren Buffet's mentor.

5. If the shares get put to you earlier than expiration date, two possible outcomes:

Put outcome #2: You are ok with keeping them. Nothing further: you keep them.

Put outcome #3: You don't want them put to you early (you are not ready to get married! You need more time!). In this case, sell them back to the market and open a new put at the same strike. 99.9% of the time (don't take it literally), this trade will be at a profit straight away, the reason being that the premium will be higher due to something called *time value* that you are very familiar with at this stage.

Conclusion

☆ By selling a put option, we can buy shares in the future at a discounted price.

☆ For that reason, our RoI will be higher than if we buy them day one at the price the shares are trading at in the market.

☆ Whether the put options are assigned or not, we get to keep the premium, which is ours the second we sell the put option.

☆ We sell put options at a particular price, called *strike price* in multiples of 100 shares (*contracts*). The put option contract expires on a particular day, mostly the 3rd Friday of the month, at 4 pm o'clock New York time.

☆ We can choose the strike and the expiration date.

☆ At expiration (or before), it might happen that the shares are put to us (therefore, we would be buying them at a discounted price equal to the strike minus the premium) or not.

☆ The command to sell put options is *sell to open* (STO).

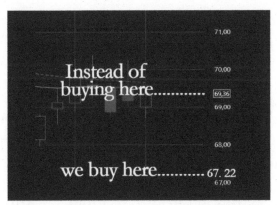

☆ Comparison between selling puts and buying and selling: the higher the volatility, the more advantageous it is to sell puts to make a profit for a given increase in share price.

In our CVS example, this is the *return on capital employed* (ROCE) on the 70P:

	Price
Price today	69.36
Put	70.00
Premium	2.78
Contracts	1
Total premium	278
ROCE, %	4.0

If the shares get put to us at 70, we would be buying them at a 3.1% discount as calculated before:

$$Discount = \left(\frac{70 - 2.78 - 69.36}{69.36}\right) * 100 = -3.1\%$$

Let's now calculate how much the share price must increase for us to make the same 4.0% return; this time, RoI:

Buy & sell at:	Profit	RoI, %
70	64	0.9%
71	164	2.4%
72	264	3.8%
At 72.11	7211	4.0%

We would need for the shares to go to $72.11 to make an RoI equivalent to the ROCE we get by the shares just being at $70 at expiration (let's say $70.01 to make sure they don't get assigned).

- If the shares <u>go up</u>, higher than $72.11, we would have made more money buying and selling.

  As a teaser, know that when shares go up, we can apply a strategy we'll see in chapter 4, called *bull put spread*, which will allow us to collect more premium in a similar fashion as if recycling. Intrigued??

- If the shares <u>go down</u> and we choose not to keep the shares, we can apply strategies to keep collecting premium on top of the initial premium at the same time we decrease the strike.

Let's see an example of a calculation made when the VIX was higher on a stock that was trading at $33.86 and the premium of the 35P was $4.20:

	Price
Price today	33.86
Put	35.00
Premium	4.20
Contracts	1
Total premium	420
ROCE, %	12.0

If the shares are assigned at 35, we would be buying them at an 8.3% discount as follows:

$$Discount = \left(\frac{35 - 4.20 - 33.86}{33.86}\right) * 100 = -8.3\%$$

Let's now calculate how much the share price must increase for us to make the same return of 8.3%; this time, RoI:

Buy & sell at:	Profit	RoI, %
34	14	0.4
35	114	3.4
36	214	6.3
37	314	9.3
At 37.92	406	12.0

We would need for the shares to go to $37.92 to make an RoI equivalent to the ROCE we get by the shares just trading at $35 at expiration ($35.01 to be sure they are not assigned).

- If the shares <u>go up</u> higher than $37.92, we would have made more money buying and selling.

  We can make extra premium by opening another position if our naked 35P put turns into a bull put spread, as we mentioned earlier.

- If the shares <u>go down</u> and we choose to not keep the shares, we can delay the process until we end up above the strike while, in the way, we'll keep collecting premium.

Tier III:

The following table summarises the results as previously discussed.

Comparison on price increase for same return	Initial price	Final price	Increase in price	Increase in price, %
High volatility				
Buy & hold	33.86	37.92	4.06	12.0%
Sell a 35P	33.86	34.01	0.15	0.4%
Low volatility				
Buy & hold	69.36	71.84	2.48	3.6%
Sell a 40P	69.36	70.01	0.65	0.9%

Some companies are more volatile than others, which means they will always offer higher premiums (%) than others.

In our examples, both companies are comparable; the biggest difference was that the VIX was at different levels when the data was collected. This difference in the value of the VIX translates into all option premiums being higher or lower as the VIX moves up and down, respectively.

As we can see in the previous table, when the volatility is high (VIX goes up), the share price must increase 12.0% for us to get the same return buying and selling that we get by selling a put and the share price just increasing 0.4%.

When the volatility is low, the share price must increase 3.6% for us to make the same return on a 0.9% increase when selling the put.

To wrap it up

In a high options volatility environment, we make more money selling options! Which we already knew.

FOMO (fear of missing out)

Indeed, sometimes we will make more money if we just buy the shares and sit on them until they grow.

In our experience, approximately one third of the puts we sell end up below the strike, one third above and one third, around the strike.

It would be fantastic, wonderful and magical, to know what companies will grow up fast, so we could buy those shares directly and puts on the rest to make some premium and/or buy the shares at a discount.

If you figure out how to tell when shares will shoot up fast, please, let us know! That being said, to increase the chances of some shares you really want to have been assigned to you, sell a more aggressive put, that is, a higher strike.

If, still, your beloved shares trade above the higher strike at expiration, sell a new put on them the next time the chart and indicators show we are at a low. If it sounds like you are chasing the company, it is because that's exactly what it is.

You can consider selling some puts and buy some shares also. And selling puts at different strikes, if your account is big enough to handle the asset allocation. As you get more experienced, you might want to try other combinations.

Other options

Some tickers, apart from the monthly and the weekly options, they also offer *daily options*, like QQQ:

QQQ is a popular *Exchange Traded Fund* (ETF) that tracks the performance of the Nasdaq-100 index, and index mentioned before.

An ETF is a type of fund that is traded on stock exchanges. It pools together the money of multiple investors to invest in a diversified portfolio of assets, such as stocks, bonds, commodities, etc. ETFs are designed to track the performance of a specific index, sector or asset class. Other examples: SLV (it tracks the price of silver), GLD (gold), SPY (SP-500), IYR (real estate), JETS (airline industry), etc.

We've seen that premium consists of time value plus intrinsic value (this latter could be zero).

Before we go any futher, we need to know what *volatility* is.

More about volatility

When comparing to the insurance example we have been using, intuitively, you would say that the older lady's driving habits and behaviour would be less volatile than those of a young man riding a motorbike. Based on her historical record, her premium would be lower than that of the young man's.

However, the conditions now are to be considered, such as weather conditions, state of the roads, density of traffic, etc. They could be the same or different for our drivers.

In turn, time value consists of two components:

Time value = Historical vol + Implied vol

Where:

- Historical vol = historical volatility. Its value takes includes the past price fluctuations of the underlying asset: the bigger the fluctuations, the higher the historial volatility. Normally, the calculations are made on the data corresponding to the last 12 months.

- Implied vol = implied volatility. Its value includes the market's expectation of the what the volatility of the underlying asset will be during the lifetime of the option. It is inferred from everything that is going on in the world, therefore, it can change fast due to sentiment, news or significant events.

The VIX measures the Cboe volatility index, that is, it shows the volatility of the options.

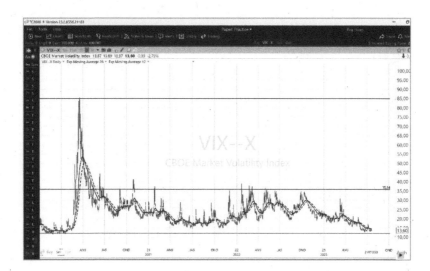

The big peak you on the left, that reached 85, in case you wonder, corresponds to March 2020.

When the VIX goes down, the SP-500 goes up and viceversa. Different scales, but same movement, mirroring each other.

Taking this information into consideration, the ideal moment to sell put options would be when the shares are down, as we know, and the VIX is high.

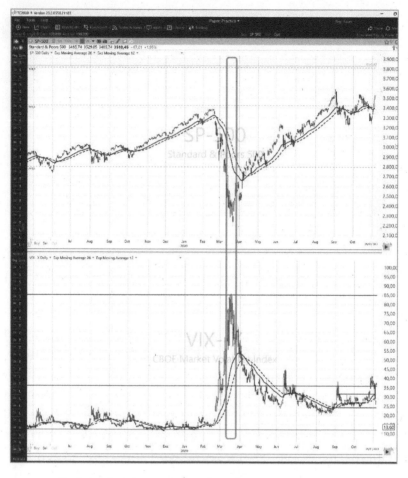

Going back to March 2020, we can see how while the SP-500 was falling approximately 35% in one month, the volatility index increased more than 4x. On average, the puts we sold at the end of March and beginning of April were giving us 4x with respect to what we used to be getting before.

We can now learn a bit more about how volatility behaves.

In the example of CVS, we saw how the maximum time value (at this stage we know that time value equals historical volatility plus implied volatility) is found at the strike closer to or ATM and that its value decays with time.

Using the data we collected for CVS:

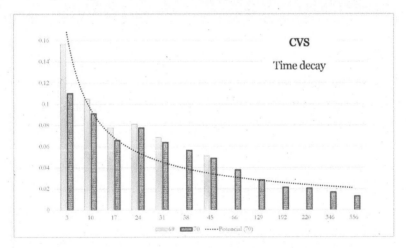

The strike closer to ATM when the data was collected is 69. However, since there are more data points for 70, all the time values available for this strike have been included in the graph.

As we can see, the closer to expiration, the faster the decay. The decay per day, the cents (or fraction) the time value decreases per day is a know parameter known as *theta* (θ).

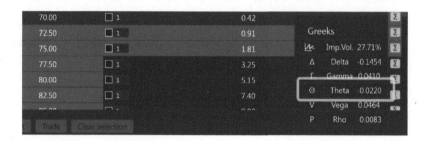

In this example, a theta of -0.0220 means that, provided the share price remained unchanged, the premium would decrease $0.022 per day.

The closer we are to expiration, the bigger θ is, which means that the premium decreases faster.

This is very important to know because, as sellers of premium, the faster the decrease, the better for us (more cents per day). If we were to buy options (and we will under very determined conditions), we want to buy options that keep the value of their premiums longer. But that's another story…

3.4 Selling dearer: calls

A bit of recapitulation. We have learned…

☞ To pick high-quality companies.
☞ To pick good value companies (high-quality and low price).
☞ To establish when to sell:
  o In a 3- to 5-year window.
  o In an 18-month time window.
☞ To refine the entry points by using charts and indicators.
☞ To sell put options to buy shares at a discount in the future.

Whether we bought shares or we got puts assigned, we now are the proud owners of a bunch of shares, such bunch being a multiple of 100.

Let's take CAH as an example, which is now trading at $94.36.

For the sake of argument, let's say we got CAH shares at an average open price of $51, which makes perfect sense, when we look at the situation of CAH when it was trading at $51: the odds stacked in our favour.

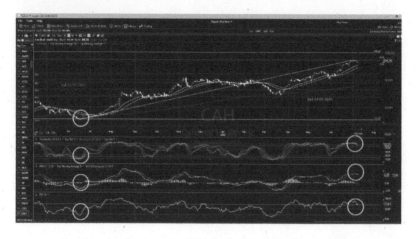

Let's see how we *stacked the odds in our favour:*

- We chose a company that was a 3x4.

- The stochastics where under the 30-line and starting to turn around.

- The MACD histogram crossed the 0 line on its way up.

- The RSI just turned around from under the 20-line.

- The longer-term EMA crossed over the shorter-term EMA when the shares were trading at 54-ish. They are *confirmation* indicators.

At this moment in time, we are very close to the top of the 18-month projections. This is the information we have:

- The company is now a 3x3.

- The stochastics are above 80 and they seem to be just about to cross this line on their way down.

- The MACD histogram has just crossed the 0 line on its way down.

- The RSI is already touching the 30-line on its way down.

- The EMAs... Join the party later.

It would make sense to think of selling.

This is what the profit would be:

	Price	Profit
Buy	51.00	
Sell	94.36	
Gain	43.36	
Profit		**85.0%**

85% profit in 13 months. That would be an average of 6.5% per month.

We could, however, make some extra profit by selling a *call option*.

When you **sell a call option**, you give the buyer the option to <u>buy the shares off you</u> at an agreed price between the moment of the sale and expiration.

To continue with a vehicle scenario, like we did with put options, this time we own a car dealership. A couple walks in and show interest in a classic model we've had for a while. We bought it at a 40,000 and we know we could sell it for 50,000.

This is the profit we would make:

	Price	Profit
Buy	40,000	
Sell	50,000	
Gain	10,000	
Profit		**25.0%**

No one can guarantee, though, what its price could be in a month or two, as price is dictated by supply and demand, which is moved by human emotions, as we have learned. On the other hand, we have read a very well-informed publication in which there are strong indicators for classic car prices to go down.

The couple would agree to buy the car at 49,500 no later than 37 days from today. Would we be ok with it?

For that option of them buying the car within the next 37 days, they will pay an unrefundable deposit of 1,000.

Time to bring out our beloved spreadsheet to do some calculations:

	Price	Profit
Buy	40,000	
Sell	49,500	
Upfront	1,000	
If they buy, we sell	49,500	**26.3%**
If they don't, we keep the car		**2.5%**

We can make 1,000 right now, which is 2.5% profit straight away. If these guys don't come and buy the car withing the next 37 days, we would have made the money and still have the car, which we can offer for sale to other people in the future.

If the couple comes and buys the car, we'll be receiving 49,500, which will make us a total profit (adding the 1,000 at the beginning) of 26,3%, which is more than if they buy the car today at its selling price of 50,000.

With all the information in front of us, we decide to sell the option to the couple.

Tier I:

What stock

1. We only sell calls on shares we have in our portfolio. We sell, thus, *covered* calls, meaning that we have the shares if they the call options are *exercised*. When you have shares of a company, you say you are *long*; it's a long position.

   At the car dealer, if we sell an option to someone to buy a car we don't have and they decide to buy it, we would need to go to another dealer and buy it from them so we could deliver as per our contract. The price of the car could be way, way more expensive than the price we'll be selling it for, thus causing us to even file bankruptcy.

   No exaggeration is enough when it comes to stress the fact that we <u>only</u> sell **covered calls**.

2. We sell calls on stock that is in profit (at least, to begin with).

3. Also, when the chart shows that we are at a high…

4. and the indicators point towards the price being at resistance and very likely to move to the next support.

What month

5. For the moment, let's allow a minimum of 5 weeks.

I'm typing this on July 12ᵗʰ, making the August option the choice.

Like put options, the most popular options are those expiring the 3ʳᵈ Friday of the month. Thus, the expiration date for our call options will be August 18ᵗʰ of this year.

What strike

6. At this Tier I approach, we could use the Fibonacci levels as an indication of what share prices our stock can visit on its way down.

In our CAH example, when drawing the Fibonacci levels, we could expect the shares to visit the following prices:

84.45

78.08

The closest strikes would be 85 and 77.5, as we can see from the table of available strikes for August:

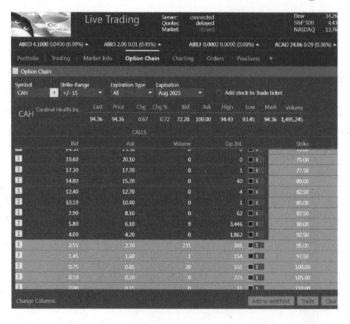

We could sell the shares directly to the market **or** we call sell a *call option* to the market for them to call the shares off us at a concrete price (strike price) by a certain date (expiration date) –you are getting the hang of it, right?–.

As stated at the beginning of this section, when we sell a call option, the buyer can exercise this option and call the shares away from us at the agreed strike price any time between them moment that we sold to open the option until expiration.

Like put options, call options are traded in multiples of 100 shares and each bundle is called *a contract*.

The reason behind you selling a call option would be, at this Tier I stage, that you think the shares have reached the selling area, you are considering harvesting the profit.

However, instead of selling them straight away, we could get some extra cash from –you know what's coming– a call option. Of course, this premium has two components that we already know of. No harm in quickly review them here again.

<u>Real value:</u> Or intrinsic value, which, is the difference between the price today and the strike price of the call option.

In our CAH example, the shares are trading today at $94.36 and we are considering selling at $85. The market is giving us $10.10.

What's the real value? The difference between the strike of $85 and the price today of $94.36, because the shares could be called off you and be sold to the market at $85.

$$Real\ value = \$94.36 - \$85 = \$9.36$$

Time value: You are more of an advanced student now, so you know the drill: the rest of the premium is time value.

$$Premium = real\ value + time\ value$$

If we sell the 85C, we will get $10.10 per share as we open the position. At expiration, the shares will be trading either above or below the strike. Let's see what the profits will be:

	Price	Profit
Open price	51.00	
Price today	94.36	
Sell today		85.0%
STO 85C	10.10	
If call not exercised		19.8%
If call exercised		86.5%

Note: in the case of call options, even though they can be exercised any time between the opening of the position and expiration, they are hardly ever exercised until the expiration weekend. An exception, that is, shares called *early*, would be when dividends are paid.

As we can see, whether we are called out or not, we are making a profit.

Whenever there is a put, there is a call and viceversa. As a refresher, let's remember that the most common expiration dates are the 3rd Friday of every month, although there are some companies that offer weekly options and some tickers, even daily options.

Another reminder: only the strongest companies offer options.

Although we have been through some information about call options, let's focus on key points for you to bear in mind as a novice call option seller you are:

What stock

1. As we already stated, but I'm not sorry to repeat, you **only** sell call options on stock you have in your portfolio, that is, you only sell *covered calls*, as opposed to *naked calls*, in which case you are

exposed and could be asked to deliver shares that you don't have and which could be trading at very high prices, so for you to deliver them, you would have to buy them at a higher price. Very fast track to getting wiped in the market.

If your account is less than $100,000, you won't be able to sell naked calls by accident. Relax.

When

2. You will sell a call option when your stock is in profit (for the moment, at least).

3. By looking at the chart and the indicators, confirm that it is at a high point.

4. Before placing the trade, do your calculations and make sure you are pleased with the RoI both if you are called out and not called out.

What strike

5. If you are at the highest point of growth, you could consider selling the next strike down or use the closest approximation to the Fibonacci levels.

What month

6. In general, the highest time value will be offered in the options expiring the next month out.

7. My personal preference is two or three months out. The reason: to give the shares more time to go down, thus reducing the probabilities of being called out in case you wish to keep the shares long-term.

How does call premium move with share price?

8. Share price and call option premium move in the same direction, which is the same to say as when the share price goes up, the call option premium goes up and viceversa.

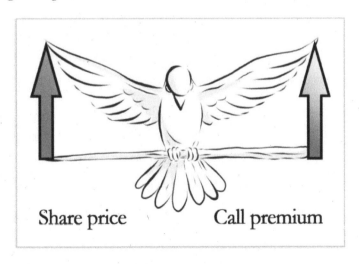

Share price   Call premium

How much goes the call option premium up for every \$1 dollar that the underlying asset goes up? The answer is: Δ. (You already know this symbol; it is read *delta*).

As an approximation, just like in the case of the put option premium, delta is approximately 50 cents at the trading price.

What if?

9. *The share price has gone up since I sold the call! I've been called out!!* So what? You could have made more money? Hear me out: You will **NEVER** sell at the absolute highest or buy at the absolute lowest.

10. *The share price has gone down below the strike I sold.* Meaning... That you could have sold a lower strike and made more money? Indeed. If we all knew what shares would do in the future, what a wonderful world ♪.

11. Reminder: we do the calculations of our RoI's of the possible outcomes and come to terms with them. Place the trades and enjoy life.

12. *There are so many strikes and so many months I don't know what to pick.* We need to introduce a few new concepts here: ITM, ATM and OTM.

ITM, ATM, OTM

In call options, we are:

In the money, ITM when we sell a strike under the current share price.

In the money we have: Real value, also called intrinsic, remember? And, on top of that, we'll also have some time value.

At the money, ATM when we sell the same strike as the current share price. Obviously, we don't always have ATM strikes available because shares trade at any given price, not only at the round prices options are offered.

Out of the money, OTM when we sell a strike above the current share price. Needless to say that the chances of being called out when you sell an OTM call are the smallest of all of them, but I'll say it anyway.

OTM there is no intrinsic value.

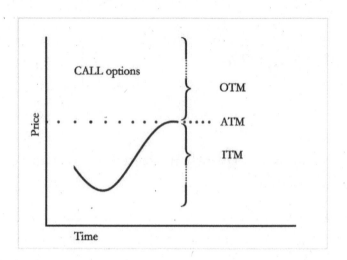

Let's see what's available for CAH at the moment of writing this chapter:

Price: 94.36	14 Jul	Jul 23	28 Jul	4 Aug	11 Aug	Aug	25 Aug	Sep	Dec	Jan 24	Jun 24	Jan 25
Strike	2	9	16	23	30	37	44	65	156	191	345	555
70	23.5	24.1	23.9	25.4	23.5	24.3	23.3	24.9	25.3	25.7	27.5	29.4
71	22.9	23.2						22.3				
72	21.6	22.1	22									
72.5									23.5	23.6		27
73	20.5	21	21.1									
74	19.7	20.2	19.8									
75	18.8	19	18.5	19	1.1	19.6	19.1	19.9	21	21.3	23.4	24.9
76	17.3	18.2	17.9									
77	16.9	17.3	16.8									
77.5	16.4					17.3		17.6	18.8	19.1	21.4	23
78	15.5	15.8	16.1									
79	14.8	15.1	15									
80	13.9	14.2	14.2	14.2	14.2	14.8	14.3	15.3	16.6	16.8	19.3	21.5
81	12.4	13.3	13	13.2								
82	11.8	12.3	12.1	12.4	12.4		12.8					
82.5		11.7				12.4		12.9	14.4	14.9	17.6	20.2
83	10.7	11.4	11.2	11.1	11.2		11.8					
84	9.5	10.2	10.2	10.5	10.2		10.5					
85	8.9	9.2	9.4	9.3	8.9	10.1	10.2	10.7	12.5	13	15.6	18.3
86	7.7	8.2	8.3	8.3	8.6		9.4					
87	7.2	7.1	7.2	6.9	7.6		8.5					
87.5		6.9				7.9		8.6	10.6	11.1	14.1	16.7
88	6.1	6.4	6.2	6.1	6.9		7.6					
89	4.7	5.4	5.4	5.8	6		6.8					
90	4.3	4.5	4.7	4.9	5.1	5.8	5.9	6.6	8.8	9.3	12.2	15.2
91	2.9	3.6	3.8	4.1	4.3		5.3					
92	2.4	2.9	3	3.3	3.5		4.5					
92.5		2.35				4		4.8	7.2	7.7	10.4	13.7
93	1.55	1.95	2.25	2.55	2.85		3.9					
94	0.8	0.94	1.6	1.95	2.2		3.3					
95	0.3	0.95	1.05	1.35	1.6	2.55	2.65	3.3	5.7	6.2	9.3	12.4
96	0.05	0.35	0.65	0.9	1.1		2.15					
97		0.15	0.35	0.55	0.8		1.75					
97.5						1.45		2.1	4.4	4.9	8	11
98		0.05	0.2	0.35	0.5		1.35					
99				0.2	0.3		1.05					
100			0.1	0.2	0.75	0.8	1.25	3.3	3.8	7.1	9.8	
101					0.1		0.6					
102							0.45					
103							0.25					
104							0.15					
105						0.1	0.05	0.35	1.75	2.2	4.9	7.6
106							0.05					
110								0.05	0.85	1.1	3.5	5.8

The dotted cells correspond to ITM calls.

94 is the closest to be ATM.

Above 94, all the prices are OTM.

The row with the numbers 2, 9, 16, etc. show the number of days till expiration.

If we plot the time value of all the premiums, this is the chart that we get:

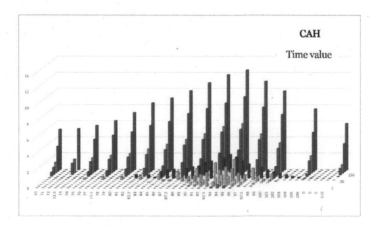

As expected, the time value increases as time increases. Also, just like it happened with put options, the time value is higher closer to the trading price *because that is where the probabilities are higher.*

Let's now plot the time value per day, which we get simply by dividing the time value by the number of days till expiration.

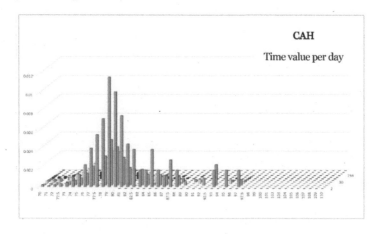

The maximum time value per day is higher the closer we are to expiration.

There is also some time value at strikes far from the trading price, which happens quite frequently and we are now very familiar with this occurrence: *the smile*.

Let's see what the time value of the options expiring on the 3rd Friday of August looks like.

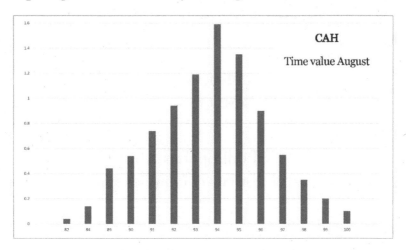

The maximum time value corresponds to $94, which is the strike closer to the trading price of $94.36.

I'm sure you remember the old proverb:

The more probabilities of an event to happen, the higher the premium.

In this case, we can observe that the distribution of the time value is a bit biased towards the ITM strikes, which indicates that those prices are more favoured by the market than the OTM prices, that is, that, as of the 3rd Friday of next month, there seem to be more probabilities of the shares to trade lower than $94 than above this strike.

Let's compare the results in RoI that we get for the ITM, ATM and OTM calls of our CAH example for August.

There is not ATM, so we picked the *94C* ($94 call option), as the closest to ATM, since the shares are trading at $94.36.

You will sell call options when you are at high points, that is, at resistance. However, there is nothing written in stone and, in the market, *never* and *always* don't apply.

Shares trading at 94.36	Premium	If NOT exercised	If exercised
ITM			
90	4.90		0.54
Gain, $/share		4.90	
RoI		5.2%	0.6%
ATM (approx)			
94	1.95		1.59
Gain, $/share		1.95	
RoI		2.1%	1.7%
OTM			
98	0.35		3.99
Gain, $/share		0.35	
RoI		0.4%	4.2%

This is an exercise to be done every time you sell a call option, since you want to have a clear vision of what are the possible outcomes, that is, what are the RoI's you'll get whether the call option is exercised or not, which is the same as to say *whether you are called away or not.*

ITM: If you think that the shares will trade underneath the strike after you sell the call, this is the best alternative, as you will get highest returns. You get to collect the potential decrease in share value as real value before the share price goes down.

Also, if you wish to sell some or all the shares of a particular stock, you will sell an ITM call to gain some extra cash from the time value and increase the probabilities of being called. If you don't get called out, you can sell another ITM call again in the future.

Graphically:

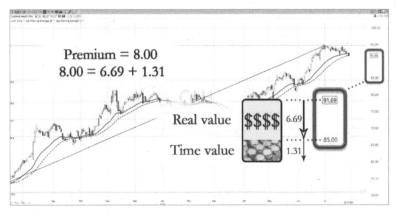

The premium is different... Because I put together this figure on a different day, which is great training: that's exactly what happens in real life, that share prices and option premiums change every second.

To do the calculations, we'll still assume we got the shares at $51.00.

At expiration, the share price could end up above or below the strike price.

a) If the share price ends up **below** the strike at expiration: The call option won't be exercised and you will keep the shares.

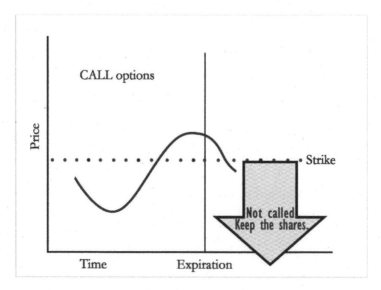

$$RoI = \left(\frac{8.00}{51.00}\right) * 100 = 15.7\%$$

You would have made a 15.7% return on your investment and still keep the shares, which you can sell a call on at the next high.

By repeating this process, you will end up owning the shares for nothing, as you can get the money back by selling option premium repeatedly.

b) If the share price ends up **above** the strike at expiration: If the price to close the position is <u>less</u> than the premium you obtained when opening it, you could BTC for a total gain.

If the price to close the position is <u>greater</u> than what you obtained when you opened it, you could allow the shares being called away from you or BTC and STO a new call for a future month. If the shares haven't gone up too much, this rolling forward could work.

ATM: the RoI is in the most similar in both cases. When we are exactly *at* the money (shares trading at the same price as the strike we are selling), the RoI will be the same whether the call option is exercised or not.

If the shares are at resistance and you wish to make the maximum time value, at the expense of less intrinsic value, and you wish to decrease the chances for the call options to be exercised, an ATM would be the preferred choice.

OTM: You get a high return if the shares end up above the strike and you get called away. You might want to STO an OTM call if you want to make some money on your assets (your shares) and decrease the probabilities of the option to be exercised even more than when selling ATM.

If you have enough shares to do so, you could consider selling some contracts ITM, some ATM and some OTM. Or whatever combination you decide.

Review

At this introductory stage of **selling** call options, you will:

1. Sell calls in companies you own: you will only *write* (sell to open) covered call options.

2. Receive premium for the call options you sell.

3. Set the strike price that you agree on being called away.

4. Set the expiration date of the options you are writing.

5. If the options are exercised, you will receive money from them equals to the strike times the number of contracts times one hundred (minus costs).

6. Both with the premium and with the cash you receive in case the call options are exercised, you can use it to buy more shares.

7. Calls and puts: are they related?

   Whenever there is a put, there is a call and viceversa.

   Calls and puts are *delta neutral*. That means that when you add up the deltas of a call and a put of the same ticker, date and strike, you get zero.

   Put option deltas show a negative sign to point to the fact that their growth is the opposite to the share price (remember the see saw). Since call options and share price increase and decrease together (remember the bird flapping its wings), deltas for call options are positive.

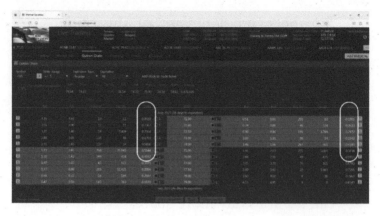

In both cases, the more ITM we are, the closer to 1.

Conclusion

☆ By selling a call option, we can sell shares in the future at a higher price than if we sell them today.

☆ For that reason, our RoI will be higher than if we sell the shares straight to the market.

☆ Whether the call option is exercised or not, we get to keep the premium the very second we sell the call option. We can use this cash to buy more shares right away, if we choose to.

☆ We always sell *covered* calls, meaning that we have the shares to deliver would the market exercise its right to call them off us any time between the selling of the contract/s and expiration. We are long in the positions.

☆ We sell call options in bunches of 100. Each one is called *contract*.

☆ We can choose the strike and the expiration day.

☆ At expiration (or before), the shares could be called away.

☆ The command to sell call option is STO (*sell to open*).

Let's see the figures behind this image.

Trade	Price	Profit
Average open price (initial price)	51.00	
Price now	91.69	
Shares sold now		40.69
85C premium	8.00	
Shares called at 85		42.00
Difference in profit		1.31
Difference in profit, %		2.6%

In our last example, we bought the shares at $51.00. Since the price now is $91.69, the profit would be $40.69 (which is a 79.8% profit).

We sold an 85C, so if the shares are called at $85, the profit would:

$85-$51+the $8.0 premium = $42.00

That means $1.31 more than selling the shares directly, which is a 2.6% increase plus the chance of still keeping the shares if they trade under the strike at expiration and the call is not exercised.

Time decay also apply, of course, to call option premium. Again, the closer we are to expiration, the faster this decay is, represented by our Greek friend theta (θ).

Please, find below a graphic representation of time decay using the data of CAH:

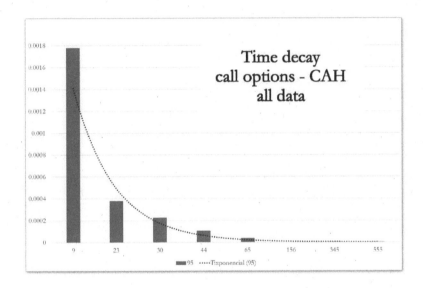

In fact, the decay is so large with just 9 days for expiration, that we can hardly see what's going on with the rest of the days.

Removing this first data point, we get the following chart, where we can see the elegant logarithmic decay with more detail:

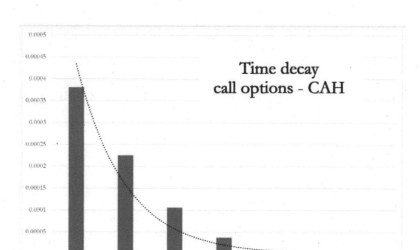

A present for you: a video on how calls work. After everything you've learned in this section, you'll love it!

Call options
very clearly explained

How to get an income from our shares and sell them dearer

3.5 Accelerated RoI's: ride the waves

Some visual recapitulation:

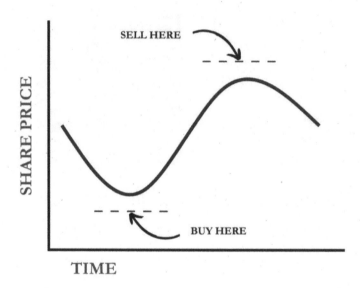

By selling put options instead of buying the shares directly from the market, we buy them at a discount in the future; it is as if we were buying them at a lower price than the shares are trading at *today*, that is, the day we STO the put option.

By selling call options instead of the shares directly to the market, we make some extra profit; it is as if we were effectively selling them at a higher price than the shares are trading at *today*, that is, the day we STO the covered call option.

We have seen that we sell puts at the low points and we sell calls at the high points.

Since share prices go up and down all the time, very often describing the Elliot waves, with practice, we could get very good at reading charts and *ride the waves*, or *do the wheel*, which is nothing more than selling puts at the bottom and selling calls at the top, reivesting the money we get in premium into buying more shares (allowing more shares be put to us).

Tier II: Even though the emphasis so far has been on **selling** options, we sometimes buy them.

For the moment, we will only buy options, which we do with the command *buy to close* (BTC), when we want to cancel the contract.

As we've seen before, we can STO both call and put options whenever we choose to, of course, always applying our system. When we sell a contract, we are obligated to fulfil the commitment that we sign for:

a) Take delivery of the shares if the put option is assigned.

b) Deliver the shares if the call option is exercised.

Also, we can choose to get out of the commitments that we incur in by closing our contracts. How? As mentioned before, by buying our contracts back.

We know that option premium moves as follows:

1. With the shares in the case of call options (the bird)

2. Against the shares growth in the case of put options (the see saw)

With these *what-colour-was-George's-white-horse* type of clue, the best moment to buy back the options that we sold will be as follows:

1. When the share price goes down in the case of call options.

2. When the share price goes up in the case of put options.

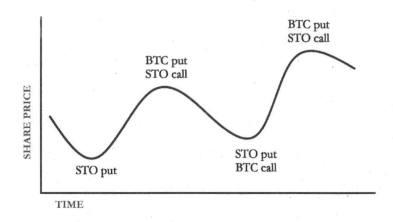

Thus, the same way that we can buy shares at the bottom and sell them at the top over and over, when we use options, we can sell puts at the bottom and calls at the top, making further profits due to the extra money that options give us thanks to the time value.

We learned that we can buy back the put options at high points. Surprise! We can buy back the call options at low points.

When we get good at this, we can sell puts at the bottom and buy them at the top. For shares we have, we can sell calls at the top and buy them back at the bottom and repeat over and over.

In case you haven't realised, this is making money from selling time.

What if... I get called out? Yes: it is likely that you will be called at some point. At a profit!!!

When to sell ITM, ATM or OTM? Already discussed.

The more familiar you get with selling puts at the bottom, buying them back at the top (BTC or open a bull put spread), selling calls at the top and BTC at the bottom... The more money you will make!

(ツ)

4. INCREASING THE RETURNS EVEN MORE: OPM

Business, that's easily defined:
It's other people's money.
Peter Drucker

We started our journey of investing in the stock market by using our own money, that we could refer to as *seed capital.*

As a first approach, we picked shares of high-quality at a good price, wait for them to increase their value (this is called *price appreciation*) and sold them for a profit. With this profit, we now have more disposable cash to buy more shares.

As a second approach, we sold puts on shares we wanted to buy and have the cash to acquire. For these trades, we received premium money which we could use to buy more shares. This premium money was *other people's money* (OPM).

When our shares mature, we can get some extra cash from selling calls on them, which, again, is OPM.

You get the idea: when tapping onto more cash than the cash we actually have, we can make money on that extra cash, thus increasing the profits way more.

Easy principle: the more money we can use, the more money we can make.

4.1 Margin and buying power

When we want to buy a house, the word *mortgage*, its ethimological meaning being *dead pledge*, comes to mind.

We go to the bank, ask for a credit and, if we tick all the boxes, we will get some borrowed money to pay the house instalments. At the beginning, these payments, as we are all aware, consist of mainly –if not completely– interest and, over time, they will correspond to more capital and less interest.

At the end of the 25 years or so, it wouldn't be unreasonable to say that you would have paid nearly double the price that the house was quoted for.

I can only talk about the brokers that I have personally been working with since 2012, now called Planner Securities LLC, already mentioned before. I would imagine, though, that what I am about to tell you would be common practice for all brokerage firms.

Through them, if you wish, you will be provided with a line of credit that corresponds to 100% of the cash you have. The only requirement is that your account value is $2,000 dollars or above.

Please, watch this video on buying power before and after you are done with this section and feel in your body the empowerment of understanding a lot more the second time around. Then, celebrate!

Account value, buying power & option drag

The summer and winter of options

<u>Tier I:</u>

Buying power

Let's dig into what we said in the last paragraph a bit more.

As an example, you have opened an account, funded it with $50,000 and you do want to make use of this line of credit, which you would have stated when submitting the forms to open your trading account.

When you open your trading platform, you will see these figures in your trading platform:

Net Liq Value	50,000.00
Buying Power	100,000.00

Translation: you sent 50,000 to the account, your seed capital. However, through the broker, you get an instant credit from the clearing firm of some other 50,000. They give you a $1 credit for every $1 of yours, no questions asked.

Now, you can trade *as if* you had 100,000 (you have a *buying power* of 100,000) instead of the initial buying power of 50,000 if you handn't requested this line of credit, that is, if you don't have a *margin* account.

I call this line of credit *ghost money*, because for every dollar we add, we get the use of another dollar just like that.

(Note: if you have been trading your account and you have open positions in it, you can access the margin facility as well when you reach $2,000 in account value).

On paper, with double the amount of disposable cash and applying the same principles and strategies we've been going through, you could make twice the profit than if you use the initial 50,000 only.

HOWEVER, WE WON'T. We won't use the whole line of credit.

Tattoo this on your hands, so you can read it before placing trades:

We shall not use all our buying power.

Why? Like everything in life, balance is called for: the more buying power we use, the more money we can make… And the more money we can lose if things go the opposite way to anticipated.

If you overcommit selling puts and share prices go down fast, you would be required to face those commitments… And you would see how you run out of money, because you would have sold more than you could buy.

When this situation happens, you incur is what's called a *margin call*: your buying power has gone negative and should restore it either by sending fresh money to the account, by closing positions options or by selling shares. If you don't do anything, the clearing firm will close positions as they wish until the buying power is restored. (They want to protect the money they lent you).

Having a margin call is not the end of the world at all. When we don't squeeze the buying power too much, our *asset allocation* is set properly (not overexposing yourself to any one particular position) and the puts are sold over many months ahead of you (6-8 or even more months ahead), repairing strategies can be applied and the buying power restored easily enough.

Talking about asset allocation, please, watch this video:

Asset allocation and diversification

Allocation and diversification with the 4x4 System

When these boxes are not ticked, and I've been there myself, you could witness how your account decreases 90% (that was my case) in front of your very eyes and the recovery afterwards could take a very, very long time because you are left with very few positions to bring it back to the splendour of where it was before.

During 2022, the SP-500 went down 19.4% and NASDAQ (an index that aglutinates mainly technological companies), 33.4%.

Out of the approximately 30 accounts I was involved with during that year, **none** of them ever incurred in a margin call during such a *bear market* (down market). And they made an average of above 60% on premium on the average account value.

And... This is where another million-dollar question arises: *How come that we made so much money and our account value has gone down? Where is all that money gone? I can't see it!*

Time to talk about who Santa really is.

Account value

First of all, it is important to know what our account value consists of:

$$Acc.Value = equities + cash + options$$

Where:

Acc. Value = liquidation value. If you close all your positions, you can bring back home the account value amount (minus the commissions for closing such positions, in case you wonder).

Equities = value of the shares.

Cash = amount of cash in the account.

Options = <u>negative</u> value assigned to put options

When we sell put options, these positions will hold a negative value. When the *underlying* stock (the stock that we sold the put on) goes down, the negative value of the options increases; it is more negative, so to speak. Likewise, when the underlying goes up, the negative value of the put option is less negative, closer to zero. But… It's always negative.

Let's look at a couple of examples:

Note: Trading prices on the 14th of June at close:

FND: $96.14
INCY: $61.44

Even though FND is trading above 96 and we sold a 75P, meaning that we are $21 above the strike and, therefore, the probabilities of having this put assigned within the next 30 days are close to zero (never say never in the stock market), it still has a negative value.

INCY 70P, with 177 days to expiration, is now trading at $61.44, $8.56 underneath the strike. It makes sense for the clearing firm to give this position a greater negative value, since we are borrowing money from them. They place themselves in a worst-case scenario to make sure we can always give them back the money we borrowed from them and have enough to honour the commitments we've made, hence their daily evaluation of positions to make sure we can pay our loses, if we get there, with what we have. Better safe than sorry.

When prices go down, this margin call system protects us from losing more than what we have.

In case your hairs are standing, remember that applying the system to the very letter and ticking all the boxes can get you through down markets perfectly fine. We have proved it.

Let's continue with the pursuit of the simingly disappearing money we generate as premium.

It's all hidden in plain sight in the formula of the account value that we saw before:

$$\text{Acc. Value} = \text{equities} + \text{cash} + \textbf{options}$$

For learning purposes, imagine the cash doesn't move for a month and the options either. Let's call these two terms together C.

$$\text{Acc. Value} = \text{equities} + C$$

In this pretend scenario, the account value would go up and down as share prices go up and down: the higher the prices of the stocks, the higher the account value and viceversa. Visually:

Acc. Value = equities + C

$$\text{Acc. Value} = \text{equities} + C$$

Part of the money we would have used to buy those shares would be coming from the premium resulting from selling put options. Now, stick to the *viceversa* in the previous paragraph: *The lower the prices of the stocks, the lower the account value.*

We are buying assets that go up and down in value. When they go down, even if we used money we didn't invest directly from our pockets, the account value goes down.

On top of that, we have a negative term in the equation, the **option** term, which we refer to as *option drag* precisely because it drags the account value down.

The option drag comes from the options and we know the price of options has two components: real value and time value. The real value is what it is and is directly correlated to the share price, as we saw before. However, the time value component decreases as we get closer to expiration until it disappears at expiration. (For the nerdy: the decrease is not linear, but it accelerates as we get closer to expiration. We've seen that in the examples of CAH and CVS.).

In the example of the car insurance, the insurance depends on the value of the vehicle and also on the amount of time you want to cover: the value of the vehicle is fixed and you would pay less the closer you are to the expiration date of such insurance.

Now that we have found the "missing" cash, you might be thinking: *So… We've cashed in all these dollars and made no progress at all? Because the account value is not moving/ is going backwards!*

Some gratitude and appreciation could be in place now.

Imagine that you invested 100,000 worth of good quality shares when they were at a good price at the beginning of 2022.

The day you buy them, the account value is pretty much 100,000.

At the end of 2022, it would make sense to estimate that your account value would be 75,000. You are 25% down.

When the shares go back to what you paid for them, and they more than likely will, your account value will go to 100,000.

However, if you had sold puts over the whole year, you would have been able to collect 50,000 of put option premium with which to buy 50,000 worth of shares.

When the shares go back to what you paid for them, and they more than likely will, your account value will go to 150,000.

This, by the way, is a real example of one of our accounts (the figures have been rounded up to make our point across).

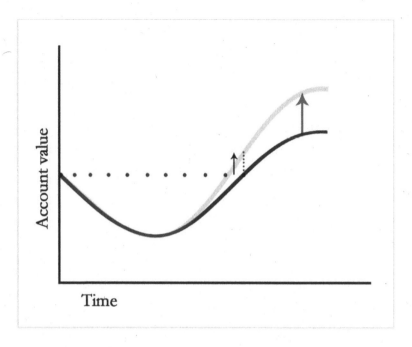

As we buy more assets on the way down, when they go back to the prices we paid for them, the account value will increase more than if we just buy and hold. Over time, the difference in account value will be even more noticeable.

We have observed that when applying the 4x4 System in a down market, our accounts tend to go down less than buy and hold only and when the market goes up, our accounts grow much faster than buy and hold only.

We mentioned that for every $1 of cash we have in our account, the clearing firm gives us, if we have a margin account, another $1 of buying power (the ghost money).

When we have shares, this could be the case, like in ATUS below: the market value is 882 and the *maintenance requirement* (Maint. Req) is also 882.

You can read this as follows: *For every dollar my ATUS shares are worth, one dollar of buying power is required.*

On the next line, we can see AEO. In this case, we would read: *For every dollar my AEO shares are worth, only ¼ of a dollar of buying power is required.*

This is where this statement is coming from: the market value of the AEO position is 7,032; the maintenance requirement is 1,758. If you divide one by the other:

$$Maintenance\ requirement = \frac{7,032}{1,758} = 4.0$$

We can say that the clearing firm gives us $4 for every $1 we have invested in AEO. Yes: shares are more valuable than money!

The minimum ratio I have seen is 1, which means that the shares are as valuable as money and the maximum, 4. Other ratios. 1.6, 2, 2.3, 3…

The ratio is fixed for every company… Until it is changed. Thus, when you observe a noticeable change in your buying power to account value ratio overnight, it could be because the maintenance requirements have changed.

How much buying power to use?

Another one-million-dollar question.

As a Tier I approximation, I would say stay between 80 and 100% of the BP to account value ratio.

Let's go deeper into this ratio as a Tier II approximation.

<u>Tier II:</u>

When we divide the buying power by the account value, we get a ratio.

Let's see some real examples:

Account 5DP***48:

Net Liq Value	103,884.64
Buying Power	106,112.41

$$BP\ to\ Acc.Val\ ratio = \frac{106.1}{103.9} x100 = 102\%$$

The ratio is above 100%. The buying power is not being fully used; more put options could be sold.

(The reason why this ratio is so high is because cash was added to this account this very week —the week of the 19th of June 2023—, a very bullish week, which means that shares have gone up, the indicators on their way to the overbought position or already there. The VIX is at a low point as well. The sensible thing to do seems to be waiting for better opportunities; what goes up, comes back down).

Account 5DP***49:

Net Liq Value	139,555.08
Buying Power	90,086.29

Ratio: 64%

This seems quite a reasonable ratio.

Account 5DP***06:

Net Liq Value	68,430.99
Buying Power	30,981.48

Ratio: 45%

This would be, in my opinion, on the edge.

I tend to use a ratio between 60 and 70% buying power to account value. However, I would apply also other ratios depending on the circumstances:

1. In accounts that add money every month, 50%.

2. In accounts that are there for the long long-term and have low risk tolerance, 80%.

3. In small accounts (between 25 and 50k), I prefer to keep the ratio between 70 and 80%.

4. I am more conservative the third week of each month (expiration week) because some puts will be put to us, some won't, some calls will be exercised and some won't. For these reasons, the buying power will change over the weekend and I prefer to take decisions about selling more puts when the buying power has settled on Monday.

5. If the market is at a low and all points for it to turn up, I would go lower in the ratio, because as share prices increase, the ratio will also increase (less buying power is required).

6. The opposite applies: when the market is up and it looks like it could go back down, I'll keep the ratio higher, because as the share prices go down, the buying power will be higher and, therefore, the ratio will go down as well.

Margin calls

If our buying power goes negative, we incurred in what's known as *margin call*. It means, pretty much, that at that point in time, we could not hold all the positions, that is, that we can't honour all the commitments we had at the time.

As mentioned before, if we don't do anything, the clearing firm will close positions, quite randonmly, to go back to a positive buying power (they need to ensure the money the lent us is safe!).

In my experience, this situation happens when:

a) We are overlevereaging our buying power to account value ratio **and**

b) The whole market (including our shares) goes down very quickly.

We have two or three days to restablish the balance. Here you are some things that can be done to increase the buying power:

1. Send cash to the account.

2. Turn our naked put positions into *bull put spreads* (BUPs).

   We'll see more about BUPs in our next section. In the case of reparing the buying power, bear in mind the second leg might have to be opened more OTM than in a regular BUP as in our next section.

3. Sell call options, which brings cash into the account.

4. Sell shares. Preferably, at a profit.

5. BTC put options.

In conclusion

We are selling put options on money that we might or might not use in the future to buy the underlying shares. In everyday words: we sell put options on shares that could be put to us, meaning, we'll *have to* buy them, for which we will use cash.

If we have the cash, the shares will be bought with it. If we don't have it, we can use the line of credit to buy the shares.

In our platform, we will see that the cash is negative. And because we are using some other people's money, we will pay a percentage for the number of days that we use it. This rate changes with the price of money, obviously. What I've seen over the years is an interest rate between 4% and 7% per year, depending on volume and interest rates.

My preference is to keep the cash above zero. However, puts can be exercised earlier than expiration and, from one day to the next, we'll see that we have some shares we didn't have and our cash is now in the red.

What can we do?

Clue: we don't do panic; we apply rules.

Tier III:

If your cash is negative, most likely it is because you haven't been as conservative as we recommend our new traders to be.

No worries, though: everything can be learned and there are solutions and strategies to reverse the negative cash into positive, that is, if that's your choice.

How to bring cash into the account, that is, if you prefer not to use the line of credit? Some investors are happy to use the line of credit because they predict that the profits they will make with the increase in the share prices will surpass the tiny interest rates they will pay for borrowing the actual money. We don't pay anything for just using the margin facility.

If you prefer not to borrow money, though, this is what you could do:

1. Add it from outside sources, that is, sending more money to the account.

   It is a great habit to send more money to invest periodically. If we know there will be some more money on the way, we can just use the borrowed cash, pay the little interest and cover it with the new money on its way.

2. Sell new puts, if feasible. I mean, if we have enough buying power and there are candidates to sell puts on.

3. Sell calls, preferably on shares that are in profit and at a high point in the charts.

4. Sell shares. Again, in profit, at a high point in the charts. It could be part of the shares we have on a particular stock to balance the portfolio.

5. Release buying power. This is a strategy that, in my opinion, deserves a separate heading.

4.2 Releasing buying power: lids

We have learned that when we sell a put option:

1. We receive premium (money) that is automatically added to our cash and we can instantly use it.

2. We commit to accept (to buy) the shares being put to us any time between the moment of selling the option to expiration.

3. We are using buying power to hold the position open.

Wouldn't it be great if we could decrease the use of this buying power? This way… We could reuse the released buying power to sell other puts that bring in more premium, which is cash that gives us more buying power and with which we can buy more shares, which, in turn, give us even more buying power... And so the story goes.

It would, certainly, be great.

You might be thinking: *Is that possible? And since everything has a price, much does it cost to realise buying power?*

Yes: it is possible and yes, it does have a price. How much you will pay depends on your patience.

We'll talk about this strategy in more detail in the next chapter, *Managing puts*. However, no harm whatsoever to see some examples here to prepare our neurones for new connections.

Let's explain it with an example.

INFY is now a 3x4 company that has recently gapped down. Experience tells us that gaps tend to get filled both on the way up and on the way down.

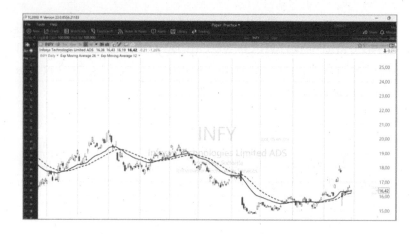

Today is the end of July and we plan to STO an 18P for January. We are given $2.00 on the bid.

To make calculations simple, we'll assume 1 contract. Therefore, the exposure in the market will be $1,800 ($18x 1 contract x 100 shares/contract).

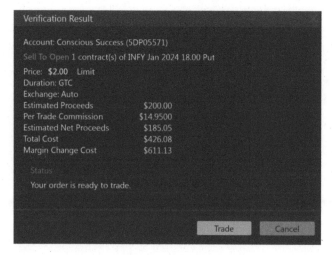

We'll bring in $185.05 and the BP required will be twice the *Total Cost*, that is, $852.16.

If we wish to reduce our exposure and we want to do it now, we can BTO (*buy to open*) a January 17P. The two trades together conform a bull put spread.

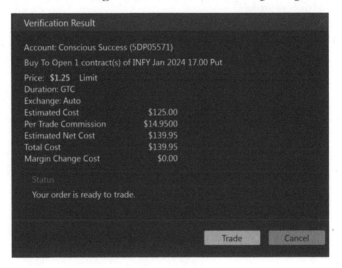

The price we pay per share is $1.25 and the total, commission included is $139.95.

By placing this trade, we would only be exposed for $1, since the shares could be put to us at $18 and we could sell them at $17. The value is not linear, so we cannot calculate it, but going from an $18 exposure to a $1 exposure reduces the BP... Big time!

To do the calculations, we are going to dismiss the commissions, to make it simpler and because they get percentually smaller as we increase the number of contracts.

INFY	Premium	Exposure	Difference
STO Jan 18P, 1 contract	2.00	1,800	
BTO Jan 17P, 1 contract	-1.25	100	
Difference in strikes			1.0
Difference in premium			0.75

These are the three possible scenarios that we will encounter at expiration:

1. The shares are trading above $18: There is no assignment of shares. We would have made a return as follows:

$$ROCE = \left(\frac{0.75 * 100}{1,800}\right) * 100 = 4.2\%$$

The profit is 0.75 per share and there are 100 shares, thus the 0.75x100.

The commitment is $18/share x100 shares, thus the 1,800.

2. The shares are trading below $17 (as low as it may be): The shares are assigned at $18 and then sold at $17, so we end up with no shares.

$$ROCE = \left(\frac{(-18 + 0.75 + 17) * 100}{1,800}\right) * 100 = -1.39\%$$

We'd lose money.

3. The shares end up between $17 and $18: They will be assigned.

   Since we buy them at $18, got $2.00 for the naked put and paid $1.25 for the lid, it is as if we had a discount of $0.75. Effectively, we would have bought them at $17.25.

   Since the shares are trading today at $16.42, this strategy doesn't seem like a smart move at all. Not only that, we've also seen we would be in the red if the shares end up underneath the put we bought.

   You could say: *Perhaps it is this case in particular, in which we only make money if the shares end up above the strike of the naked put, but the strategy would work if we chose another company or different strikes or months.*

   To save you time, know that the strategy will work when **the difference in premium is greater than the difference in strikes**. Let's see with an example.

   Now, instead of buying the put underneath straight away, we just place an order to BTO the Jan 17P for a 10% of the premium we got when we sold the 18P:

INFY	Premium	Exposure	Difference
STO Jan 18P, 1 contract	2.00	1,800	
BTO Jan 17P, 1 contract	-0.20	100	
Difference in strikes			1.0
Difference in premium			1.80

Time to compare the three possible scenarios at expiration:

1. The shares are trading above $18: Equally, no assignment of shares. The return will be:

$$ROCE = \left(\frac{1.80 * 100}{1,800}\right) * 100 = 10.0\%$$

The profit in this case is $2.00 - 0.20 = 1.80$.

2. The shares are trading below $17: Just like before, the shares are assigned at $18 and then sold at $17, so we end up with no shares.

$$ROCE = \left(\frac{(-18 + 1.8 + 17) * 100}{1,800}\right) * 100 = 4.4\%$$

3. The shares end up between $17 and $18: The shares will be assigned.

Since we buy them at $18, we got $2.00 for the naked put and paid $0.20 for the lid, it is as if we had a $1.80 discount, so we would be buying the shares at $16.20, which is a discount of 1.34% with respect to the price today.

I agree that it isn't much of a discount, but I'll give you three reasons why. I would consider this to be a <u>Tier III</u> information:

First: The VIX is at a low that we haven't encountered since before March 2020, and we all know what happened then.

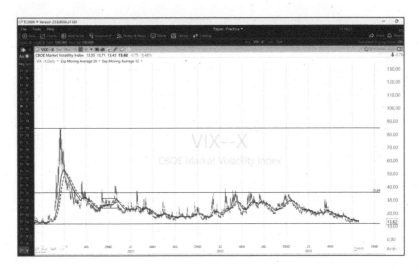

Second: INFY's volatility is very low, which translates into low time value in its options.

Third: I wanted to show you a gap, a great opportunity to make some real value, and INFY just happened to have one.

Let's witness some bigger discount that we could get when we choose a more volatile stock, such as INCY. Similar ticker, different behaviour.

INCY is at support and now it's trading at $62.04.

We could STO the INCY Dec 65P and get $4.40 per share:

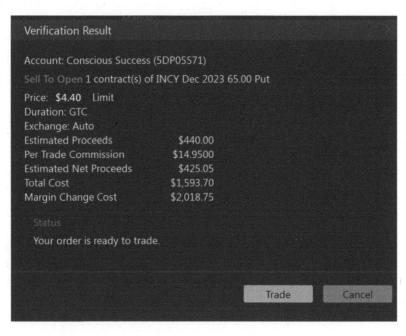

Verification Result

Account: Conscious Success (5DP05571)

Sell To Open 1 contract(s) of INCY Dec 2023 65.00 Put

Price: **$4.40** Limit
Duration: GTC
Exchange: Auto
Estimated Proceeds $440.00
Per Trade Commission $14.9500
Estimated Net Proceeds $425.05
Total Cost $1,593.70
Margin Change Cost $2,018.75

Status

Your order is ready to trade.

Trade   Cancel

8% of $4.40 is 35 cents.

INCY	Premium	Exposure	Difference
STO Dec 65P	4.40	6,500	
BTO Dec 62.5P	-0.35	100	
Difference in strikes			2.5
Difference in premium			4.05

1. If the shares trade above $65 at expiration, we get to keep the $4.40 − $0.35 = $4.05 and this would be the ROCE:

$$ROCE = \left(\frac{4.05 * 100}{6,500}\right) * 100 = 6.2\%$$

2. If the shares trade below \$62.5 at expiration, no assignement either and the ROCE will be as follows:

$$ROCE = \left(\frac{(-65 + 4.05 + 62.5) * 100}{6{,}500}\right) * 100 = 2.4\%$$

3. If the shares end up between both strikes, the shares get assigned and, effectively, we would be buying them at \$60.95 (\$65-\$4.05). Since they are trading at \$63.04, that's a \$2.09 discount, that is, 3.02%, 2.3 times bigger discount than in the case of INFY.

How to increase the ROCE?

<u>Tier III</u>

- Look for more volatile companies.

- Sell options when the VIX is high (or higher).

- Sell some intrinsic value. That means that you will be more aggressive in your put selling. At this stage, you will be able to discern what companies, what strikes, what months, how many contracts.

How much for the lid?

As a guideline, we offer 10% of the premium collected for the naked put when the difference in strikes is of $1, 8% when it is $2.5 and 6% when it is $5. Of course, the orders are rounded up or down to the nearest 5 or 10 cents, depending on how the options are priced.

Therefore, we need to make sure that we are getting more than $1.1 per share when selling a put whose options are offered at $1 increments, more than $2.7 when the difference in strikes is $2.5 and more than $5.3 when such difference is $5.

Difference in strike	% of premium received	Minimum premium
$1	10%	1.1
$2.5	8%	2.7
$5	6%	5.3

If the puts are assigned early, what do we do with the lid?

A put option that we sell can be assigned to us at any moment before expiration.

When we sold the put, we also would have placed an order to buy a put under the strike that we sold (what we, at home, call *a lid*).

Now, the option is assigned, which translates into us having the shares of the underlying asset and an order to buy a lid ready to get triggered when and if the shares trade high enough for the premium to go down to the limit we set.

What do we do with this order? Cancel it? Leave it?

In general, we tend to leave the order on. Know that if expires, you can also place another one for the future at the same strike and offering the same limit price.

If the order gets triggered, these will be its effects:

➢ It releases buying power that can be used to open new puts, thus bringing more cash/premium to the account.

➢ It fixes the buying power needed to maintain this position, regardless of the trading price of the underlying stock.

4.3 Managing puts

We have seen how put options are a fantastic way to buy shares in the future at a discount.

At this point, it is very likely that you have realised that selling put options can be used to buy shares cheaper and also as a way of generating an income from our portfolio, haven't you? ☺

Think of it: you can sell put options and, at expiration, if they are not put to you, you would have made money… Out of thin air. Well, you need to have assets behind (shares, cash or both) to be able to respond to the possibility that you are assigned the shares, but you would have never had the asset; it's like people you insured never reported an incident and just kept your premium.

In my experience, when selling put options at support at the next available strike above the price the shares are trading at and allowing at least 4 months for expiration, no more than 40% of the puts are exercised, on average.

Obviously, the percentage goes up in a bearish market and down in a bull market.

You might think: *But… 40% of the options being exercised is quite a lot! I won't have enough money to buy them all!* Good job we know how to manage this situation in the eventuality that more shares that you want get put to you. Also, that 40% goes down when selling strikes closer to the trading price. Sometimes, when the volatility is high enough (either for a stock in particular or generally in the whole market), we can sell OTM puts (below the price the shares are trading at) and still get enough for the limit price to be within the limits we established in the last table you can find when turning the pages back/scrolling up.

This especially high volatily is often encounter in the options of a particular when there's extra uncertainty around the stock. Sometimes, no clue when this uncertainty is going to happen or why (rumours, scandals, news...), but there are four times a year we know about, and that's when the *earnings report* is released.

Companies are obliged to submit a truthful (or they will literally go to jail) report on their sales and earnings every quarter. Around the time of the earnings announcements, the volatility tends to increase due to the uncertainty of the results about to be presented. A *rally* before the announcement is quite common (shares going up), which presents an excellent opportunity to sell calls both because the shares are at a high and because of the added time value. After the announcement, gaps happen regularly.

This is an example of a company gapping up and down on earnings. If you take a closer look at the dates, you will notice that these gapping happens at intervals of 3 months:

And if you can't read the months because they are small, know that the earnings announcements are public. We tend to use both the Value Line web to find them and also the Earnings Whispers or Nasdaq websites.

In these websites, we can also find very interesting information about what are the past results both in earnings and sales and the expected results for the coming quarter. When results are lower than previous quarters and years, it is very likely that a gap down happens. The opposite also applies.

These gaps down offer an excellent opportunity to enter a position: low point meets high volatility and give birth to a beautiful, high premium put option family.

Note that gaps tend to fill, so a next high or low are made evident with neon lights.

Going back to puts, point at which I was before I started rambling about earnings reports, a couple of reminders:

Number #1: When you open your account, you **do** want shares being put to you. That's the whole point, remember? Shares are assets. Wealth = assets.

At the early stages of creating a portfolio, it will take months, sometimes years, to get our cash invested into shares. At these early stages, we could choose to be a bit more *aggressive* when picking the strikes for our puts. No need to bite off anyone's nose or push and shove to sell our puts – we have as many puts available for us as we wish.

By aggressive, I mean that we can sell a higher strike. These are the effects of selling a higher strike (ITM):

- We will get a higher premium consistent of more intrinsic value than the put underneath, although also less time value than it. All in all, though, more money in our account.

- We increase the chances of the shares being put to us. No mystery here: the higher the strike, the higher the probability of the share price to end up below this strike, which means assignment.

However, when we are invested in shares, our portfolio is built and we can now change our strategy by selling more *conservative* puts, not Victorian nor prude, but at lower strikes. Because, at this point, the objective is to sell puts to generate an income rather than to purchase shares at a discount. We will keep buying some, of course, with the new money coming in from selling options.

What a powerful machine!

Number #2: When we step up to this stage of selling puts with the intention of income generation, we should have a very clear vision of what are the possible scenarios we can encounter throughout the life of those puts.

Let's visit those scenarios, some of which we have already seen before.

The framework is that we have sold a put, which, of course, we have carefully chosen: on a 3x4 or 4x4 company, at support, the indicators in the *right place*, etc.

The following picture sumarises all the scenarios we can face during the life of our put – and beyond. You might not follow everything right now, but wait and see and everything will make sense when we go through each one of the outcomes.

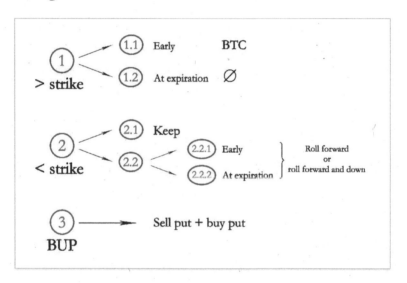

Alert: You are going to see a few formulas coming up. Before you freeze or start chanting in your head *I'm not good with numbers*, let me tell you that they are very easy once you know what they mean.

These formulas will express the **returns** obtained.

Going to the vegetable kingdom, think of apples.

a) One scenario is when you buy something. Let's say you bought a tree for a *price* and got apples that you sold.

Because you have invested money in buying the tree, you will be talking about *Return on Investment*, that is, how much money you got out of the money you invested.

$$RoI, \% = \frac{sale\ of\ apples}{price\ of\ the\ tree} x\ 100$$

We use the %, per cent, as we are interested in a figure that we can compare with others. If a red jumper offers a $20 discount and a green jumper offers a $15 discount doesn't mean that the first one is cheaper, right? If the red jumper initial price is $200, the discount is (20/200)x100 = 10%. If the initial price of the green jumper is $70, the discount is 21%.

Now we know that the red jumper, even though the discount is greater in dollars, offers a smaller percentual discount than the green jumper.

b) A different scenario is when you don't buy anything. This brings us back to being the insurance company.

You collected a premium from a customer. Two things might happen: the customer reports an incident or not.

If they do, you pay.

If you don't, which is where I wanted to get to, you would have made money (the premium you received from your customer) on a promise to pay for the repairs of their vehicle. The money is put aside; you have it. But you never used it.

In this case, we'll be talking about *Return on Capital Employed* (ROCE): it represents how much money you've made from the money you put aside but never used.

$$ROCE, \% = \frac{premium}{money\ put\ aside} x\ 100$$

Easy, right? It's always the same thing: money made from money either used (RoI) or put aside (ROCE).

Let's now translate these concepts into stock market concepts:

Sale of apples = premium
Price of tree = investment
Money put aside = buying power (BP)

Note that the premium, in the case of options, can be obtained over several trades and it can include expenses as well. The premium is positive if we STO a position and is negative if we BTC it.

The total premium will be the premiums of all the STO positions minus the premiums of all the BTC positions of the trades on a particular put.

Every formula you will see in this section will be an adaptation of the following general one:

$$return, \% = \frac{gains}{BP \ or \ cash} x \ 100$$

Which you can internally read as: *My return (*on capital employed *if I didn't buy anything or* on inverstment *if I did) is the money I gained on the money that I promised to use or the money I used. Then I multiply by 100 to express this return as a percentage.*

Tier I: Going back to the summary in the figure above, as a Tier I, we have two possibilities when we sell a put option: The shares trade above or below the strike price. We'll go now through the possible scenarios and what we can do in both cases.

1. Share price > strike Ø or BTC

1.1 The share price goes up

You see how the share price has gone up since you sold the put and the expiration date is not happening for a good while. You are the one to decide how long a *good while* is. For me, more than 3-4 weeks.

Since puts move down when shares go up, the premium of the put you sold is now much cheaper than when you sold it.

We tend to consider *cheap* a premium that's 20% or less of the premium that we got when we opened the position.

You can BTC (buy to close) the contract for a profit. Your software will allow you to set an order to close the position at the limit price you establish. If you sold a put and got $10, to do the math simple, you can set an order to BTC at $1. Or $2. Or $1.6. Whatever the exit point you decide to get the return you want.

You can place the order to BTC at any time. Just be aware of making a GTC order (good till cancel), so the order remains active until the conditions you've set are met. Obviously, if they are never met, the order won't get triggered.

$$ROCE, \% = \frac{Total\ premium}{BP} x\ 100$$

The total premium in this case will be the premium you got when you sold the put minus the premium you paid to close it.

The immediate effect of closing a put is that the BP increases. Therefore, you could use it to buy a new put.

1.2 The share price is above the strike at expiration

Even if it just by one cent, if the share price ends up above the strike at COB, the shares won't be assigned.

We've made money on buying power, because we never used any money at all.

$$ROCE, \% = \frac{premium}{BP} x\ 100$$

2. Share price goes down

2.1 The shares are assigned and you buy them

If you choose to keep the shares, whether they are assigned before or at expiration, you buy them.

In comparison with the price the share was trading at the day you sold the put and you decided it was a good entry point, you would have bought them at a discount.

$$RoI, \% = \frac{Premium\ per\ share}{Strike} x\ 100$$

This would be the return of investment *per share*. Since it is a percentage, it doesn't matter that you calculate it per share or per position.

2.2 The shares are or will be assigned and you don't want to keep them

2.2.1 The shares were put to you early

You wake up in the morning and discover that you have some shares you didn't have the night before.

We told you: the contract you sold involves that such contract can be exercised at any time between the sale and expiration.

The customers you insured can report an incident any time during the period the insurance is valid. You pay, end of story.

In the stock market, however, after we have paid for the shares, we can sell them back to the market at any time and open a new put at the same strike for a profit.

By doing this, we give the shares more time to end up above the strike and we accumulate some more premium.

$$return, \% = \frac{Total\ premium}{BP} x\ 100$$

The total premium will be all the premium collected when we sold the puts minus all the premium we paid to sell the previous positions.

You might wonder: *Why would there be a profit when selling shares at a loss and selling a new put?*

Refresher: option premium has two components: real value (it is what it is) and time value. The time value of the option we buy back is smaller than the time value of the option we are selling in the future. We are selling *time!*

<u>Tier II:</u> The shares have been assigned to us and still we don't want to keep them. We sell them

back to the market, but, in this case, instead of selling a new put of the same strike price, we sell a put at a lower strike price.

CAKE (40P)	$
Buying price	-40.00
Premium	7.30
Selling price	31.03
Minimum premium to get	-1.67

If we just sell the shares at the price they are trading today, 31.03, the overall position would be at a 1.67 loss per share.

All we need to do is to find a new put that gives us at least 1.67.

Which, in our case, did find: we sold a CAKE 32.5P, for which we received 4.50, which means we are now in profit by 4.50 − 1.67 = 2.83.

Why 32.5 instead of the same strike of 40?

This is entirely up to you: you can go for the same strike, thus collecting a higher premium (the intrinsic value will be higher) or you can go for a lower strike and although you are receiving less premium, you are decreasing the buying power, because a 32.5 position on a company requires less buying power than a 40 position on the same company.

We chose the lower strike for this reason, to decrease the buying power requirement, plus to give the shares more time to recover, since they had gone down during the period between selling the first put and the moment that the shares were put to us and we've decided not to keep them long-term. The aim is to be in profit as soon as possible, which we'll achieve faster by lowering the entry price.

It could happen that at expiration of the new put, the shares will be trading above the new strike of $32.5. In this case we won't have the shares, but we'll always have the premium money.

Don't know about you, but, for me, this was a big eureka moment: not only we can roll the puts forward, but also *down*!

The return in this case would be:

$$ROCE, \% = \frac{total\ premium}{BP} x\ 100$$

This is why my preference is to accept any puts at expiration, even if cash goes negative, and proceed to sell the shares back to the market and open new positions at a lower strike later, either the day after or months later; anytime.

For those who are visual, this is what happens:

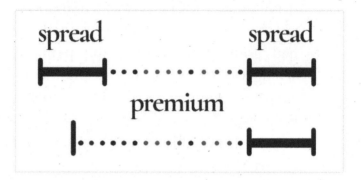

If we close a put and open a new put, there are two spreads and the premium we get is the difference between buying one and selling the other. However, if we get the shares put to us, we are buying them at the strike, therefore, no spread. That gives us more premium and if enough to move to a lower strike (usually this is the case), that's what we do.

2.2.2 The shares will be put to you

(Back to Tier I).

We are now getting closer to expiration and the shares are trading below the strike. Unless we take action, they will be assigned. Remember that we are operating under the assumption that we don't want to keep the shares.

In this case, we can buy back the option and open a new one in the future at the same strike.

We call this process *roll forward*.

If you are thinking: *What's the point on buying and selling the same thing?*, remember that we are closing a put with little time value and opening a new put with more time value, because we can say we *sell* time.

Bear in mind we can continue repeating this process of buying back and selling again over and over; it's not a once off thing.

$$return, \% = \frac{Total\ premium}{BP} x\ 100$$

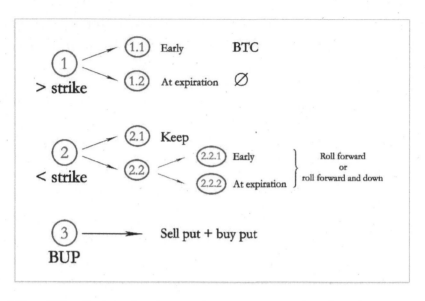

<u>Tier III</u>: Going back to the summary in the figure above, as a Tier III, we can apply a strategy that has made us hundreds of thousands of dollars. This wonder is called *Bull put spread.*

3. Bull Put Spreads (BUPs)

Apart from the brief introduction to BUPs in section 3.2 of this book, all we would have seen was *one-legged* trades. However, there are many strategies that can be used that are created with more than one trade that work in combination.

Let's see how we build the two legs that a Bull Put Spread (BUP) consists of.

The story begins with us selling a put, that is, STO a put option. This is the first leg. This is a trade we are very familiar with at this stage.

As we know, we'll get some premium.

We will be using part of this premium to build the second leg of the trade.

This second trade consists on *buying* a put below the strike we sold. It could be any. However, we tend to choose the one at the immediately lower strike price at which we sold the first one because this is the one that frees up more buying power. We'll come back to this.

Since options are offered most commonly at 1, 2.5 and 5 intervals, we'll buy the option that is 1, 2.5 or 5 dollars under the one we sold, respectively.

Both puts, the one we sold and the one we bought, must have the same expiration date.

As we know, when we sell a put, we give the buyer the option, the opportunity, to sell the shares to us.

However, when we buy a put option, as buyers, we can sell the shares at the strike we had chosen.

Up until now, we sold options, either covered calls (we have the underlying asset in our portfolio) or naked puts. Whatever buying of puts we did would only be with the purpose of closing the positions we had opened previously.

Here we are buying a put one strike interval under the strike we sold. Why? There are various reasons, not listed in order of importance.

I'll be using an example throughout the explanation because I think it'll be easier to follow.

Why buying a put at a lower strike

1. To reduce our exposure

   The moment we sell a 60P, we are blocking $60 to buy the shares in the future, as a first approximation (because we can roll forward and down as well, as we have already explained). Commitment = $60.

   When we buy a 55P, that gives the option, but not the obligation, to sell the shares at $55.

   Thus, on the one hand, we have a $60 commitment to buy shares, but, on the other, we can sell them at $55, which means that our commitment has been reduced to $5.

We reduced out commitment from $60 to $55, that is, our commitment is now only $5. Or our exposure if of $5, if you will.

The way I explain this sometimes is as follows: Imagine you are naked on the rooftop of a 60-storey building and there is no baranda and by *naked*, I mean you don't have any protection in the eventuality that you fall from a height of 60 floors (it's meant to be the equivalent to a $60 naked put). Picturing yourself with your clothes on or off it's up to you.

However, if you install a net around the windows of the 55th floor, if you fall from the rooftop, you would only be falling five floors, and then, you would safely land on the net. *Only* five floors 😊. (In the image, I used another building instead of a net because it was easier to copy/paste. Thank you for accommodating).

It might be a bit of a gore and over the top comparison, pun intended, since we sell naked puts knowing that the shares could be put to us and, even in the event that we decided not to keep them, we can always sell them back to the market and open new puts at the same or lower strike, over and over, until we get to an expiration date in which the underlying shares end up above the strike.

My desire is that you get the idea that by buying a put under the put we sold first, we reduce our exposure in the market.

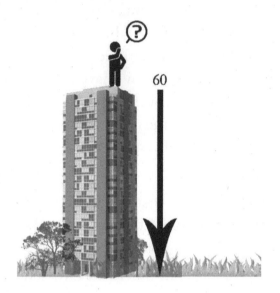

2. To reduce the buying power

The 60P we sold, as an example, needs buying power for the whole $60 that we are naked (it's a *short* position).

The moment we buy a 55P and our exposure is reduced to $5, the buying power requirement will be reduced (the equivalent of $55 worth of buying power).

3. To use the released buying power

Following with the previous point, since we have now a release of buying power, we could use it... To sell another put!

For some reason, this image comes to mind:

Perhaps because we are reusing for a new put the same buying power we were using for another one.

4. To hold the account value

When we have a BUP in place, the use of buying power is fixed to those $5 (in our example). It could be $2.5 or $1 per share, but that's it, that's the limit.

Thus, even if the share price goes down whatever number of dollars, even if the shares traded at $1, our account value wouldn't be affected more than the equivalent to those $5.

If we have a naked put, for every $1 that the shares go down, the buying power goes down $2.

How to place the trades

Now we know the reasons behind BUPs. We are now ready to learn how to place these trades.

As stated before, the first leg is the selling of a naked put. In our example, a 60P.

In the real world, we did sell a KRFC Jul23 60P from which we got $8.50 of premium.

We could have bought the KRFC Jul23 55P straight away, but we didn't! I didn't record the price back then, but it would have been around $6.

Why pay more when you can pay less?

A little recapitulation here: *when the share price goes up, the put option premium goes* _____.

Exactly: when shares go up, puts go down. (Mental cue: puts–see saw). Therefore, we just place an order to get filled when the put we are buying, the second leg, is cheaper. How much cheaper? We tend to apply the following rules, rounding up or down a bit to the nearest 5 or 10 cents. As we have already seen:

- For a $1 strike difference, 10% of the premium received when selling the first leg.

- For a $2.5 strike difference, 8% of the premium.

- For a $5 strike difference, 6% of the premium.

Very important: for the BUP to work, the premium we got when we sold the first leg minus the price we paid to buy the second leg must be greater than the difference between the strikes. I know I'm repeating myself, but experience tells me this is not redundant.

This is the same as saying that the premium we received minus the premium we pay for the second put must be more than $1, $2.5 or $5, depending on what the difference on strikes is.

As soon as we got the $8.50 for selling the KRFC Jul23 60P, we placed a GTC (good till cancel) limit order to BTO (buy to open) a KRFC Jul23 55P at 50 cents, as this is approximately 6% of $8.50.

Some time later, when the KRFC share price went up enough for the 55P to cost only 50 cents, the order got filled.

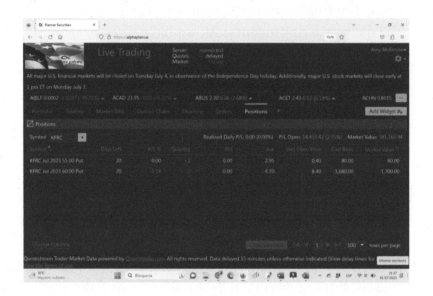

In fact, it got filled at 40 cents. The reason for that being that if the share price noticeably increased overnight, the premium gapped down, thus getting filled at an even lower price than the established limit price.

This is the way our platform works: if we place a limit order to buy something, we will be buying at that price or less; when we place a limit order to sell something, we'll get that amount or more. Thank you, Planner!

Do the second leg always get triggered?

No.

Placing a limit order trade doesn't mean that the order will be filled. It just means that *you would like it to be filled.*

As long as you place it GTC (good till cancelled), the order will stay in ready to get triggered until expiration.

We always place an order for the second legs, that we refer to as *lids.* Always. They don't always get filled.

Because we sell options with 4-6 months to expiration, or even more, and we sell at support, the chances of the share prices to go up at some point and for the order to buy the second leg to get filled increase, even if the share price goes down afterwards.

What happens at expiration?

If the conditions to buy the put a lower strike were met, like in our example, we have the following pair of positions that constitute a BUP:

- Leg 1:
  STO KRFC Jul 60 Put = 8.40

- Leg 2:
  BTO KRFC Jul 55 Put = -0.40

What happens at expiration, when both of these positions will cease to exist?

The share price can be in three places: above the highest strike, below the lowest or in the middle. Let's analyse what happens in the three different scenarios:

1. The share price ends up **above** the highest strike

   You know what happens: nothing. If the shares are trading above the strike of the put we sold, the shares are not assigned.

   Money made = premium when we sold leg 1– premium we used to buy leg 2.

   In our example, if KFRC trades above $60 the third Friday of July, we would have made:

   $$\$1,680 - \$80 = \$1,600$$

1,680 is the total premium received when we sold 2 contracts of the 60P at 8.40/share:

$$\$1,680 = \$8.40 \times 2 \times 100$$

80 is what we paid when we bought 2 contracts of the 55P at a cost of 40 cents per share:

$$\$80 = \$0.40 \times 2 \times 100$$

2. The share price ends up **in the middle**, between both strikes

The shares will be assigned.

In my opinion, this is the best place to get shares assigned, because they are not that far from the strike we sold the put at, therefore, close to be in profit.

In any case, if you don't want to keep the share, you can do what we have learned before: sell them and open a new put at the same or at a lower strike.

We will be buying the shares at the strike we sold with a discount that equals the premium we got when we sold leg 1 minus the premium we paid to buy leg 2.

We would be buying each share at a net price of $52.00 as follows:

$$\$60 - \$8.40 + \$0.40 = \$52.00$$

You will see that the signs in the platform seem to be the other way around than we would expect them to be, that is, negative when we buy (because we have less money) and positive when we sell (because we make money).

In the platform, the naked put is considered a *short position*, thus the negative sign, and the put we bought is considered a *long* position, thus the positive sign.

3. The share price ends up **below** the lowest strike

   Because we are below the highest strike, the shares will be assigned at expiration. We went short at $60, the share price is less than $60, consequently, we are *forced* to buy the shares.

   However, because we are also below the lowest, the put that we bought, because it is part of a BUP, will be exercised. Thus, the shares will be sold at the strike of the put we bought. We were long at $55 and the shares get sold at this price.

   The money we would made per share would be:

   $$\$8.40 - \$0.40 - \$60 + \$55 = \$3.00$$

What happens if leg 2 doesn't get triggered?

I have already answered this question, under the title *Does the second leg always get triggered?* I'll go through it again because this is a question that we get all the time and it proves to be quite confusing a concept.

Placing an order doesn't mean that it will happen in the future, let alone immediately. We are just being proactive. It *might* happen. It *might* get filled. But there is no certainty.

For the second leg to be filled and, this way, complete the BUP (otherwise we would only have a naked put, like in Tier I), the share price must go up; only when share prices go up enough to reach the limit price we established does the order get fil.

Note: placing orders is free. The trading fee is charged only when orders are filled.

What happens if the shares are assigned before expiration?

We know that when we sell a naked put, the shares can be assigned at any point in time before expiration.

If they are assigned and we haven't cancelled the order to buy leg 2, it could happen that the share price increases enough for its order to get filled.

Now, we can see shares (they act as leg 1) and the lid (leg 2).

At expiration, the share price could be either above the strike or below the strike. Remember that now we only have one put; the other leg has *mutated* into the shape of shares. These are the two possible scenarios:

1. The share price ends up **above** the strike of the leg 2

   Leg 2 expires worthless. We keep the shares.

   We would have bought the shares at a discounted price equal to the strike minus what we received when we sold leg 1 plus what we paid for leg 2.

2. The share price ends up **below** the strike of the leg 2

   The put gets *activated*. Whether we have shares or a short position on those shares (leg 1), when the shares trade below the strike at expiration, leg 2 does its thing, which is selling the shares at the strike price.

   The shares that had been put to us early will be sold at the leg 2's strike.

   The money we make will be the premium we got when selling leg 1 minus the money we paid to buy leg 2 minus what we paid for the shares plus what we got when selling them at leg 2's strike.

Visualisation of a BUP

When we have built a BUP position, that is, a STO put at a particular strike and a BTO put at a lower strike, we can imagine it is a meatless hamburguer within two buns of bread.

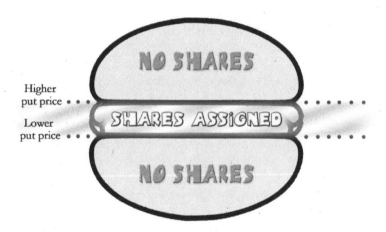

The top and bottom of the hamburger represent the two strikes.

At expiration, the trading price of the stock could fall in one of three places: on the top part of the bun, on the meatless content or on the bottom half of the bun.

- If we fall on the bread, either top or bottom, both positions will disappear over the weekend after expiration.

- If we fall on the meatless part, we will be assigned the shares.

4. In conclusion

Please, look at the difference scenarios we can encounter after selling a put:

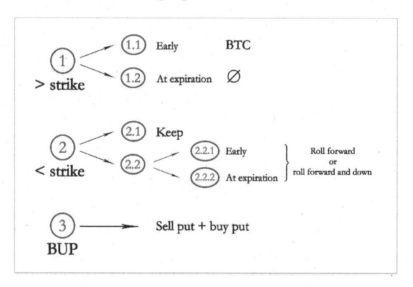

Although we have gone through a lot of information, all the different scenarios can be dealth with by you just asking two simple questions:

1. *Above or below?*

2. *If assigned, do I want to keep the shares or not?*

Tier I:

If we are above the upper strike, question 2 doesn't apply.

If we are below the strike, answer question 2. If the answer is YES, you are done; if the answer is NO, turn the shares into a new put to give them time to end up above the strike the next time around. Or the next. Or the next…

Tier II:

When rolling forward, if the share price has gone down significantly since we sold the put, you might find that the spreads don't allow for the rolling forward to be executed for a net credit. However, since we got premium with our first trade, even if we don't get a credit on the rolling forward, the overall position would still be in profit because the first premium is still higher than the cost of the subsequent trade/s.

In my experience, picking companies with a strong Value Line report reduces this possibility

☺

drastically. In 11 years and thousands of trades, I have encountered this situation a handful of times.

Please, watch this video about BUPs:

Bull Put Spread: Zero risk, zero cost trade

How to build a zero cost, zero risk trade one leg at a time

5. MISTAKES I MADE

Calm seas never made a good sailor.
Franklin D. Roosevelt

Applying the strategies I have shared with you so far, I made, pretty much, all the mistakes that can be made.

This chain of mistakes used to make me think that I was especially stupid, until I realised that it was just the normal process of mastering a skill, as Roosevelt reminded us in his famous quote above.

I confessed at the very beginning of this book, the direct effects of the over confidence derived from knowing just a bit, but believing I knew a lot: my personal Dunning-Kruger effect that we have already mentioned before. As a reminder:

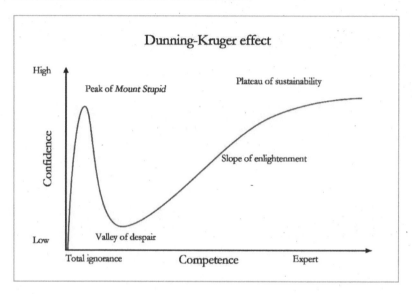

I will be sharing with you all the mistakes I've made that I can think of. Nothing will be hidden on purpose.

The order in which I'll be presenting them doesn't mean some are more important than others: they all add up!

If you think education is expensive, try ignorance. Benjamin Franklin (and many others after him).

I didn't know what I didn't know. Not only about the stock market, but, above all, about myself both as an insolated individual and as part of other bigger systems.

Feel free to laugh at all these sins (*sin* as 'miss the mark', which is its ethimological meaning) I committed; I don't mind at all. The reason why I am compiling them here is for you to learn from them and that's why each one of them will be followed by a valuable lesson afterwards. By *valuable* I mean that you can put a price tag on it, sometimes in the tens of thousands of dollars.

Background

The stock market was so well known to me as the metabolism of bacteria living at the bottom of the Mariana Trench: All I know is that these bacteria exist.

I started trading at the end of 2012. Take a look at what the SP-500 did since then until August 2015:

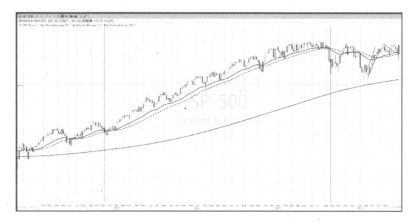

Probably, this was the worst that could have happened: a rookie in an uptrend market.

With what you know now, just by looking at the line under the trend, which is the 200 DMA, you would be able to tell me: *Since values tend to the means, it looks like the market is due a correction.* From what I know now, I would have said: *We are far from the 200 DMA, so the market is going to go down to the mean at some point. Careful!*

5.1   No awareness of the bigger picture

I was pretty much oblivious to what the SP-500 was doing. During the support webinars I attended, I did notice that they always started with various indexes: our very well-known SP-500, NASDAQ (an index mainly of technological companies and companies in the growth stages), the DJ-30 (30 of the top companies trading in different stock exchanges operating in the US) and the VIX (volatility of the options market).

I was unable to realise what valuable information these indexes were giving us, because, instead of paying attention to them, I focused only on the following comment: *What is relevant is what our individual companies do.*

My excuse could be that it was too much information to be learned at the same time, although it certainly was a lot of information on a topic I didn't know anything about all at once; many new concepts I had never heard of which were called names for which I didn't even know the word in my own language, let alone in a foreign one.

Learning: Indeed, when we take an investment decision, our focus the single company we have in front of us. If we are thinking of buying that company (or selling a put on it), we will do the 4x4 analysis, study the charts, the indicators... The lot.

We must, however, have the big picture in mind or, even better, right in front of our own very eyes to put our single company in context of what's going on in its world.

A mental image to get this point across: You are at the beach with your toddler and find this shallow spot surrounded by sand, meters away from the sea. You might think this is the perfect place for your kid to play and go back to your chair to read a book. Would you do that? No! You will take into consideration what the tide is doing, whether there are sea gulls that could peck on your child's eyes and, if you have had the experience before or you are extra careful, you would check for any approaching tsunamis.

Thus, your individual stock might be doing its own thing, trading low when most of the other stocks are at a high. Still, your baby (your stock) is part of a larger system and it a tsunami happens, your baby is likely to be, at least, splashed.

During March 2020, the vast majority of companies dropped down to supports they hadn't been at for 10 or 20 years. Some companies, however, continued trading as if nothing had happened or even thrived. In the middle of the earthquake March 2020 was, I'm very confident that most investors had an eye on the overall situation rather than just enjoy the bliss of their one single stock doing well in its little flower power garden.

5.2.   The whole elephant in one bite

I was too much in a hurry to get rich, so I dived into all the modules, books and webinars with my mouth full opened. I didn't learn using a tiered approach, but all the tiers at once, which resulted in a mixed salad of information of such proportions that I couldn't tell the carrots from the lettuce, that is, I had no awareness of what was important and what wasn't so much.

Looking back, it feels like a student of Medicine in their first year of studies conducting and appendectomy. I won't exaggerate saying brain surgery; an appendectomy seems enough reasonably far fetcthed.

Learning: One foot after the other and baby steps. Understand fully what you are doing, what you want to get, define what is your contingency plan and your exit strategy; practice and practice until you become confident and only then move to the next level. Before practicing with your money, join a club or consortium and do paper trading. There is a link in the bibliography chapter where you can open a demo account.

The main reason why this program has been born is to take you into the journey of mastering the stock market one step at a time. It is crucial that the concepts we are learning are built over the solid foundation of understanding well the previous layer of knowledge... And practice!

5.3.   Financial thermostat

It is said that we all have a financial thermostat that is set at a certain financial temperature (amount of money and wealth) in such a way that when we deviate from that level either up or down, we tend to go back to it.

Mine was set at the *always have enough, but never can afford everything I'd like to get* temperature. Thus, food, shelter, (basic) clothes, a few holidays here and there, an average car… were never an issue and there was absolutely no doubt in my mind that that would always be the case.

The next level up, however, made me feel uncomfortable, even though that was exactly where I wanted to be. I used to imagine a time in which I could walk in any shop and buy anything I'd like whatever the price, go on holidays and get the whole experience rather than avoiding going here and there to save some money, attend any seminar in the world any time… You get the picture.

Back in 2012, I could handle this much amount of money (picture my index and thumb spread out about an inch/3 cm). When my account crossed the line of 25,000 and I was able to sell naked puts, I looked at it as if it were the highest pile of money ever. I had gone over the line between a beginner trader and an advanced trader with all the tools in my pocket ready to reach the next level of 100,000. A completely arbitrary level, of course, based just on the fact that it had one more digit.

Although I had the experience of buying things in the 5- and 6-digit price tag (cars and two properties), since the installments were less than my wages, I could handle them easily.

Living in a 4 figures universe could only get me to 4 figures experiences. Simple as.

We need to grow as a person to grow our accounts. More money requires a bigger vessel just like a big plant needs a big pot and huge trees need no restrictions whatsoever of where and how to grow their roots. They live their ultimate freedom of accepting that they deserve as much space and soil as they want... And even more! We've all seen how roots lift even roads.

The financial thermostat is set by our circumstances, events and beliefs that we go through while growing up, mostly.

The good news is that it can be modified. Obviously! We create our own lives!

Being a millionaire... A billionaire even...

They might look like romantic ideas that some will fantasise with, but others will make come true if you have:

a) A strong reason for you to become a millionaire.

b) A plan to execute and follow through no matter what.

Of course, this is a simplification of your personal hero's journey.

My journey started setting myself up with just 6 digits. I still remember my body's reaction the first time one of the clubs I was involved with reached 100,000: sweaty hands, shaky feeling, sleeping patterns altered… Now, however, anything less than 200,000, I delegate because it's too little and my experience is better use in larger accounts that other vessels can't hold yet.

In my book *Empowered*, there is a full chapter about money in which the topic of wealth is treated in depth. I strongly recommend that you read it… over and over. Become familiar with a lifestyle that you can make yours. I don't mean tomorrow morning, but it could be as fast as you grow with it.

If your mind is already thinking *I'm making x,xxx a month and even a promotion wouldn't increase my salary so much* or *there's only one of me and I only have 24 hours a day to produce my products/ deliver my services*, be open to the idea that there are many ways that money can find a way to you that you can't even fathom.

Just by joining a community with a mindset different to the people surrounding you now, you are multiplying your chances of getting to places that were out of reach for you before.

Learning: Know what your financial thermostat is and feel gratitude for it. At a pace that's slightly uncomfortable for you, move it up.

Something that helped me a lot was the use of splitting the money I got for different concepts, in particular the one named *thithing* and the one named *leisure*. I had tagged envelops to do this. The first one, thithing, hughly increased the feeling of gratitude and fulfilment when a donation makes a difference in the life of whoever is receiving it. The *leisure* money helped me enjoy pleasures money can buy, linking positive, guilt free experiences with money, which was new for me.

5.4. Investing too much money

In my *investing* envelop I had around 6,500 that I used to buy my first (NOK) shares. After that, and seeing that the account was growing noticeably, I sent to the trading account every coin I could put my hands on. I cut expenses so I could send more money to make it grow, to the point that I even trim my hair myself, quite unevenly at the back, as expected.

Fear and greed found a fertile ground to show me, magnified, what my decisions took me when basing them in these two emotions that, of course, were in me.

Let's add scarcity to the pile.

My *fear* of not having enough in the future, because mine was a mentality of *scarcity* thanks to my childhood programming at home, meant that I wanted to make more and more and more (*greed*) until there would be a day, who knows when, in which I would have enough, that *enough* being an undefined amount.

I wanted to have enough in the future, which meant that I believed I didn't have enough in the present. *Not having enough in the present* is what the universe brought me: exactly as requested.

And that's how my first 6,500 was topped up with 30,000, which was everything I made plus everything I could salvage by cutting out expenses. Needless to say how the fear of losing money that I had worked so hard to get and that could impact my children's lives could cloud my thinking process when trading. And, as we know, when emotions go up, intelligence goes down; it's a physiological fact that, thankfully, can be controlled by repeatedly using tools at our disposal.

36,500, a small fortune that I traded with all my unexperience and ignorance until it reached a bit over 100,000, exactly my mental milestone towards riches.

What happened? In July 2015, the market pulled down and, with it, the price of all the stocks I had and all the underlying stocks of my put positions, reaching the bottom on the 24th of August. My account value went down 84% and, what's worse, I lost many positions, which meant that going back to where I was before wasn't just a matter of time of my shares going up, because I had lost most of them.

Remember that it wasn't only that the market went down: I was making all the mistakes we are going through in this section *at the same time!*

Learning: Never, ever, ever, ever, ever, ever, ever invest money you need to live.

Invest a percentage of your income and adjust your expenses to it. Invest from abundance. Know that you can survive even if your account gets wiped overnight. If it helps, lie to yourself and think that taxes have increased, but if you make this money grow, you will be granted access to it when you are xx years of age. Whatever it takes.

Learn how to make your heart and brain produce coherent waves. It could be through breathing techniques, meditation, exercise, focussed activity… But do it.

5.5.   Poor asset allocation and diversification

Understatement.

In a bullish market as it was when I started my journey, it's very easy to make money.

My limited knowledge, little experience and inflamed confidence spiced up with a fistful of greed were my trading team taking all the investment decisions.

It makes sense that those decisions were based on their objective: making a lot of money as quickly as possible.

Oil was at low prices back then and it was highly volatile, which means there were many opportunities in the oil industry to sell puts and obtain high premiums.

Making the quick buck was priority number one of my unqualified trading team. The quick buck was in oil.

I sold way too many puts in oil, thus going way above the 5-10% rule of asset allocation I now religiously follow.

Not only that, the number of contracts of any puts I sold was calculated on the buying power used, instead of on how much money would have to be invested if the puts were assigned.

Learning: Respect the asset allocation rules. Calculate the number of contracts based on how much it will cost to buy the shares if the put is assigned.

When the volatility of a particular stock is high, look into the reasons: is it the usual behaviour of this stock? Where is the VIX? What is going on with the SP-500?

Some stocks or assets, like ETFs (exchange traded funds), like SLV, GLD, etc. are more or less volatile by nature. Oil stocks tend to be more volatile than SLV, for instance, which offers only a small amount of time value. INFY would be an example of a strong company that also gives little time value. These less volatile assets will eventually go back up when there is a gap down, which gives us a great opportunity to sell intrinsic value.

5.6. The homework

Doing the mindmaps was something I found really tedious and, in my (brainless) opinion, since things didn't change that much from one quarter to the next, it should be ok to just take a glance at the reports a couple of times a year, but no need to run the system with the spreadsheet. It was a waste of time.

The horrors!!!

Funny to look back to witness how I couldn't find the time to run the 4x4 System analysis of the maybe 30-40 companies in our watchlist back then and now I keep updated the quality and price Excel of over 100 companies. Myself. Because if someone does it for me, I wouldn't get to know the companies so well. Imagine sending someone else to date and get to know a possible romantic partner for you. Same here: get to know the companies you will or do invest in yourself. Be intimate with them.

You might say: *It takes a lot of time and I don't have it! This why I invest in the stock market: so that I can make money without investing an awful lot of time.*

And if I got sucked into your complain, I could even agree. With a calculator in your hands, though, these are the numbers:

100 companies x 20 min/company =

$$= 2,000 \text{ min/quarter} =$$

$$= 11 \text{ hours/quarter} =$$

$$= 3.7 \text{ hours/month}$$

Hand in heart, would it be reasonable to say that you spend more than 3.7 hours a month watching movies, news, videos, etc.?

That's if you were to do the quality and price study of all 100 companies.

I don't. I do keep them updated, yes, but I would only do the quality and price study of the companies which are at low points. If they are midway on their journey from the bottom to the high of the next 18 months, I might study them less regularly. I do, however, update the 18 months projections of all the companies in my watchlist.

20 min is just an average. Some companies will show red flags and you can discard them just there and some will belong to industries you already have your full allocation on.

You will do some mindmaps at high points to evaluate whether you wish to sell call options on them.

Realistically speaking, the 3.7 hours per month can be reduced to half the time or even less. If you think half an hour a week is too much dedication into your financial improvement... Continue enjoying your 40 hours a week!

Learning: Do the homework! Get to know your companies well. Follow them. If you own a company, follow its progression by reading and studying its quality and price every quarter. You might have fallen in love with one and, some time later, its quality went down for whatever the reason. Is that reason a deal breaker for you not to hold it long, long-term?

The quality might change or the geo-political circumstances around a particular company, country or industry. As an example: Taiwan Semicondutors, a very strong 4x4 company, is an asset Mr. Buffett himself wouldn't invest in, as he said in Berkshire Hathaway's 2023 AGM... Because of its location: Taiwan.

5.7. The buying power to account value ratio

When you don't have a clue, you don't have a clue. So, if someone tells you a 20% buying power to account value ratio is enough to cater for potential down movements in the market, you just believe it to be true.

And that's how I was able to make 12% of premium every month for some few happy 6 months at the beginning of 2015: the combination of squeezing the ratio to 20% with selling puts on volatile (oil) stocks made the magic happen.

In a bullish market, using a lower ratio would be a great decision because you will be making money on a lot of money that's not yours. HOWEVER, big however, the tables turn drastically in a bearish market. And even more so in a *bear* market!

Learning: Know your risk tolerance limits. Adjust your buying power to account value ratio in accordance with them and with the availability of fresh cash that you could transfer to your trading account if you wish to restore your buying power without closing any position.

As Tier II and Tier III ideas, adjust your ratio depending on the market conditions (in a down trend, keep it higher), on the week of the month (be more conservative on the week of the 3rd Friday), take into consideration whether you are planning to add more cash to the account or if you will require to withdraw some money, which reduces the account value in an amount equal to the dollars withdrawn and reduces the buying power twice that amount.

5.8. Negative cash

Since the cash we can borrow from the clearing firm could be cheaper than the potential growth of the assets we could buy with it, it could make perfect sense to use this line of credit to buy stock and pay a bit out of the profits.

Once again, this works wonders in a bullish market. After an SP-500 not making progress for the second half of 2021 and all of 2022, this idea of the previous paragraph could have been not so profitable, after all.

Tier II: if you just have shares, no puts, and the market goes down, you might think you wouldn't get a margin call because all that could happen is that your shares go down and, that's fine, they'll go back up again. The news is that you could get a margin call if your cash position is negative. So that you know. I've been there too, of course! That's why I know!

Learning: Keep your cash positive. Simple!

Tier II: Be aware of the put options that might be assigned and whether you have cash to honour those commitments. If you don't, or you prefer not to hold shares put to you and you don't know what to do, go back to the section in which we talked about the possible outcomes when we sell puts.

Check your call positions: if you are going to be called away, that will bring money into your account that you can use to buy shares.

Tier III: Remember that shares give more buying power than cash, so having the cash invested in shares gives us more buying power to sell more puts and, thus, get more premium.

You will learn to get a balance that you feel comfortable with over time, with practice.

5.9. Time allocation

In 2015, when I took my most expensive class ever, the time allocation I was using was poor, to say it with elegance.

Most of my puts were expiring within the following 1 or 2 months. A few would expire later; those would be the ones that I had rolled forward and I allowed some extra time for the shares to trade at higher prices, although, due to my ignorance, I would sometimes picked the first month available in which the rolling forward would work, that is, would be possible to do for a credit rather than looking at the chart and allowing a reasonable length of time for the shares to recover.

Why would I do this? Because time value decreases the further we are from expiration. Thus, an option of a particular company at a given strike will hold more the highest amount of time value in the option expiring next month, followed by the next one, and the next one…

This is what greed does to you. And lack of experience, of course. But… Mostly greed.

Learning: Sell puts for the next 4, 5, 6… 9 months or more.

Calculate how much money you would need to have at your disposal if you were to take delivery of all the puts expiring every month.

Tier II: In our professional dashboards, we have this feature that shows us how much money we would need to buy all the put options that we have sold for the coming months. See an example:

Cost to buy all the shares we have puts sold on, $	Estimated cost, $	Month
18,600	*11,585*	Aug
141,400	*88,069*	Sep
180,000	*112,110*	Oct
131,300	*81,778*	Nov
162,950	*101,491*	Dec
217,550	*135,497*	Jan
67,400	*41,979*	Feb
19,000	*1,134*	Mar
53,500	*33,322*	Jun
20,000	*12,457*	Jan

The amounts in italics give us an estimation of how much we would need if all the put options of each month were assigned taking into consideration what has happened in the past, that is, what was the percentage of all the puts sold that were actually assigned.

Tier III: This is the history of this account. The calculations above are made using the following data:

	Cash	%
Puts sold with a total value of	3,926,000	
Total cost to BTO & BTC puts and buy shares	2,445,241	62.28%
of which buying shares was…	*2,277,068*	58.00%
Cost of BTO & BTC puts	*168,172*	4.28%
% of value from puts spent		**62.28%**

From the moment we opened this account, we've sold puts corresponding to 3.9 million worth of shares. Out of this amount, it is only 62.28% of the put options that have been assigned.

To take into consideration:

- This account has been trading for 34 months.

- At the beginning of any account, we sold more aggressive put options to increase the probabilities of the shares being put to us.

- The 34 months include the whole of 2022, in which the SP-500 went down nearly 20% and the NASDAQ, more than 33%.

- The cash invested in this account has been a total of $474,397.14 including the amounts withdrawn, with an average invested (time weighted) of $237,593.

5.10. Straight roll forward

I wouldn't say this was a big mistake I made; not even a mistake. It's just that I know better now, and by *better*, I mean a more profitable way of doing things, as it is explained in the section 3.3 Managing puts.

The week containing the 3rd Friday of the month used to be one with a lot of activity, because I used to roll forward all the puts I didn't want to be assigned.

We have already seen that roll forward consists in a two stepped process done in a trade with two lines of orders as follows:

Line 1: BTC the active put option we have.

Line 2: STO a new put in the future at the same strike.

The condition to be met is that there should be a credit when combining both trades, that is, that the price to BTC was less than the STO. Indeed, there would pretty much always be an option that would give a premium higher than the price to close the first option, even if we would go one year ahead.

Learning: Allow the puts to be assigned and proceed to sell the shares to the market and open a new put at a lower strike at a later stage.

<u>Tier II</u>: Hold the shares until the VIX is at a high point and proceed with the selling and opening a new put then. A high VIX means high volatility in the options, thus getting higher premiums.

<u>Tier III</u>: Instead of placing both trades at once (selling the shares and opening the new put), we can:

1. Open the new put when the VIX is high, so you can get a high premium. When the VIX is high, the SP-500 is low: chances are our stock is at a low point.

2. Wait for the shares to go to a high point and sell them then. If you get it right, that is, that the share price goes up, your profits will be even higher, as you would have made more money on selling the shares than if you had sold them at the same time that you sold the new put.

    I always do both trades at the same time. Just me being more conservative, because no matter what the circumstances are and what the indicators point at, share prices can still move the opposite way.

5.11. Beliefs and ego

Even though, in my opinion, my first motive to make money was laudable —to give my children a very complete education— as my account kept growing, so did my shadow.

The *shadow effect* is a term coined by Carl Jung. It refers to the unconscious part of our personality that doesn't match the ego ideal, which leads the ego to resist and project the shadow. It's a blind spot and could show both what we consider positive traits and negative ones.

Scarcity was something I kept in the shadow. Believing that whatever we have today could disappear tomorrow, making it a priority to build for that empty future was a pure fact. Because that was the cauldron in which I was conconcting my daily manifestations, they all showed exactly what they were made of: lack. Although the list of inhabitants living in my Shadow World is extensive, let's just focus on Scarcity Village for the moment.

My unconscious programming's commands were: *Whatever you have can be taken away from you, you need to work very hard to make money, rich people take advantage of others, we don't belong to the wealthy classes,* etc.

With those bricks, no way you can build up a strong and beautiful home!

Betraying those beliefs would have meant being untrue to who I was. Little did I know that was **not** who I was, but who *I played to be* to belong.

That was at the bottom of it all: I had to play a game with a set of rules that gave me more chances to gain acceptance from my tribe, the ultimate price being receiving love from them.

My first tribe: my parents. The little girl they produced sought love and attention from them. She couldn't get it at home, so she kept looking for it.

Once I left home, I continued finding people who represented the same role my parents did to give more the opportunity to learn the lesson, once and for all, and move one.

It was not that long ago that I got it: *We are showing you scarcity, fear and limitation to give you clues of what your soul wants to experience in this life: abundance, trust and infinite manifestation.*

It could seem a bit twisted, but effective. Because it was dark, Edison was pushed to invent the light bulb, which he did based on the research of others before him: Alessandro Volta, Humphrey Davy and Joseph Swan. If it had been bright all the time, he wouldn't have bothered!

The part where Edison made use of what others had figured out before is crucial: we can always take advantage of other people's experiences.

I used to believe in scarcity, even if I wasn't aware. All the decisions that I made would agree with this pattern of scarcity: the mould that I had become couldn't make cakes of any other shape. Thus, whatever I did, will present itself with scarcity and lack. Even if I managed to manifest some extra money, for instance, I would (unconsciously) figure out a way to make it go so the reality around me would match with the pattern, the blueprint, inside.

Learning: When you see something in others that catches your eye, you judge, you envy, pushes your buttons... Try and turn it around. When you catch thoughts of the type: *Look how he shows off his new big, expensive car. He can't be up to any good!*, consciously ask yourself questions around them, like: *What a beautiful car! I wonder what is it that I could do to have one myself... What do I have and know now that I could monetise? Would it be other ways of driving a car like that without buying it? How could I get it cheaper? What if a group of us buy one together? What if...? How...?*

If you are serious about knowing what experiences your soul chose to go through this life time around, no need to travel to the other side of the planet and spend months eating little and sitting on your ass in silence: go back to your childhood, as painful as it may be (I strongly recommend assistance, someone to *hold the space* for you, so you feel safe).

If you think about it, it makes perfect sense that you are placed in the perfect environment for your soul to get those chosen experiences and learn from them. That's what nature does: it places creatures in the environment where they can develop, even though their first experience might mean death.

Nature also provides with tools to survive in the environment creatures show up. What tools were you given? What traits? What do you love doing? What are you good at?

I love learning, teaching and writing. I learned tons from my parents (particularly, how *not* to be!), turned around —work in progress— many of those lessons so I could enjoy the other side of the same coin and now I have lots of material to share. Thank you very much!

By *the other side of the same coin* I mean that, for instance, scarcity and abundance are the exact same thing, not two like this dualistic fantasy we live in makes us believe. Scarcity is nothing else but little or no abundance. Light is a tiny percentage of darkness. Love is no fear.

5.12. Placing the trades wrong

I must admit this didn't happen that often, but it's quite easy to slip a finger on the wrong key or choose a different item to the one desired out of a drop-down menu.

Learning: These are mistakes easy to avoid, yet, some systems must be set up in place to make sure the orders on the screen match the orders in our minds.

Some ways to achieve this *zero error* when typing:

- Work in a team. Ideally, of three people: one will be calling out the trades from the paper or spreadsheet, another one will type in the orders and a third one will be making sure everything is correct.

- When the team is smaller: You can choose your trades from our support webinars, so they have already been filtered, or you can do your own research and apply the 4x4 System from beginning to end.

    Something I do when I'm trading by myself is that I prepare the trades I intend to place on a spreadsheet in which I write down everything: ticker symbols, strikes, months, amount, P, C,

B, S (put, call, buy, sell), the premium or price, the buying power…

Then, when I place them for real, I compare the actual prices, premiums and buying power to the on-paper ones and they should all match withing certain small limits due to the ever-changing live prices.

- Focus. When you are trading, do nothing else. Don't chat, don't sing along or watch a movie, don't eat… Also, when you start a trade that involves several steps, make sure you finish them all before you engage in any other activity.

  I'd advise to always follow the same order in doing things. This is not the best time to be creative.

- Practice, practice, practice. On a demo account, watching videos of people placing trades, in your mind… Know your stuff well before you try for real.

5.13. No awareness of the bigger picture

In my tiny little world, when money started to pour in, all I could see was a day in which I could buy anything I could think of regardless of the ticket price. I could see myself travelling to places, learning new things, having lots of free time to write books, living in comfortable houses around the world in which everything was done for me…

All these images were placed sometime in the future and seasoned with the fear of never getting there. One foot on the accelerator and the other one on the brake. I didn't realise that I could enjoy them *now!*

I can go to the supermarket and buy any article there whatever the price (I'm talking about groceries, not top shelf whiskey). I do travel, even if it is 20 km from home. There are books, courses, videos… to learn from one click away. We can make the time to do something we enjoy, even if it is for twenty minutes. We can delegate stuff and choose not to do chores or do them a lot less regularly. (The pleasure of not ironing anything at all! Well, just some shirts at hotels).

My understanding is that the big picture is just the little picture enlarged. The environment where we are born has all the ingredients for us to thrive and we are also given the traits to turn what appear to be challenges into pure power. I give it to you: we are better off when we work on those traits to master them. That power energises our purpose.

Learning: The purpose of learning how to make money was not to be able to buy expensive stuff, but to bring light to the darkness: to bring the abundance that we are (undeniable: we are part of Nature) to what we call *lack* or *scarcity*. Abundance of life experiences, of wisdom, of laughter, of health… And, yes, wealth as well.

Since everything is energy, so is money. Energy can be transformed. What can we transform money into something else? Apart from the obvious big car, huge house and quit work, what else can we do?

Last summer, I had the privilege of do volunteering work at an orangutan's sanctuary with my partner and my sons and give them a donation. I suppose that larger picture started when by placing a feeder for wild birds, leave cat food outside the house for whatever creature wants to help itself and giving carrots to our neigbor's mares. There's always something we can do to make our dreams come true.

Then, watch how the magic unfolds in front of your very eyes.

5.14. No awareness of the bigger picture, part II

My journey started with me, myself and I, playing the victim, rescuer and persecutor roles in a loop: I knew was the only one who could save myself from all the fear in pain my mind was feeding me with, but feeling helpless and wondering *why me* at the same time. Quite some acting in a Stephen K's drama triangle movie[2].

As I went along, more actors where introduced, as I started blaming others, my particular villains, of all my woes. More perpetrators were added to the plot and some rescuers were hired in an attempt to get out of the mess and find peace.

The plot thickened when the bad guys turned out to be victims themselves and the superhero who had the ability to save the day was... Me! Like Superman, my powers come from the sun, that is, the light, a light that embraces and connects us all, and speaks to us

---

[2] The *Karpman drama triangle* is a social model of human interaction proposed by Stephen B. Karpman, which describes a type of destructive interaction that sometimes occurs among people in conflict, each one representing the archetypes of victim, rescuer and persecutor (poor me, let me help you, it's all your fault).

through our hearts. A light that makes all darkness disappear and shows that what we think we are immersed in, so called *reality*, is… just a movie.

I call my hero inside of me Empowered Supernova and her discoveries are summarised in *Empowered*, therefore, there's no need to rewrite them here. Let's just say that very simple and powerful tools can be used to rediscover who we are and the power we harness inside.

Learning: I am perfectly aware that, at this stage, you would have heard this idea of how powerful we are and that all we need is inside us a gazillion times. As an intellectual concept, we could all give talks about it and even write books (hint, hint). Another million-dollar question is: What is the trick to make it travel from the brain to the heart? How can we manage to really, trully, deeply embrace this concept and, in this 3D world, put it to work for us?

I am about to share with you how I understandood it all with my heart. For you, it will be different: It could be given to you as a flash, as a vision, as an all-body snake of energy going through your anatomy, as a several days kind of being in a high experience, as a slow and steady flow that grows inside, as mixtures of all of these…

My *understanding of how it all works* moment happened in a commuter train to London. Not that glamorous, I know.

We were travelling to the city after a visit to a psychic surgeon. No comments on his job, the main point is that, whatever he did, it set off a conversation with God himself.

The caller was, of course, floating amongst clouds. I could only see his bust. Right beside him, it was my father, biological, earthy father, whose body stopped functioning in 1995.

I have already described how I mentally buried him in a deep pit and poured concrete on top to seal it, as if the body were radioactive waste material. When I saw his face beside God's, I wanted to run away from inside my mind to… I don't know. Where can you hide from your own mind?

Not only he was there together with the source of everything, he was smiling (big effort for my imagination if I were to make up this image by myself), both busts, somehow translucid, move side to side, overlapping each other's face. The non-verbal message that they were one and the same, both full of love for me.

Even as I type this message again, tears come to my eyes. Probably because back in those days where the catholic religion representatives around me repeated over and over how much my heavenly father loved me (although didn't I dare not to comply with all his rules or I would be literally damned!), he *was my father*. My father.

No need to be a genius to figure out how the message the young version of me received by putting together these two fathers who, allegedly, loved me so much came across: **Father equals danger**. Whatever and whoever was behind the description of *father*.

Doubting God's goodness was a place I couldn't go to through reasoning due to the severe implications this act of rebellion could bring onto me upon migrating to his heavenly realm, but the unconscious belief was there, anyway.

They both, as pals, were showing me that it was all a plan that the three of us had agreed on before, the last time we were together among the clouds. We had teamed up to make it happen, in a relaxed, smiling and loving atmosphere.

Those two semi translucent floating ever moving faces (they were also white, like the clouds around), insisting on the idea that they were just one, showed me then how it all worked in images my earthly bound self could make sense of.

I was shown a big wave. It as tall, single, a bit comic like wave, because although there was movement, it was a wave that stood up, without crashing down.

I was induced to understand that big wave was The Source. Once I understood that my childish equation of father = God, I could drop the idea of the bearded man on a cloud.

Around the big, tall thin wave, there was, obviously water, but also other waves like the big one, just smaller in size. It's important to remember that there was movement, so the shape of all the waves was always different somehow.

One drop of the big wave split apart from it and moved through space to planet Earth. A drop of The Source, a piece of God, was sent to this planet and it entered my heart.

A drop of divity was implanted in my heart, or the place where the heart is, in any case.

The wave made me understand that It had the potentiality to be anything and everything, but just that, the potentiality, the capability, rather the factuality To become actuality, drops of It were sent across the universes to make happen those infinite potentials. The body where the drops were implanted (any creature) would then produce experiences and stuff that, when the life cycle of such creature ended, would go back to the big wave, adding the information to it and feeding the other little waves and every single drop conforming the whole amount of water.

All the experiences of all creatures. As such, the beingness of a lettuce will add whatever it is, different to the beingness of a ladybird, of a rock, of a fairy, of a human. All of them, though, add to The Source. All the information will be passed onto every single drop that, in turn, will be sent to other creatures.

I say *in turn* because it's easier to think in linear terms of time. But it's all happening at the same time, which I suppose is part of the pluripotency of The Source.

The drop implanted inside me knew exactly what body to land in (can water *land,* even if metaphorically?). It was a body born in a particular household —the one with the human actor representing a frowning father the smiling father in heavens above agreed on playing— and the seed of some powers that, when worked on them, will have a multiplying effect on other creatures with their own drops inside. And that's how we all add to The Source as a big organism.

Clearly, I wasn't given the power to run fast or draw comic books, for instance. I've always had this inclination for the written word and the sharing knowledge with others, even if the others were some markers, my first pupils.

It makes a lot of sense that if we pursue the talents that we are inclined to develop, we would be able to add a lot more to our fellow creatures and, ultimately, to The Source than if we go after a type of life for which we haven't so nicely equipped for.

Does this ring a bell? You love music and spend the best of your life in front of spreadsheets?

Be honest with yourself. What are your gifts? What are your talents? What do you love doing? What would you do if time and money were not an issue?

....

....

....

6. TRICK OR TREAT

Vision is the art of seeing what is invisible to others.
Jonathan Swift

If you have read so far, congratulations! Persistance works.

I sincerely hope you have learned from my mistakes and also from my wisdom in the sense of knowledge plus action.

Apart from facts like *you will make more money selling options when the VIX is high* or practical and quick tips of adding the score and date of the Value Line reports on the charts, along with the high and low of the 18 months ahead and comments for you, I would love for you to have seriously reflected on why you are doing what you are doing. And, what's more important: Do you want to continue doing what you are doing the way you are doing it now?

We are constantly bombarded with the idea of changing and reinventing ourselves. Change is something our minds don't like. Point blank. It's scary because it can take us to places we haven't experienced yet and that could kill us, either our egoes, our bodies or both.

That being the case, **mental rehearsal** seems like a fantastic way of introducing ourselves into experiences we want to have, and that's where our heart is and our ego mind doesn't. Since the mind, albeit clever, can't tell real from fiction, go crazy living adventures and experiencing new sensations with your mind's eye. Of course, and more importantly, feel the feelings associated with your mind movie.

If you are one of the people for whom seeing pictures with your eyes closed is tough, create a mind movie with an online program, draw with colour pencils what you want to get or cut out photographs from magazines or the Internet.

Look at them and feel... Strong, empowered, calm, at peace, blissful, happy, joyful, rich... Whatever it is you want. Note: you don't need to pick one option; you can pick them all.

Then... Go multiply your money!

I would like to invite you to take a very close look at your parents and your relationship with them, whether you have them or not, whether you had them or not.

A good few times, I have stumbled across this concept of comparing all males with our fathers and all females with our mothers, whether they were present or not. Unless we realise we are trying to look for love, acknowledgment, acceptance or whatever from those around us playing the dumb down version of our progenitors, we won't be able to snap out of it and start creating a new movie in which we can play our role if not freely, much freer.

Rather than the changing or reinventing, I believe in reconnecting. Reconnecting with the divine drop we were gifted with and the set of tools that came with the delivery, namely talents.

Still, because we live in a 3D world in which potatoes are not exchanged by hugs and smiles, money becomes quite handy, since it buys us resources and time.

Going back to the father/mother thing, it seems that *father* has to do with money and *mother*, with the creativity to generate it. I'm not stating here that this is an absolute truth; this is an invitation for you to dig deeper into your childhood, your parents, your relationship with them, money in your childhood, your relationships now, especially the romantic ones.

Here is an invitation for you to let out your innermost thoughts regarding your partner or spouse. Breath deep with your eyes closed, feel calm inside and start writing whatever comes to mind when you ask yourself the questions: *How is my partner just like my mum/dad?* No judgement. It could be what the mind adjectivises as good or bad. Doesn't matter. Everything goes. *How is my partner just like my mum/dad?*

....

....

....

....

....

....

I suggest you do this exercise with both: mum *and* dad.

Now, this one for the champions: *How am **I** just like my mum/dad?*

_____

_____

_____

_____

_____

_____

_____

_____

_____

_____

Once you have integrated all these inner thoughts you might not even know you had, which had most likely become beliefs, here's another exercise for the bravest of you: First with one of your parents and then with the other, picture them in front of you and tell them:

1. *Thank you for giving me life.*

2. *If I were you, I would have done the same thing.*

3. *I am who I am thanks to you.*

4. *I honour you and respect you.*

5. *If I were born again, I would choose you as my father/mother, since you are the father/mother my soul needs to evolve in this incarnation.*

I know, perfectly, believe me, that saying the words could be challenging, but it's very doable. *Feeling* them, actually feeling gratitude for the gift of life when one of your thoughts could very well be *I wish I had never been born* or be in a state of gratitude when your parents were abusive and violent seem quite a stretch, not to mention that you honour and respect some people who made your life miserable!

The *I would repeat with your, folks* is where I draw the line. For the moment…

Something I am extremely grateful for to both is that they taught me how *not* to be a parent. Thanks to them, not despite them, I had a very clear idea of what I wanted to <u>avoid</u> while rearing my own children.

We don't tend to stop and feel gratitude for being in a painless body. However, when we have a pain, as small as it might be, all we can think of is how good it feels to be pain free.

What if we were born in conditions which seem to be the opposite of what our soul wants to learn so we bring our attention to that determined issue so we can grow out of it? That and the seed of what will be the set of tools for us to learn the lesson and move (remember the drop of Divine Essence, not a parfume?).

If you are reading this book, learn to live in abundance could be one of the subjects this time around. If you had made millions, you would probably be reading *My 10th Billion,* rather than this beginners' book.

As I already shared, I couldn't feel any gratitude for my parents at the beginning, so I used the alternative routes of making them children or very small. Figure something out if you want to release the pain of living with your parents over and over again, if not through them directly, through all the volunteer actors life generously places in our way so we can reenact those passages or our lives we would like to change to a Hollywood happy ending. Know that you are the one hiring them, not by placing an ad on the Internet, but by the signal you emit. Whoever comes, matches the signal.

If our signal is *I'm not good enough*, the actors will play the nasty guys who remind us this is true by giving us unrequested feedback on the value of what we do or that we have (in this case, very little or none).

If our signal is *I'm abundant and money comes to me easily*, we would have attracted this book and, with it, a community of likeminded individuals who will add to the abundance of our life experiences.

The trick is to pick the thoughts and replace those one that don't make us feel growing with others either neutral or that do make us feel empowered.

I'm not good enough might not be there as such, but it shows up when you compare yourself with others and feel inadequate and less than them. This could be a good time to recall heroic acts you made come to fruition, like preparing the meal in time or land a business deal. Or… Being born! It's quite a challenge to get through a tiny space and start doing something new with no help or instructions: breath.

I'm abundant can be reinforced all the time by feeling abundance around us and in us: abundance of cells, air, water in the tap, food in the fridge, toilette paper in the supermarket…

I would also say that a nice trick is to use the buying power wisely. I know, quite an abrupt change of topic. Or not… Our personal buying power could be our energy and resources: spending time and energy mulling over events that happened in a past that only exists in your memory and who knows how adulterated they are might not be the wisest way of using your energy. Although your mind stubbornly takes you there, actively find something you could build, create, experience that you would like to attract to your life. Tame your monkey mind.

With the *other* buying power, yes, same idea: use it wisely.

Put options of different companies consume different amounts of buying power. The lower the requirement of buying power, the better for us, as we can use it for other trades. I think of it in terms of *cheap* and *expensive* trades. Since this a general statement, I take a spreadsheet and calculate what is the ROCE of each trade before I place it and then I compare the trades with one another.

In the next screenshot we can see some proposals for put option selling.

Acc value	101,000.00		Initial cash	101,000.00
BP	202,000.00		Final cash	115,075.00
Ratio	200		Cash made	14,075
			Cash made,%	14%

PUT Ticker	# contracts	Month	Strike	Premium	Total cost	Total premi	If assigned BP'	New ratio	ROCE
3.0 FL	2	NOV	30	4.7	1400	925	6,000	2800	197%	33%
3.4 MXL	2	DEC	30	6.6	2250	1,305	6,000	4500	195%	29%
4.0 WBA	2	JAN	32.5	3.85	1500	755	6,500	3000	190%	25%
4.4 EEFT	1	FEB	95	10.1	2200	995	9,500	4400	185%	23%
4.8 HAIN	4	FEB	14	1.4	1300	545	5,600	2600	183%	21%
5.0 RHI	1	DEC	80	7.8	1900	765	8,000	3800	179%	20%
5.2 DIS	1	DEC	95	9	2300	885	9,500	4600	175%	19%
5.3 GOLD	3	JAN	18	1.67	1300	486	5,400	2600	172%	19%
5.6 IVZ	3	OCT	18	1.6	1300	465	5,400	2600	169%	18%
6.1 NEM	1	NOV	45	3.75	1100	360	4,500	2200	167%	16%
6.1 LUV	2	JAN	35	2.93	1750	571	7,000	3500	164%	16%
6.4 INCY	1	DEC	67.5	5.5	1700	535	6,750	3400	160%	16%
6.5 INFY	3	OCT	18	1.35	1270	390	5,400	2540	158%	15%
6.6 EW	1	FEB	85	6.5	2100	635	8,500	4200	154%	15%
6.9 CNC	1	JAN	70	5.1	1700	495	7,000	3400	150%	15%
7.0 VZ	2	OCT	36	2.3	1700	483	7,200	3400	147%	14%
7.3 JNPR	2	NOV	29	2	1400	385	5,800	2800	144%	14%
7.4 GDXJ	2	NOV	38	2.64	1900	513	7,600	3800	140%	14%
7.6 CPB	1	FEB	48	3.3	1200	315	4,800	2400	138%	13%
7.9 AUDC	5	MAR	12.5	2.7	5300	1,335	6,250	10600	128%	13%
8.6 CAG	1	JAN	34	2.05	1700	395	6,800	3400	124%	12%
9.7 TTEC	1	JAN	40	5.5	2600	535	4,000	5200	119%	10%
						14,075	81,600			

The columns contain the following information:

Column on the left: *expensiveness* of the trade as per the paragraph before. The higher the ratio, the *more expensive* is the trade, that is, the less money we make on the buying power used.

Some would base this calculation on cents per day, but since it is impossible to know the future, we cannot know how many cents per day we will be making. For example: if the underlying share gaps up tomorrow, we might BTC the position when the market opens and we would have made all the profit of this position in one day. We don't know either when the second leg will get triggered in the case of building a BUP, which releases buying power before expiration (but we can't know when a priori). This way, an expensive trade turns into the cheapest of all because time has been reduced.

Just simply divide the buying power consumption by the the total premium we would get when placing the trade (calculation made on the bid as it is). The higher the ratio, the more expensive the trade is, because it needs more buying power to collect the same amount of premium.

A visual aid to burn in our brain the idea that, at the same price, the higher the buying power used, the worse off we are in the same time period.

More columns: Ticker, number of contracts, month, strike, premium per share... You already know what these are.

<u>Total cost:</u> We get this figure when we place a trade. It is shown in the trade preview window:

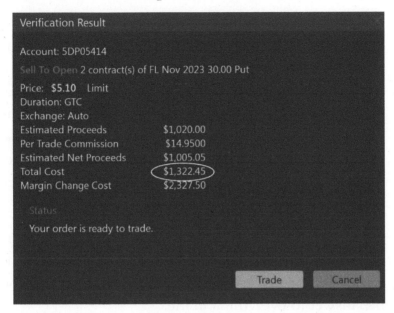

<u>Total premium:</u> Number of contracts x premium per share x 100.

<u>If assigned:</u> How much cash we would need to take delivery of the assets.

<u>BP':</u> Buying power that is required for the position. It is the result of multiply the total cost by 2.

<u>New ratio:</u> Buying power to account value after placing the trade as suggested. Reminder: this ratio, depending on the conditions, will go from 50% to 80%, in general.

<u>ROCE:</u> Return on capital employed. We know this! The lower it is, the more expensive the trade.

To wrap up this chapter, a cheap trick: prime yourself in the morning to have a wonderful, peaceful, blissful, meaningful, *easyful* day. Thank The Source or your higher power in advanced for the wonders that await your day. Ask for help and assistance to find the answers you need, sort out problems in the best way possible for all the parties and to find joy. Also offer your vessel to be the highest expression of the Source for the day.

Just like us, Spaniards, start saying bye ten full minutes before we depart, let me tell you the end of the story with the wave, the little waves and the drops and the answer to everything in life.

As the story continues, we arrived in London and I had some time to enjoy walking around. So, I did.

Then, at some point, I felt the urge to follow a command that no one else could hear, but me: *Find a park.* I have learned to do as I'm told when this voice talks, so I grabbed my phone and looked for a park.

I found one only a couple of blocks away from where I was.

Now what?

The next instruction came: *Find a bench and sit down on it.* You got it: I did.

I sat down, looked up… And this is what I saw:

7. REAL EXAMPLES, BULL MARKET, BEAR MARKET AND BOTH

For those properly prepared, the bear market
is not only a calamity , but an opportunity.
John Templeton

Stating that all positions in all accounts are always in profit is something not even Mr. Warren Buffet can affirm.

Likewise, account values go up and down with the movements of the share prices. There's nothing static in the market (nor anywhere in the universe, to be more precise).

What we can state, however, is that applying the system we are describing in this book, we can make money in bull markets, bear markets and sideways markets.

Needless to say that account values move up faster in bull markets than in bear markets. However, a bear market, like 2022, is an excellent opportunity to make money and to bring down the average open prices of our positions, which is know as *dollar cost averaging*, as so wisely John Templeton reminded us.

I could write pages and pages, but I thought it would be much simpler and faster to show you examples of random accounts so you can judge by yourself.

Popcorn time!

8. CONSORTIUMS VS GOING SOLO

Teamwork is the secret that makes common
people achieve uncommon results.
Ifeanyi Enoch Onuoha

You can start investing in the US market for as little as $500 and you can sell call options when your account is $2,000. To sell naked puts, your account value should have a value of at least $25,000. Above $100,000, you can apply any strategy under the sun.

Another way of starting your career as a trader is together with other people.

In our investment groups, the members invest the equivalent to €100 to €200 per month as a minimum and there's no upper limit. They invest together and meet online once a month, where all decisions are taken democratically.

It's a genius idea! From a very small amount of money and in full control of the group. Very little time and massive empowerment. We learn with others and from others, tapping into other people's strengths. A mastermind group, in short.

In this environment, we learn a system to find the best quality companies, identify when they are at a good price and treat shares as the assets they are, i.e., turning them into powerful money machines that generate an income and tap into the 8th wonder of the world, according to Einstein: compound interest.

You can also do both: be part of an investment group (or more) and have your own account/s. Let's see why you would want either option.

Investment clubs and consortiums

Under this title, we include groups of people that invest together. Depending on the way they organise themselves, the structure could be that of an investment club or that of a consortium.

We'll go through the points they both have in common and we'll list the differences at the end.

- The investment per person starts at €100 per month. Depending on how much you wish to invest, there would be a group for you, no upper limit.

- The group meets once a month online and the members take their investment decisions there and then. Occasionally, there could be other meetings mid month.

- The group is regulated by a set of norms established in their Club Constitution and everyone follows them. Some are: one person, one vote; the members commit to take education; whatever level of investment agreed by the group should be honoured.

- Each member has a share of the account.

- Having more money together allows to allocate resources (cash and buying power) to more positions, thus enabling a wider range of diversification.

- Since optins are available in contracts, one contract representing 100 shares, a higher account value provides allows for higher strikes to be sold. In numbers: if the goal is to allocate 5-10% of the portfolio to each position in multiples of 100 shares; when our account is 25.000, we'll only be able to sell put options with strikes up to $25. If our account is 200.000 and above, we can sell put options with strikes up to $100.

- The trading commissions are diluted.

- More people are looking after the account, so you know that if you decide to go on holidays for a month, someone else will be making sure your money keeps working for you.

- Discipline: there are actions to be taken each month. Because you are part of a bigger organism that is counting on you for investing and doing your bit, you have way more chances of taking action than if no one is looking.

- New relationships: you are very likely to establish a strong bond with some of your peers, not only in relation to the stock market, but also in relation to other aspects of life. The fact that you met through your interest in thriving already sets a common ground on which to build on.

- Even when you are tired of waiting for the results you wanted for yesterday, the group will assist you in keeping your focus and persistance.

- Emotions get mitigated: When we panic because the price of a stock has gone down, someone more analytical will be able to put into perspective the effect of that particular black dot we found in the white canvas has on the overall portfolio and a good strategist will share what can be done that we maybe we could have thought of if we were in a calm state.

- The strengths of every individual in the group are available for the whole group.

- Those strengths can be used on the different parts of the trading process and management of the group: treasurer's report, quality and price evaluation, charts, trades, general strategy, asset allocation, expiration dates, diversification, etc.

A note on people's strengths and weaknesses: iMA behavioural styles. www.ticnima.com

This is a very simple to use yet powerful tool that helps us understand the way people tend to behave, starting by ourselves, of course.

This system classifies the behavioural styles that humans tend to exhibit most of the time and assigns them four colours: High Red, High Yellow, High Blue and High Green. By knowing what colour an individual is more comfortable in, we can understand better why they do what they do and how they do it.

A fluid relationship among the members of the group is much easier once everyone is aware that High Yellows are very creative with not that much of an attention spam, High Reds move fast and show very little patience, High Greens love attention to detail and won't give a chance to risks and High Blues are more interested in peace and harmony and would go with what the group decides.

You can find a longer description of each colour in *Empowered* and at the website. A one liner of each style in the context of an investment group could be as follows: the High Yellows would come up with ideas, the High Greens would analyse them thoroughly, the High Reds would make the call to take the decision to go ahead and the High Blues would make sure there is peace and harmony within the group.

As for the differences between clubs and consortiums, there are two: number of individuals and investment.

Number of individuals: Clubs are limited to a maximum of 20 members (in Europe. It depends on the country). Up to this amount, a club is not considered as a taxable entity, which means that each member is responsible for their own tax affairs and cannot impact on the rest of the group.

Consortiums can have any number of individuals. Equally, each person's tax affairs are for them to sort out.

Investment: In clubs, every member invests the same amount both per month and in total. Thus, whenever a new member joins the club, they should catch up with the rest of the members.

In consortiums, there is a minimum to invest and no maximum. As long as the minimum is reached, the periodicity of the investments is any the member decides.

Going solo

At this moment, we are only opening accounts of a minimum of 200,000, amount which can be invested over a few months. With this amount, we can choose to invest in any of the companies in our watchlist, which trade between $5 and $100, observing the 5-10% asset allocation we aim for.

We have clubs that invest in this range that were put together for various reasons, so the amount is not the determining factor of going solo versus being in a group.

Some reasons why our clients prefer to go solo:

o The account is in the name of a company, or is a joint account, or a joint account with rights of survivorship, or a pension account... In short: other types of accounts that could fit their needs better.

o To have the total and complete freedom to move money in and out of the account.

o To keep their privacy.

o To have one on one sessions with us, the trading team, thus making the learning process more individualised and tailored to the person.

o For other reasons I won't tell you because I would have to kill you. (Joke).

If you are still confused with clubs, consortiums or going solo know one thing: we can procure for every pocket size and need.

Also know that... You can have it all! You can be in clubs, consortiums and have various accounts.

*Where attention goes,
energy flows and results show.*
You *choose what results you want to achieve.*

9. MORE ADVANCED STRATEGIES

Intellectual growth should commence at birth
and cease only at death.
Albert Einstein

Apart from the strategies you have learned so far, know that there are many other strategies with names that will make you look very clever if you casually drop them during conversation: ion condors, iron butterflies, straddles, bear call spreads, bull call spreads, central pivotal range strategy, calendar spreads, trading the *volatility smile*...

It is vey likely that if you apply *only* what you have learned in this book, after some time you will get bored.

Wait –you might say–. *Are you suggesting that making money in the market a few hours a month is "boring"? Try a 9 to 5 for 40 years!*

I am just saying that, in my experience with hundreds and hundreds of students, some never seem to have enough when it comes to learning new ways of squeezing some more cash out of the billions that change hands every day in the markets.

If there is demand for it, I'll be happy to write more books about other strategies. You, reader, let me know whether you have interest in it and I will be happy to provide.

In my humble opinion, the greater the focus, the better the results.

To get really good at the whole lot covered by this book will take you years. I'm not saying you are especially thick in the head, it's just a fact: you need to experience at least one bull market and one bear market, including sudden drops, to test yourself. It's all about experience, as with everything else in life.

From here, I would recommend mastering the base of knowledge laid out in this text. I can promise you that all situations can be handled once you know how to pick companies, read charts and use calls and puts. The rest of the strategies are all based on the same foundations you now have; they are combinations of the same elements you will get to understand so well.

So that you have a fair idea, in my own accounts, I would have one of these other strategies going on for every $100,000 worth of account value. And not even all the time.

I would, though, encourage everyone to always keep working on the emotional and psychological part of the equation. Work on *yourself*. See the results you are witnessing in your life and seach for the unconscious reasons that make you manifest them. Find the patterns you repeat over and over, study what pushes your buttons, improve your relationship with yourself, observe and modify the thoughts and behaviours that don't make you feel better, be kind to all…

Special mention for our relationship with our parents, whether they are or were present or not, as repetitive as I may sound. They were the main characters in writing the code that programmed you to live in a certain way and, unless we do something to snap out of the pattern, we will continue to reenact the same play with slightly different actors, always unconsciously looking for the same thing: the love of our parents.

Our parents carry themselves the information their parents passed onto them and created their own patters which, in turn, came from the generation before. We are, therefore, the recipients of information from many generations before and will be the conduits for the next generations. Consider what you are willing to pass on.

And because people interact with people of other family trees, some information will be shared by many others, linking us all in a megapattern dynamic. I think that's why we can see how people from a certain area or country in a particular time would exhibit common behaviours based on the group's belief system.

Some people would refer to this kind of conversation as tree-hugger stuff. No problem!

I have read books and watched videos of scholars and PhD's[3] who, applying the scientific method, have come to conclusions that other scholars and PhD's either don't know about or refuse point blank. PTSD (post traumatic stress disorder) is the most commonly occurrence in the studies; when you move to other authors, like Bert Hellinger and those who practice Integrative Medicine, you can conclude that the basics of information transfer evidence is all around us.

---

[3] Rachel Yehuda, Bruce Lipton, Mark Wolynn, to name a few.

The whole point of this outloud thinking is that we, as humans, have a strong belief in scarcity, and that's why most of the wealth of the planet is in the hands of 1 to 5% of the global population. If, during pregnancy, the mother is under severe stress[4], their newborn babies' levels of cortisol are lower than the average (chronic fatigue, weakness, low weight, low blood pressure, difficulties to handle stress, etc.)

Whatever the case, I would suggest you do your own research. I'd just turn to Mother Nature for examples and, of course I could be wrong; but they make sense to me.

A kitten is born and it looks pretty much like its parents. Its claws haven't retrated yet, its eyes will be closed for a few weeks, can hardly walk and its ears are on the side, rather than at the top of its head. Other than that, it could be considered a miniature of the mother it just came out from.

No one discusses that DNA is responsible for all that: half of the DNA strand of the little one comes from mother cat and the other half, from father cat and boom! You have a new creature made from the genetic information of two other individuals.

---

[4] Studies conducted on pregnant women in or around ground zero on 9/11.

What happens with the rest of the traits the kitten is born with? You can argue that they learn everything from their mothers, and I would agree that many behaviours are learned by imitation. But, what happens with those behaviours kittens were never exposed to and still exhibit?

Our cat Mixta was quite prolific. She came to live with us at 5 weeks old. The first time she had kittens, she knew perfectly what to do, how to be its own midwife and look after the newborns without any pre birth classes or assistance of any kind.

Where is the manual in which she learned all that? It would make sense to think that the instructions were somehow passed onto her from her own mother via DNA. It would not be a physical trait, but a *behavioural* one.

We've all seen images of sea turtles that hatch in large numbers, all of them at the same time, to cross the beach that takes them to the sea, where they will spend years. They've certainly never seen or experienced breaking a shell, crossing a sandy beach or swimming. Nevertheless, they do it.

I know this is called *instinct*. That doesn't say where it is recorded, though. I think it is recorded in the DNA, because no cow is born and runs to sea, right?

The same way, it would make sense that our ancestors passed onto us certain information that inclines us to some behaviour. This way, scarcity could run in a family. Not deserving. Poor health. I agree that there are many other factors that add to the pot, but the information travelling from our past would be one of them.

We also need to embrace the *100th monkey effect*, which describes how when a behaviour, knowledge, etc. is reached by the square root of 1% of the population of consideration, the whole population afterwards will show this trait.

The more of us start believing that we *are* abundance, therefore, we *deserve* to live an abundant life in all areas, the more opportunities will appear in front of us to bring to this material world the abundance we are and deserve. And the more of us that climb on this wagon, the more the new belief will spread out until we reach the 100th monkey threshold.

Consequently, we could say we have the obligation to do everything in our power to change the paradigm of scarcity to free the new generations so they can make grow their seed of greatness into whatever they are called to be and do, thus adding more to the whole creation.

Today is the perfect day to take one step towards this new present that you wish and can live in. There are many of us like you out there to walk by your side and hold your hand on your journey. Some of those around you now will project this hindering shadow that can get you stuck, so perhaps you might consider parking them somewhere to continue your journey with others who will pull you and celebrate the new discoveries ahead of you. They are invaluable, as they point towards what we need to learn, outgrow, let go or all the above.

Where to start?

- Find a strong reason to step up.
- Follow your heart and feed it with gratitude.
- Give your monkey brain a banana and tell him who's in charge.
- Take action.
- Rinse and repeat.

Bear this in mind:

NO ONE IS GOING TO DO IT FOR YOU.

Yours to serve at:
ana@ticn.ie and empowered.supernova@gmail.com

10. ACCESS TO INFORMATION

*Knowledge is power. Information is liberating. Education
is the premise of progress in every society, in every family.*
Kofi Annan

Value Line

You can access the Value Line reports, as well as all the
other TICN Tools, via subscription, as follows:

- 1 year subscription: :
  https://tinyurl.com/TOOLS300

- 2 year subscription:
  https://tinyurl.com/TOOLS540

Other TICN Tools you will have access to:

- The TICN Research Sheet

  Information on all the companies we have found to be 4x4 applying our 4x4 System, such as: ticker; industry; date of the next earnings report; quality score (52 being the maximum); price score (ib.); total score (quality and price added up); the low, medium and high ranges we expect the company to trade at; credit ratings, etc. It also includes the date that the company was found to be a 4x4. The list was first created in 2001.

- Educational webinars

  The following webinars run every week:

  See The Trends on Sundays. View of some indexes that show a global view of the stock market and a review of the most likely trends of approximately 100 companies in our watchlist.

Secrets of Successful traders on Mondays. Analysis of two companies using the 4x4 system.

Bottom Fishing on Wednesday. Finding the companies of a watchlist of around 100 tickers that are at support.

- The Mindmap

Excel spreadsheet to assist us with the 4x4 analysis.

Demo account

You can create a demo account, free of charge, at demo.alphaplan.us

Opening your own trading account

Our brokerage firm is Planner Securities LLC. They act as our intermediaries with the clearing firm, Apex Clearing Corporation.

They are third party organisations and we don't financially benefit from using them.

You decide what type of account suits your needs better: personal, corporate, trust, investment club, limited company, joint account, joint account with rights of survivorship, etc. Whichever the case, you also decide the terms, such as whether you wish to open it with a *margin facility* or not.

The margin facility refers to the use of the line of credit we discussed previously. In the case of pension accounts, for instance, they must be traded based on cash only.

All the forms you need to open your account are here: www.plannersecurities.com/download.php

Education

There are, at least, seven ways that you can educate yourself on the 4x4 System:

1. Online education

    You can start your education at your own pace with the online MMCP course, divided in 8 modules. We recommend you start with Module 2 and move up.

    We are also working on an update to match more precisely this material you have in your hands, including not only the mechanics, but also the psychology of investing.

2. Free online videos

    We have a series of short videos that explain what we do... Very well! You've seen them throughout the book and we put them all here together for your convenience:

Option premium clearly explained

| Time value | Volatility | Delta |
| Real value | Premium | Theta |

Simple interest versus compound interest

Bull Put Spread: Zero risk, zero cost trade

How to build a zero cost, zero risk trade one leg at a time

Call options very clearly explained

How to get an income from our shares and sell them dearer

Account value, buying power & option drag

The summer and winter of options

Asset allocation and diversification

Allocation and diversification with the 4x4 System

Make sure you subscribe to our channel to work on both sides of the making money process, the physical and the non-physical, and to connect with more like-minded individuals.

You will also be able to listen to other content about empowerment that you can use as inspiration: if they could, you too!

3. Face to face events

   We regularly hold face to face educational events in any part of the world. Contact us at ana@ticn.ie if you wish to organise one in your area.

4. Through the online support webinars

   As stated previously, we hold three support webinars per week. You can attend these webinars live or offline during the following 48 hours.

5. Attending online club meetings

   Either clubs or consortiums. They tend to take place once a month and most of them, if not all, welcome guests during the meetings.

6. Reading some other of our books, that can be found at www.ticn.ie/books

7. Practicing with a demo account, your own funded account or both. This is something to be done at the same time that any or all the rest of the previous six options are chosen.

Reach out:

ana@ticn.ie

empowered.supernova@gmail.com

LinkedIn: Linktr.ee

(?)

11. FAQs

Sometimes, the questions are complicated
and the answers are simple.
Dr. Seuss

If it's so good, why isn't it more popular?

What can I say? The hundreds of people I surround myself with, they all have a fair idea of the 4x4 System!

I understand that selling options is not a topic of discussion on the everyday news. The fact that not everyone knows about them doesn't mean at all that they are less real or that the results are what they are when you learn how to use them to make money, the same way that axolotls continue growing missing limbs whether you know about them or not.

You might have a gold mine in your back garden, but unless you go out and start digging, you won't find it.

Those who study finances tend to learn more about *buying* options, rather than selling them. When you buy an option, you can lose all the money you invest; we only buy options under certain, very specific conditions, some of which have been covered in this book.

In my experience and the experience of some people I personally know, those selling financial products or services tend to be people working for wages. For that very reason, I completely understand that it would be included in their job's description to sell their employers' products and services. I have nothing against this practice, it's just that I prefer to learn from someone who is financially free who, of course, deserves to be paid for the value added, they wouldn't rely on a payment at the end of the month to look after themselves and their families.

The information is there… If only you look for it.

(?)

There is also a component of ego: *How come that I, being as clever as I am, have never heard of these strategies? Who are you to know more than me?* Not precisely with these words, but nearly, have I been the object of such comments. *I've been working in a bank for 30 years and never heard of this! Options are very dangerous! You don't know what you are doing!* These words are more similar to what my delicate ears have been exposed to. Being a woman with a background in science, unrelated to money, adds insult (or salt) to injury.

I fully understand that anything new is perceived as dangerous by the mind and anything challenging our identity makes our ego go ballistic. I've been there too!

I would just say that if you want to experience something you haven't experienced before, you would have to learn things that you ignored and do things you've never done before. We all know what Einstein said about doing the same thing and expect different results; that only works with electronics – you switch them off and on, do the same thing, and this time, it might work where it didn't before; anything else, you always get the same results.

(?)

How can I lose money?

You lose money if:

- You sell shares at a lower price you paid for them.

- The company you have shares on goes bust (no company, no shares).

- If you incur in a margin call and close put positions at a loss.

Remember that we will be buying many companies with money coming from selling options, that is, we would be buying a lot of companies *for free*. If one of them has the *disgrace* of going down, it wouldn't be the end of the world. Plus you can collect call premium every month, if you want, until the total premium equals the average open price. Then, you will have free shares... Again.

The highest risk of death if being alive. If you invest, you can always lose money. If you don't invest and keep your money under the mattress or in a bank you will lose money for sure, even if only due to inflation.

The best way to beat inflation is to make your money grow. Then, do it! We have seen how we can make progress even in a down market, so even if the account value doesn't show such progress, be patient, keep applying the system over and over and wait for the compound interest to show its true colours in all its glory.

What do I do if my shares go down?

You can celebrate! Here you are a few things you can do if your shares go down in price:

1. If you are of the opinion that the quality of the company is still high, you can buy more shares at a lower price. That will bring the *average open price* (AOP) down. This is called *dollar cost averaging*.

   It's a simple principle: if we buy more of an item at a cheaper price than what we paid first for it, the average price we would have paid for such article is lower.

   In share language, it's called *buying the dips*: same company plus same fundamentals plus cheaper price equals great opportunity.

   As the share price goes back up again, we will be sitting on a profitable position faster.

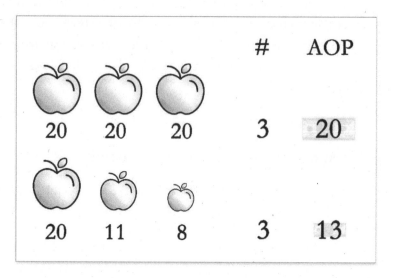

			#	AOP
20	20	20	3	20
20	11	8	3	13

2. You can sell conservative calls on the stock, at the money or even out of the money, at high points. By repeating this action, you will be able to get all the money you invested back.

3. You can sell conservative puts of the stock at the lower price the shares are trading at now. If the shares are not assigned, you get to keep the premium and the AOP goes down plus you can sell more puts at support; if the shares are assigned, you will buy the shares at a lower price at a discount, which will also reduce the AOP.

4. You can sell the shares and open a new put at a lower strike. If they end up being assigned, you would have reduced their AOP; if they don't, you would still be in a profitable position because the

trades would have been made at a profit, as explained in 3.3.

5. You can do combinations of the above.

6. Something that I've done a few times in the past is to close a position at a loss and make the profit by opening another position in another company. I did that in companies whose quality had significantly decreased (went to negative earnings, for instance) and I thought it could take a while to recover. The losses of the one company were covered by another one immediately.

7. You can apply a *current portfolio repair* (CPR) strategy, which I didn't mention in chapter 9 on purpose because I though I would give it to you as a surprise present in this section.

   This is the ideal scenario for a CPR to work at its best:

   ➤ You own shares that have dropped to what appears to be the very bottom, the ultimate support because there are signs of the price to start turning around to go back up again. This strategy works if you are not called away, and that's why we buy an ITM call, which we will see below.

   ➤ Slow recovery.

➢ Shares that offer positions at $1 intervals.
➢ Shares trading between the two option strikes.
➢ Volatile stocks.

Y can also apply this strategy when you first enter into a position.

Let's go through the steps to place the trades and the possible outcomes with an example.

Step 1: You have 1,000 shares already that you bought at whatever price; their price has gone down to $20 and it seems very likely that their price will start to recover. (You could also buy *new* shares at support of a company that has gone down and it looks like it's going to recover).

If you buy the shares at $20, this is the investment:

$$1,000 \; shares * \frac{\$20}{share} = \$20,000$$

Step 2: BTO 10 contracts of the $20 call option, for which you will pay $0.50 per share.

$$10 \; contracts * 100 \frac{shares}{contract} * \frac{(\$0.50)}{share} = (\$500)$$

Thus, the total investment will be:

$$Total \; investment = (\$20,000) + (\$500)$$
$$= (\mathbf{\$20,500})$$

<u>Step 3:</u> STO 20 contracts of the $21C option for which you get a premium of, at least, half of what you paid for the 20C you bought. Let's say that you get just half, that is, $0.30.

$$20 \ contracts * 100 \frac{shares}{contract} * \frac{\$0.30}{share} = \$600$$

<u>Outcome 1:</u> At expiration, the shares trade below the strike of $20.

You are $100 better off than before, as you spend $500 buying the ITM call options and received $600 selling the OTM call options.

The share price has dropped, which is what shares do, anyway, up and down all the time!

<u>Outcome 2:</u> The shares are trading between $20 and $21. As an extreme case, let's consider they trade at $20.99 so we can study the maximum potential of this trade.

The 21C will not be exercised.

We STC the 20C, which has an intrinsic value of $0.99. Since we bought 10 contracts:

$$10 \ contracts * 100 \frac{shares}{contract} * \frac{\$0.99}{share} = \$990$$

If we sell the shares at $20.99:

$$1,000 \ shares * \frac{\$20.99}{share} = \$20,990$$

Since we bought them for $20,000, we would have made $990 profit. Thus, the RoI would be:

$$RoI = \frac{\$990}{\$20,000} * 100 = 4.95\%$$

The total profit of the CPR consists of two terms: the profit coming from selling the shares and the profit coming from selling the call option.

$$Total \ profit = \$990 + \$990 = \$1,980$$

Thus, the RoI in this case would be:

$$RoI = \frac{\$1,980}{\$20,000} * 100 = 9.90\%$$

Twice as much for the same movement of the share price!

Outcome 3: At expiration, the shares trade above the highest strike. In our example, let's say the shares trade at $22.00.

We BTC the 21C to avoid the option be exercised. The cost will be as follows:

$$20 \ contracts * 100 \ \frac{shares}{contract} * \frac{(\$1.00)}{share} = (\$2,000)$$

We STC the 20C, which has an intrinsic value of $2.00, so we will receive the following premium:

$$10 \; contracts * 100 \frac{shares}{contract} * \frac{\$2.00}{share} = \$2,000$$

As we can see, no matter how much the share price goes up, the option we sold gets more expensive the same amount of money that the option we bought gains value. Since we are at expiration, the only component of the premium of both options is their intrinsic value.

If we were to sell the shares, this would be the profit, provided we bought them at $20.

$$RoI = \frac{(\$22 - \$20) * 1000}{\$20,000} * 100 = 10.0\%$$

When we apply this strategy to shares we bought before at a higher price, we will keep them and focus on making money on them with more CPR's, selling the shares to the market and opening new put positions at a lower strike or the same strike, but making some extra time value, selling call options on them and buying them back to avoid the calls being exercised, doing dollar cost averaging… Look at you! All the tools you have in your toolbox now! Wow!

(?)

When can I withdraw my money?

If your money is **in your own account**, you can withdraw it any time. All you need to do is to fill the form you can find at:

1. Non-US residents:
   https://tinyurl.com/Withdrawal-nonUS

2. US residents: https://tinyurl.com/Withdrawal-US

It will take one or two days to get your money in your bank account once the form is duly completed, signed and sent to the broker.

Be aware that when you withdraw cash from your Apex account, the buying power will go down twice as much.

(?)

If your money is in a **club or consortium**, it will depend on what all the members of the group had agreed to: sometimes, withdrawals are possible at the end of every quarter, but some groups encourage their members to leave the money in the trading account for several years to allow for the compound interest to mature.

Why the US markets?

For several reasons:

1. Volume: The markets in the USA, in particular, the New York Stock Exchange (NYSE) and NASDAQ, are one of the largest in the whole world. That means that they offer a very large number of companies to choose from, which, in turn, has a direct impact on the…

2. *Liquidity*, that is, the number of available buyers and sellers. A higher liquidity means that the trades get filled faster and that the spreads can be tighter.

3. Diversification: Many companies that belong to different industries trade in the US markets, which offers the possibility to diversify our portfolio.

4. Stability: In comparison with other countries, the US is a quite stable country in terms of economy

and politics. The legal framework of investing in the US is very well established. All these factors contribute to provide a sense of safety to investors.

5. Currency: The US dollar is a currency accepted in most countries and widely use in international transactions.

(?)

Can these principles be applied in other markets?

The buy and hold, of course.

The options part, yes, provided these other markets trade options.

What happens with taxes?

So that it is clear: **we are not expert in taxes**.

Each person or entity investing in the stock market is responsible for their own taxes.

Also think that if you are paying taxes is because you've made money. You could consider to be a standard bearer of prosperty and pay an expert to do the tax returns for you.

Why do you use Planner Securities and Apex?

TICN has been working with Planner Securities LLC (formerly Track Data LLC) since 1996.

I can tell you, first hand, that they are always on the other side of the email or the phone. Imagine that! A phone call away!

Anything we need, they will answer our call and assist us promptly.

They know us and we know them personally. We visit their premises every time we go to the US, which is, normally, once a year, on our way back from attending the Berkshire Hathaway AGM.

As already mentioned before, they use this *intelligent router* that scans the market and finds the best prices for us. One cent at a time times many contracts/shares… It all adds up to our bottom line!

Although we tend to place the trades ourselves, they can place trades for us over the phone if to do so. instructed

www.plannersecurities.com is the brokers' website.

Can I invest if I live in _____?

The money coming from certain countries is not accepted to be invested by the clearing firms.

Check on a one-to-one basis, please.

Some of our members are originally from countries whose currency is not accepted. However, they can invest, as individuals, by sending their money from other countries where they have it.

How do I send money to the US?

Directly from your bank account or by check.

Crytocurrency is not an option; only fiat currency.

Once your trading account is ready to fund, you will receive the instructions on how to wire the money.

Many of our clubs and investors use the services of VFX Plc, a foreign exchange currency desk of the Royal Bank of Scotland and Barclays Bank. www.vfxplc.com

What charts to use?

The support team (obviously, me included) use TC2000.

You can try this platform for free for a month and then, if you like it, subscribe to it.

(?)

What happens with the money if I die?

Your trading account will be treated just like any other of your assests, as disposed of in your will.

If you don't have a will, again, just like any other of your assets.

Let know your next of keen about this investment of yours and how to contact us. We'll guide them through the process of recovering your assets.

What do I need to do to start investing?

Contact us at ana@ticn.ie

Less than $200,000

If you wish to invest less than $200,000, the best option will be a consortium or a club. We can find one for you.

To join a consortium or a club, the following information is required:

- Current passport or photographic ID. This latter one, must be written in English as well.

- Proof of address: utility bill or bank statement dated within the last two months in which we can see what bank it is, your name, your address and the date.

- Tax identification number. It has different names in different countries: TIN, PPS, CIF, National Insurance Number, etc.

- Your occupation or job.

We can assist you with the process.

<u>More than $200,000</u>

Contact us at <u>ana@ticn.ie</u> and we will work to find what structure suits you best.

How to place trades?

In my Empowered Supernova channel, there is a playlist called *Empowered Abundance*. You can find examples on how to place trades, among other very interesting videos relating money and money mindset.

Any other questions?

Ask me at ana@ticn.ie

12. SUMMARY

In summary, all great work is the fruit of patience and perseverance, combined with tenacious concentration on a subject over a period of months or years.
Santiago Ramón y Cajal

In a nutshell, the following video summarises our 4x4 System. I'm sure that, at this point, everything will make a lot of sense to you.

Remember that:

- Every skill is learnable.

- You need to start somewhere.

- It's not a coincidence that this book is in your hands.

- To achieve different results, you need to do something different.

- Know thyself and make sh*t happen, because you are a creator.

- Use the power of the team and surround yourself with the tribe in which you can all thrive.

13.Annex

We are including here large pdf documents so it'll be easier for you to read them and use them.

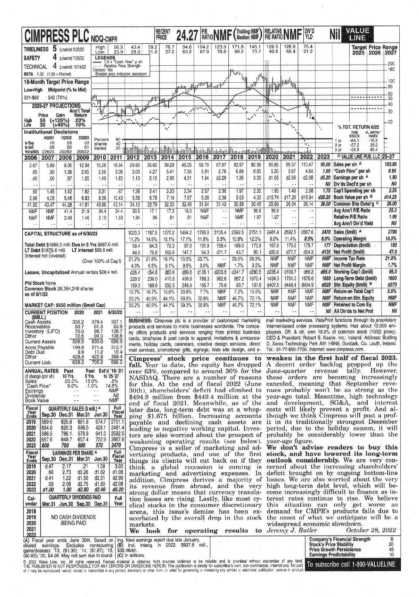

CIMPRESS PLC NDQ-CMPR

RECENT PRICE	24.27	P/E RATIO	NMF	(Trailing: NMF / Median: NMF)	RELATIVE P/E RATIO	NMF	DIV'D YLD	Nil	VALUE LINE

TIMELINESS	5	Lowered 5/20/22
SAFETY	4	Lowered 7/29/22
TECHNICAL	4	Lowered 10/14/22
BETA 1.35	(1.00 = Market)

LEGENDS
— 5.0 x "Cash Flow" p sh
- - - Relative Price Strength
Options: Yes
Shaded area indicates recession

High/Low prices by year:
Year	High	Low
	56.3	23.9
	43.4	28.0
	58.2	31.8
	76.7	37.0
	94.6	63.2
	104.2	67.9
	123.9	78.8
	171.8	99.2
	145.1	73.7
	126.5	40.8
	128.9	65.4
	75.4	21.2

Target Price Range 2025 2026 2027

18-Month Target Price Range
Low-High Midpoint (% to Mid)
$21-$62 $42 (70%)

2025-27 PROJECTIONS
	Price	Gain	Ann'l Total Return
High	55	(+125%)	23%
Low	35	(+45%)	10%

Institutional Decisions
	4Q2021	1Q2022	2Q2022
to Buy	70	59	53
to Sell	59	65	61
Hld(000)	22623	20292	20632

% TOT. RETURN 6/22
	THIS STOCK	VL ARITH. INDEX
1 yr.	-64.1	-16.9
3 yr.	-57.2	29.2
5 yr.	-58.8	45.4

2006	2007	2008	2009	2010	2011	2012	2013	2014	2015	2016	2017	2018	2019	2020	2021	2022	2023	© VALUE LINE PUB. LLC	25-27
3.67	5.89	9.05	12.34	15.28	18.94	29.90	35.60	39.29	46.05	56.70	67.97	83.97	90.36	95.86	99.57	110.47	95.00	Sales per sh A	103.85
.25	.90	1.38	2.05	2.56	3.08	3.03	4.27	5.41	7.56	5.91	2.76	6.89	8.83	5.30	3.67	4.84	1.60	"Cash Flow" per sh	8.95
.45	.50	.97	1.25	1.49	1.83	1.13	2.15	2.95	4.31	1.64	d2.29	1.36	3.00	d1.08	d2.99	d2.08	d5.20	Earnings per sh A	1.80
--	--	--	--	--	--	--	--	--	--	--	--	--	--	--	--	--	Nil	Div'ds Decl'd per sh	Nil
.60	1.45	1.42	1.82	2.31	.87	1.36	2.41	2.23	2.34	2.57	2.96	1.97	2.32	1.95	1.48	2.08	1.75	Cap'l Spending per sh	2.55
2.99	4.05	5.48	6.83	8.58	10.43	5.55	5.78	7.19	7.67	5.26	2.39	3.03	4.33	d3.74	d17.26	d18.94	d20.20	Book Value per sh B	d14.25
41.50	43.47	44.26	41.81	43.86	43.14	34.12	32.79	32.33	32.45	31.54	31.42	30.88	30.45	25.89	26.04	26.14	26.00	Common Shs Outst'g C	26.00
NMF	NMF	41.4	21.9	34.4	24.4	30.5	17.1	17.3	16.0	NMF	--	NMF	36.9	36.9	--	--		Avg Ann'l P/E Ratio	25.0
NMF	NMF	2.49	1.46	2.19	1.53	1.94	.96	.91	.81	NMF	--	NMF	1.97	1.97	--	--		Relative P/E Ratio	1.95
--	--	--	--	--	--	--	--	--	--	--	--	--	--	--	--		Avg Ann'l Div'd Yield	Nil

CAPITAL STRUCTURE as of 6/30/22

Total Debt $1686.0 mill. Due in 5 Yrs $987.0 mill.
LT Debt $1675.6 mill. LT Interest $95.6 mill.
(Interest not covered)
(Over 100% of Cap'l)

Leases, Uncapitalized Annual rentals $28.4 mill.

Pfd Stock None
Common Stock 26,354,248 shares
as of 8/1/22

MARKET CAP: $650 million (Small Cap)

	1020.3	1167.5	1270.2	1494.2	1786.0	2135.4	2592.5	2751.1	2481.4	2592.5	2887.6	2470	Sales ($mill) A	2700
	11.2%	14.5%	18.1%	17.1%	11.8%	5.3%	10.8%	12.3%	9.0%	11.4%	8.5%	8.0%	Operating Margin	10.5%
	59.4	64.3	72.3	97.5	131.9	158.4	169.0	173.8	167.9	173.2	175.7	177	Depreciation ($mill)	185
	44.0	75.8	102.6	147.7	54.3	d71.7	43.7	95.1	d30.8	d77.7	d54.3	d135	Net Profit ($mill)	47.0
	21.2%	21.8%	18.1%	10.5%	23.7%	--	29.5%	26.3%	NMF	NMF	NMF	NMF	Income Tax Rate	21.0%
	4.3%	6.5%	8.1%	9.9%	3.0%	NMF	1.7%	3.5%	NMF	NMF	NMF	NMF	Net Profit Margin	1.7%
	d26.4	d54.8	d83.6	d89.6	d135.1	d203.5	d241.7	d280.5	d235.4	d109.7	d66.2	d95.0	Working Cap'l ($mill)	95.0
	229.0	230.0	410.5	499.9	788.3	982.6	887.2	1070.4	1434.3	1751.0	1675.6	1650	Long-Term Debt ($mill)	1600
	189.3	189.6	232.5	248.9	165.7	75.0	93.7	131.8	d407.5	d449.4	d494.9	d525	Shr. Equity ($mill) B	d370
	10.7%	18.7%	16.6%	20.8%	7.7%	NMF	7.2%	10.5%	NMF	NMF	NMF	NMF	Return on Total Cap'l	5.5%
	23.2%	40.0%	44.1%	59.3%	32.8%	NMF	46.7%	72.1%	NMF	NMF	NMF	NMF	Return on Shr. Equity	NMF
	23.2%	40.0%	44.1%	59.3%	32.8%	NMF	46.7%	72.1%	NMF	NMF	NMF	NMF	Retained to Com Eq	NMF
	--	--	--	--	--	--	--	--	Nil	Nil	Nil	Nil	All Div'ds to Net Prof	Nil

CURRENT POSITION
(MILL.)	2020	2021	6/30/22
Cash Assets	335.2	378.4	327.1
Receivables	50.7	61.5	63.9
Inventory (LIFO)	70.0	96.7	126.7
Other	72.6	94.0	108.6
Current Assets	528.5	630.6	626.3
Accts Payable	199.8	271.4	313.7
Debt Due	9.9	11.2	10.4
Other	428.5	422.6	368.4
Current Liab.	638.2	705.2	692.5

ANNUAL RATES
of change (per sh)	Past 10 Yrs.	Past 5 Yrs.	Est'd '19-'21 to '25-'27
Sales	20.0%	18.0%	.5%
"Cash Flow"	9.0%	-1.0%	14.5%
Earnings	--	--	NMF
Dividends	--	--	Nil
Book Value	--	--	NMF

Fiscal Year Ends — QUARTERLY SALES ($ mill.) A
Fiscal Year	Sep.30	Dec.31	Mar.31	Jun.30	Full Fiscal Year
2019	589.0	825.6	661.8	674.7	2751.1
2020	634.0	820.3	598.0	429.1	2481.4
2021	586.5	786.1	578.9	641.0	2592.5
2022	657.6	849.7	657.4	722.9	2887.6
2023	600	700	600	570	2470

Fiscal Year Ends — EARNINGS PER SHARE A
Fiscal Year	Sep.30	Dec.31	Mar.31	Jun.30	Full Fiscal Year
2019	d.47	2.17	.21	1.09	3.00
2020	.66	2.73	d3.26	d1.62	d1.08
2021	d.41	1.22	d1.50	d2.31	d2.99
2022	.09	2.08	d2.75	d1.50	d2.08
2023	d1.00	1.00	d2.80	d2.40	d5.20

Cal-endar — QUARTERLY DIVIDENDS PAID
	Mar.31	Jun.30	Sep.30	Dec.31	Full Year
2018					
2019	NO CASH DIVIDENDS				
2020	BEING PAID				
2021					
2022					

BUSINESS: Cimpress plc is a provider of customized marketing products and services to micro businesses worldwide. The company offers products and services ranging from printed business cards, brochures & post cards to apparel, invitations & announcements, holiday cards, calendars, creative design services, direct mail services, promotional gifts, signage, Web site design, and e-mail marketing services. VistaPrint functions through its proprietary Internet-based order processing systems. Has about 12,000 employees. Off. & dir. own 18.0% of common stock (10/22 proxy). CEO & President: Robert S. Keane. Inc.: Ireland. Address: Building D, Xerox Technology Park A91 H9N9, Dundalk, Co. Louth, Ireland. Tel.: 31-77-850-7700. Internet: www.cimpress.com.

Cimpress' stock price continues to weaken in the first half of fiscal 2023. Year to date, the equity has dropped over 63%, compared to around 30% for the NASDAQ. There are a number of reasons for this. At the end of fiscal 2022 (June 30th), shareholders' deficit had climbed to $494.9 million from $449.4 million at the end of fiscal 2021. Meanwhile, as of the later date, long-term debt was at a whopping $1.675 billion. Increasing accounts payable and declining cash assets are leading to negative working capital. Investors are also worried about the prospect of weakening operating results (see below). Cimpress is a seller of marketing and advertising products, and one of the first things its clients will cut back on if they think a global recession is coming is marketing and advertising expenses. In addition, Cimpress derives a majority of its revenue from abroad, and the very strong dollar means that currency translation losses are rising. Lastly, like most cyclical stocks in the consumer discretionary arena, this issue's demise has been exacerbated by the overall drop in the stock markets.

We look for operating results to weaken in the first half of fiscal 2023. A decent order backlog propped up the June-quarter revenue tally. However, these orders are becoming increasingly canceled, meaning that September revenues probably won't be as strong as the year-ago total. Meantime, high technology and development, SG&A, and interest costs will likely prevent a profit. And although we think Cimpress will post a profit in its traditionally strongest December period, due to the holiday season, it will probably be considerably lower than the year-ago figure.

We don't advise readers to buy this stock, and have lowered its long-term outlook considerably. We are very concerned about the increasing shareholders' deficit brought on by ongoing bottom-line losses. We are also worried about the very high long-term debt level, which will become increasingly difficult to finance as interest rates continue to rise. We believe this situation can only get worse as demand for CMPR's products falls due to the onset of what we anticipate will be a widespread economic slowdown.

Jeremy J. Butler   October 28, 2022

(A) Fiscal year ends June 30th. Based on diluted earnings. Excludes nonrecurring gains/(losses): '13, ($1.30); '14, ($1.67); '15, $35.46/sh; '20, $4.08. May not sum due to round-ing. Next earnings report due late January. (B) Incl. intang. In 2022: $927.6 mill., $35.46/sh. (C) In millions.

Company's Financial Strength **B**
Stock's Price Stability **20**
Price Growth Persistence **45**
Earnings Predictability **10**

O'REILLY AUTO. NDQ-ORLY

RECENT PRICE	869.75	P/E RATIO	23.9 (Trailing: 26.0 / Median: 20.0)	RELATIVE P/E RATIO	1.38	DIV'D YLD	Nil	VALUE LINE

		High	Low
TIMELINESS 3	Lowered 3/24/23	107.1 135.6 196.8 278.0 292.8 284.0 363.2 454.3 488.0 710.9 870.9 873.9	75.6 87.1 128.2 179.0 225.1 169.4 217.6 329.9 251.5 424.0 562.9 767.3
SAFETY 3	Lowered 7/27/18		
TECHNICAL 3	Lowered 3/3/23		
BETA .90 (1.00 = Market)			

LEGENDS
— 15.0 x "Cash Flow" p sh
.... Relative Price Strength
Options: Yes
Shaded area indicates recession

Target Price Range 2026 2027 2028

18-Month Target Price Range
Low-High Midpoint (% to Mid)
$666-$1300 $983 (15%)

2026-28 PROJECTIONS
	Price	Gain	Ann'l Total Return
High	1335	(+55%)	11%
Low	890	(Nil)	1%

Institutional Decisions
	2Q2022	3Q2022	4Q2022
to Buy	464	440	571
to Sell	524	488	492
Hld(000)	53269	57151	53547

Percent shares traded 45 30 15

% TOT. RETURN 3/23
	THIS STOCK	VL ARITH.* INDEX
1 yr.	23.9	-5.8
3 yr.	182.0	99.5
5 yr.	243.2	60.9

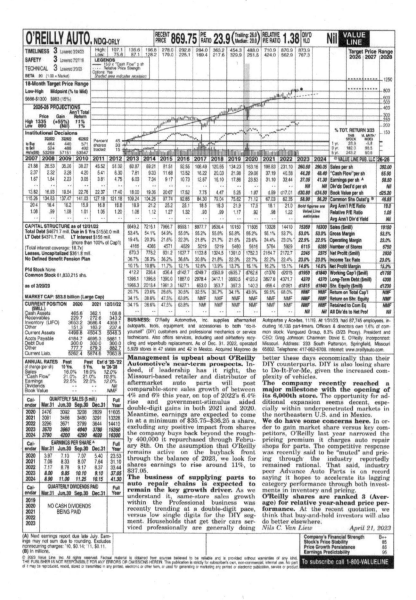

2007	2008	2009	2010	2011	2012	2013	2014	2015	2016	2017	2018	2019	2020	2021	2022	2023	2024	© VALUE LINE PUB. LLC	26-28
21.88	26.53	35.26	38.27	45.52	51.02	60.87	69.21	81.51	92.55	106.49	120.65	134.23	163.16	198.83	231.10	260.60	290.05	Sales per sh	392.00
2.37	2.32	3.28	4.20	5.41	6.30	7.81	9.33	11.68	13.52	16.22	20.03	21.98	29.06	37.19	40.58	44.20	48.40	"Cash Flow" per sh	65.50
1.67	1.84	2.23	3.05	3.81	4.75	6.03	7.34	9.17	10.73	12.67	15.10	17.88	23.53	31.10	33.44	37.05	41.30	Earnings per sh A	58.50
..	..	..	..	..	..	..	..	..	..	..	..	..	..	..	..	Nil	Nil	Div'ds Decl'd per sh	Nil
13.82	16.93	19.54	22.76	22.37	17.45	18.00	19.36	20.07	17.52	7.75	4.47	5.25	1.97	d.89	d17.01	d30.80	d34.50	Book Value per sh	d25.20
115.26	134.83	137.47	141.03	127.18	121.18	109.24	104.25	97.74	92.85	84.30	79.04	75.82	71.12	67.03	62.35	58.90	56.20	Common Shs Outst'g B	48.65
20.4	16.4	16.2	15.9	16.8	16.8	18.9	21.2	25.2	26.1	18.5	18.3	21.9	17.5	18.1	21.0	Bold figures are		Avg Ann'l P/E Ratio	19.0
1.08	.99	1.08	1.01	1.05	1.20	1.06	1.12	1.27	1.32	.93	.99	1.17	.92	.98	1.22	Value Line estimates		Relative P/E Ratio	1.05
																		Avg Ann'l Div'd Yield	Nil

CAPITAL STRUCTURE as of 12/31/22
Total Debt $4671.7 mill. Due in 5 Yrs $1550.0 mill.
LT Debt $4371.7 mill. LT Interest $155 mill.
(more than 100% of Cap'l)
(Total interest coverage: 18.7x)
Leases, Uncapitalized $361.8 mill.
No Defined Benefit Pension Plan

Pfd Stock None
Common Stock 61,833,215 shs.
as of 2/20/23

MARKET CAP: $53.8 billion (Large Cap)

CURRENT POSITION	2020	2021	12/31/22
Cash Assets	465.6	362.1	108.6
Receivables	229.7	272.6	343.2
Inventory (LIFO)	3653.2	3686.4	4359.1
Other	151.3	183.2	237.4
Current Assets	4499.8	4504.3	5048.3
Accts Payable	4184.7	4695.3	5661.1
Debt Due	300.0	300.0	300.0
Other	777.7	679.3	882.7
Current Liab.	5262.4	5674.6	7063.8

ANNUAL RATES	Past 10 Yrs.	Past 5 Yrs.	Est'd '20-'22 to '26-'28
of change (per sh)			
Sales	16.0%	16.0%	12.0%
"Cash Flow"	21.0%	21.0%	10.5%
Earnings	22.5%	22.0%	12.0%
Dividends	--	--	Nil
Book Value	NMF	NMF	NMF

Cal-endar	QUARTERLY SALES ($ mill.)				Full Year
	Mar.31	Jun.30	Sep.30	Dec.31	
2020	2476	3092	3208	2829	11605
2021	3091	3486	3480	3291	13326
2022	3296	3657	3799	3644	14410
2023	3570	3960	4040	3780	15350
2024	3970	4200	4290	4020	16300

Cal-endar	EARNINGS PER SHARE A				Full Year
	Mar.31	Jun.30	Sep.30	Dec.31	
2020	3.97	7.10	7.07	5.40	23.53
2021	7.06	8.33	8.07	7.64	31.10
2022	7.17	8.78	9.17	8.37	33.44
2023	8.00	9.85	10.10	9.10	37.05
2024	8.90	11.00	11.25	10.15	41.30

Cal-endar	QUARTERLY DIVIDENDS PAID				Full Year
	Mar.31	Jun.30	Sep.30	Dec.31	
2019					
2020	NO CASH DIVIDENDS				
2021	BEING PAID				
2022					
2023					

8649.2	7261.1	7966.7	8599.1	8977.7	9536.4	10150	11605	13328	14410	15350	16300	Sales ($mill)	19150
53.4%	54.1%	54.9%	55.0%	55.2%	55.6%	55.9%	55.2%	56.1%	53.7%	53.0%	53.5%	Gross Margin	53.5%
19.4%	20.3%	21.6%	22.3%	21.8%	21.7%	21.8%	23.6%	24.4%	23.0%	22.5%	22.5%	Operating Margin	23.0%
4166	4369	4571	4829	5019	5219	5480	5616	5764	5929	6115	6285	Number of Stores	6750
670.3	778.2	931.2	1037.7	1133.8	1324.5	1391.0	1782.3	2164.7	2172.7	2245	2375	Net Profit ($mill)	2930
36.7%	36.3%	36.2%	36.6%	30.8%	21.8%	22.3%	22.7%	22.2%	22.4%	23.0%	23.0%	Income Tax Rate	23.0%
10.1%	10.8%	11.7%	12.1%	12.6%	13.9%	13.7%	15.1%	16.2%	15.1%	14.6%	14.6%	Net Profit Margin	15.2%
412.2	236.4	d36.4	d142.7	d249.7	d350.9	d635.7	d762.6	d1370	d2015	d1950	d1840	Working Cap'l ($mill)	d1700
1395.1	1396.8	1390.0	1867.0	2978.4	3417.1	3690.5	4123.2	3827.0	4371.7	4370	4370	Long-Term Debt ($mill)	4300
1966.3	2018.4	1961.3	1627.1	653.0	353.7	397.3	140.3	d66.4	d1061	d1815	d1940	Shr. Equity ($mill)	d1230
20.7%	23.6%	28.6%	32.5%	32.5%	36.7%	34.1%	43.0%	59.5%	68.0%	NMF	NMF	Return on Total Cap'l	NMF
34.1%	38.6%	47.5%	63.8%	NMF	NMF	NMF	NMF	NMF	NMF	NMF	NMF	Return on Shr. Equity	NMF
34.1%	38.6%	47.5%	63.8%	NMF	NMF	NMF	NMF	NMF	NMF	NMF	NMF	Retained to Com Eq	NMF
..	..	..	..	..	..	..	..	..	..	Nil	Nil	All Div'ds to Net Prof	Nil

BUSINESS: O'Reilly Automotive, Inc. supplies aftermarket autoparts, tools, equipment, and accessories to both "do-it-yourself" (DIY) customers and professional mechanics or service technicians. Also offers services, including used oil/battery recycling and wiper/bulb replacement. As of Dec. 31, 2022, operated 5,929 stores in 47 states and 42 in Mexico. Acquired Mayoreo de Autopartes y Aceites, 11/19. At 1/31/23, had 87,745 employees, including 16,133 part-timers. Officers & directors own 1.6% of common stock: Vanguard Group, 8.3% (3/23 Proxy). President and CEO: Greg Johnson; Chairman: David E. O'Reilly. Incorporated: Missouri. Address: 233 South Patterson, Springfield, Missouri 65802. Telephone: 417-862-6708. Internet: www.oreillyauto.com.

Management is upbeat about O'Reilly Automotive's near-term prospects. Indeed, if leadership has it right, the Missouri-based retailer and distributor of aftermarket auto parts will post comparable-store sales growth of between 4% and 6% this year, on top of 2022's 6.4% rise and government-stimulus aided double-digit gains in both 2021 and 2020. Meantime, earnings are expected to come in at a minimum of $35.75-$36.25 a share, excluding any positive impact from shares the company buys back beyond the roughly 400,000 it repurchased through February 8th. On the assumption that O'Reilly remains active on the buyback front throughout the balance of 2023, we look for shares earnings to rise around 11%, to $37.05.

The business of supplying parts to auto repair chains is expected to remain the key growth driver. As we understand it, same-store sales growth within the Professional business has recently trending at a double-digit pace, versus low single digits for the DIY segment. Households that get their cars serviced professionally are generally doing better these days economically than their DIY counterparts. DIY is also losing share to Do-It-For-Me, given the increased complexity of vehicles.

The company recently reached a major milestone with the opening of its 6,000th store. The opportunity for additional expansion seems decent, especially within underpenetrated markets in the northeastern U.S. and in Mexico.

We do have some concerns here. In order to gain market share versus key competitors, O'Reilly last year narrowed the pricing premium it charges auto repair shops for parts. The competitive response was recently said to be "muted" and pricing through the industry reportedly remained rational. That said, industry peer Advance Auto Parts is on record saying it hopes to accelerate its lagging category performance through both investments in inventory and pricing.

O'Reilly shares are ranked 3 (Average) for relative year-ahead price performance. At the recent quotation, we think that buy-and-hold investors will also do better elsewhere.

Nils C. Van Liew April 21, 2023

(A) Next earnings report due late July. Earnings may not sum due to rounding. Excludes nonrecurring charges: '10, $0.14; '11, $0.11.
(B) In millions.

Company's Financial Strength	B++
Stock's Price Stability	85
Price Growth Persistence	85
Earnings Predictability	95

To subscribe call 1-800-VALUELINE

Q1 INDUSTRY RANK [_____]

Industry's potential for growth ⓘ
relative to other industries

- 1-25 Ideal (4)
- 26-50 High Range (3)
- 51-75 Low Range (2)
- 76-100 Red Flag (1)

[____]

Q2 TIMELINESS [_____]

How fast will the price of the stock rise
relative to other stocks in the next 12 months?

- 1-2 Ideal (4)
- 3 High Range (2.5)
- 4-5 Red Flag (1)

[____]

Q3 SAFETY

How much volatility is there likely to be on the stock over
the next 12 months compared to it's long term trends?

- 1-2 Ideal (4)
- 3 High Range (2.5)
- 4-5 Red Flag (1)

[____]

Q4 DEBT [_____] %

Debt as a % of capitalisation (Q4A / Q4B) * 100

Q4A ($B)   **Q4B ($B)**   ⓘ

[_____]   [_____]

- 0-9% Ideal (4)
- 10-30% High Range (3)
- 31-50% Low Range (2)
- 51%+ Red Flag

[____]

Q5 BETA [_____]

Volatility of this stock relative to
movement of total stock market

- 0.95-1.1 Ideal (4)
- 0.94-1.2 High Range (3)
- 0.91-1.49 Low Range (2)
- Other Red Flag (1)

[____]

Q6 GROWTH TRENDS

Q6a What has the company's sales [_____] %
growth been in the last 5 years?
Q6c What has the company's earnings [_____] %
growth been in the last 5 years?

- 15%+ Ideal (4)
- 11-14.99% High Range (3)
- 6.66-10.99% Low Range (2)
- 6.65% or less Red Flag (1)

[____]

5 Consecutive years of uninterrupted growth - Ideal(4)   Q6b Sales [____]
4 Years of growth and
  Growth up in last 2 years - High Range (3)   ⓘ
  No growth in last 2 years - Low Range (2)
2 or more years without growth - Red Flag (1)   Q6d Earnings [____]

Projected Revenues ($M)

Q6e	Ideal (4)	Range(3)	Range(2)	Flag(1)
Small less than $400m	15%+	13.6-14.9	12.1-13.5	12 or less
Medium $400-$3999m	12%+	11.1-11.9	10.1-11.0	10 or less
Large $4000m+	10%+	8.6-9.9	7.1-8.5	7 or less

Q6f Projected Sales [_____] %

Q6g Projected Earnings [_____] %

- 19-24 Ideal (4)
- 13-18 High Range (3)
- 7-12 Low Range (2)
- 0-6 Red Flag (1)

Total → [____]

Q7 MANAGEMENT

Q7a Are profits increasing? ☐
Q7b Is management solid & are they anticipating future trends? ☐   ⓘ
Q7c Have they handled past challenges? ☐
Q7d Are they operating smoothly without any pending lawsuits? ☐

- 4 Y's - Ideal (4)
- 3 Y's - High Range (3)
- 2 Y's - Low Range
- 1 Y - Red Flag

	Values	Multiply by	Total	Max
Industry Ranking		*		4
Timeliness		**		8
Safety		**		8
Debt		**		8
Beta		*		4
Growth Trends		***		12
Management		**		8
				52

The
Investment
Club Network
TICN
Copyright TiCN Ltd. 2002

- 40-52 Ideal (4)
- 27-39 High Range (3)
- 14-26 Low Range (2)
- 0-13 Red Flag (1)

TICN Guide

Name: [_____] **Date:** [_____]

P2 DIVIDENDS

		Yes, Ideal (4)
E.P.S	P2a [____]	Are last year's dividends
Last year's dividends	P2b [____]	less than 1/2 of E.P.S?
		No, Red Flag (1)

[____]

P3 ESTIMATED PRICE APPRECIATION

		Yes, Ideal (4)
Projected % growth of the high	P3a [____]	Is it over 15% per annum?
high stock price 5 years forward		No, Red Flag (1)

[____]

P4 SALES Vs EARNINGS

% of annual sales in past 5 years	P4a [____]	Earnings growth faster than sales?
% of annual earnings in past 5 years	P4b [____]	2 Yes = Ideal (4)
		1 Yes, 1 No = Range (2.5)
Projected % of annual sales growth in next 5 years	P4c [____]	2 No = Red Flag (1)
Projected % of annual earnings growth in next 5 years	P4d [____]	Earnings growth faster than sales?

[____]

P5 P/E Ratio

P/E for past 5 years			Current P/E ratio at or below 5 yr average - Ideal (4)
Current P/E	Nudge -> ↑	P5a [____]	Current P/E ratio above 5 yr average - Range (2.5)
			Current P/E ratio 2 times 5 yr average - Red Flag (1)

Average P/E for past 5 years	
Current P/E	P5b [____]

[____]

P6 BUY/SELL RANGE

Nudge-> ←

					Averages
5 Year Highs	[ ]	[ ]	[ ]	[ ]	[ ]	P6a
5 Year Lows	[ ]	[ ]	[ ]	[ ]	[ ]	
5 Year E.P.S.	[ ]	[ ]	[ ]	[ ]	[ ]	P6b

Average High/P6b [____]	Average Low/P6b [____]
P6c Projected E.P.S. [____] X	P2a E.P.S. [____] X
	for last year
P6d [____]	P6e [____]
Slice (P6d-P6e)/3 [____]	

Highest Stock Price	[____]	P6d
Highest Hold Price	[____]	P6d - Slice
Highest Buy Price	[____]	P6e + Slice
Lowest Stock Price	[____]	P6e

John McGrade Version 2.3

The Investment Club Network
TICN
Copyright TICN Ltd 2002

P7 REWARD/RISK RATIO

Estimated high price P6d [____] minus	Current Price P1 [____] minus	A divided by B = [____]
Current Price P1 [____]	Estimated low price P6e [____]	3 or more = Ideal (4)
A [____]	B [____]	Less than 3 = Red Flag (1)

[____]

	Value	Multiply by	Total	Max
Dividends		*		4
Estimated Price Appreciation		***		12
Sales V Earnings		***		12
P/E Ratio		***		12
Reward/Risk Ratio		***		12
				52

Completed By [_____]

TICN Guide
40-52 Ideal (4)
27-39 High Range (3)
14-26 Low Range (2)
0-13 Red Flag (1)

6. Thank you...

... to the men in my life in alphabetical order: Alberto, Jaime, Mario and Owen for the love you all surround me with.

... to my parents, for all the lessons I learned from them and all the teachers whose words helped me make sense of those lessons!

... to the black sheep that come out and dare to be themselves.

7. Other books by the author

This is the link in which you can find all my books on https://linktr.ee/Empowered.Supernova. I will continue updating the new titles there.

At the moment of publishing this book, these are the books that are already available in the English language:

Books about the stock market

4 steps for financial freedom

El Dorado: Optimise your options trading

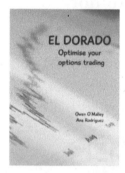 

Cash from silver

Personal development books

Empowered: Wealth, Health and You

The story I never wanted to tell: Farewell to marriage in peace and harmony

Instruction manual to live in this new era

Konversations with my kids: Keys to build extraordinary relationships with your teenagers

Konversations with my kids: The six human needs

Narcissistic mother: goodbye! Three steps to stop living under the shadow of the woman who believes she owns you

Children's books

Halloween: Palabras - Words

Fun, feelings and emotions

Rhymes, riddles and tickles

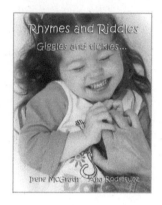

8. Bibliography and links

Books:

A great discovery: the doubling of time, Jean Pierre Garnier Mallet

Diagnostic and Statistical Manual of Mental Disorders (DSM–5), American Psychiatric Association.

The seven spiritual laws of success, Deepak Chopra

Unshakeable, Tony Robbins

It didn't start with you, Mark Wolynn

The Biology Of Belief : Unleashing The Power Of Consciousness, Matter & Miracles, Bruce Lipton, Ph.D.

MONEY Master the Game: 7 Simple Steps to Financial Freedom, Tonny Robbins.

Movies:

Sliding Doors, Peter Howitt, 1998

Links:

www.ticnima.com

www.plannersecurities.com

earningswhispers.com

www.nasdaq.com/market-activity/earnings

www.vfxplc.com

Demo account: http://demo.alphaplan.us/
https://www.longtermtrends.net/sp500-price-earnings-shiller-pe-ratio/

www.ticn.com

Warren Buffet's letters to shareholders:
https://www.berkshirehathaway.com/letters/2022ltr.pdf

www.Investopedia.com

The Dunning-Kruger effect:
https://en.wikipedia.org/wiki/Dunning–Kruger_effect

Disclaimer: the day this book was published, all the links here and throughout the text worked. If they don't when you type them, please, refer to Google.

9. Notes